LLMS SIMPLIFIED

A PRACTICAL GUIDE TO LEARN AND ADOPT GENERATIVE AI FOR YOUR ENTERPRISE

SANDEEP KAPOOR

Made with ♥ on the Notion Press Platform
www.notionpress.com

Contents

Acknowledgements

Writing a book is never a solitary endeavour, and this one is no exception. It has been a journey shaped by the support, wisdom, and encouragement of many remarkable individuals to whom I owe my deepest gratitude.

To my beloved wife: your unwavering belief in me and this project has been my anchor. You have been my partner, my sounding board, and my greatest source of strength. Thank you for your patience, understanding, and the countless sacrifices you have made to help me bring this vision to life. This book is as much a testament to your support as it is to the ideas within its pages.

To my children, who constantly remind me of the boundless curiosity and wonder that fuel my passion for AI: thank you for inspiring me to see the world through fresh eyes every day. Your questions, your laughter, and your fascination with technology motivate me to explore new horizons and to create a future where AI can serve humanity in meaningful ways. This book is dedicated to you and to the next generation, who will inherit and shape the technologies we build today.

To my extended family, whose steadfast encouragement has been a source of quiet strength: thank you for standing by me in moments of triumph and doubt alike. Your faith in me has been a foundation upon which I have built my career, and I am profoundly grateful for your love and support.

To my colleagues, collaborators, and mentors: your contributions, insights, and shared dedication to advancing the field of artificial intelligence have enriched this work beyond measure. Thank you for challenging me, inspiring me, and teaching me. This book is the result of countless discussions, brainstorming sessions, and collaborative efforts with some of the most brilliant minds in the industry. I am grateful for the privilege of working alongside you and for the knowledge that each of you has imparted.

And finally, to every reader who has picked up this book with curiosity and an open mind: thank you for joining me on this journey into the world of large language models. Your interest and enthusiasm are the reasons I undertook this project, and I hope this book serves as a valuable guide, sparking ideas, insights, and perhaps even new ventures in your own work.

Preface

We are living through a historic shift in how intelligence is created, applied, and amplified. What began as a quest to understand human language has evolved into a profound transformation of how we interact with technology—and with each other. At the center of this change are large language models (LLMs), which have emerged not only as tools of automation, but as catalysts of a new cognitive era.

This book, *LLMs Simplified: A Practical Guide to Learning and Adopting Generative AI for Your Enterprise*, is the result of years spent working at the frontier of language, computation, and enterprise innovation. It is written for leaders, builders, thinkers, and technologists who seek clarity amid the noise, and action in the face of opportunity. LLMs are no longer experimental novelties. They are foundational infrastructure for intelligent systems—and increasingly, for intelligent organizations.

Since their early breakthroughs, LLMs have rapidly grown in sophistication, scale, and autonomy. Today, we stand at the dawn of agentic AI—where models don't just respond but act, reason, plan, and collaborate. This shift expands the scope of what AI can accomplish and deepens its integration into our digital and physical environments. Yet with this progress comes complexity, risk, and the pressing need for responsible design.

This book is not a theoretical manifesto. It is a grounded, pragmatic guide—one that simplifies the science without diluting the substance. It aims to help you understand how LLMs work, how they can be adapted to real-world needs, and how to deploy them responsibly within your enterprise context. Whether you're exploring your first AI use case or orchestrating multi-agent systems across your business, you'll find principles, patterns, and practices that illuminate the path forward.

More than anything, this book is a call to thoughtful action. AI, in its most transformative form, should not be something we passively consume—it should be something we shape with intention. I invite you to treat this book as a map, a compass, and a conversation starter for a journey that is only just beginning.

Let us build what's next—not just with intelligence, but with integrity.

Introduction

Language is not just a tool—it is the operating system of human thought. Through language, we reason, dream, negotiate, build, and connect. It encodes our knowledge, expresses our values, and enables collaboration at scale. It is deeply human, profoundly complex, and infinitely nuanced. And now, for the first time in history, we are teaching machines to speak it with us.

Large language models (LLMs) represent a breakthrough in this effort—not because they perfectly mirror human intelligence, but because they reveal new ways for machines to engage with language in dynamic, context-aware, and surprisingly creative ways. They are no longer confined to recognizing patterns in words; they are now capable of generating ideas, composing responses, simulating conversations, and even orchestrating actions across digital systems. LLMs are reshaping how knowledge is accessed, how software behaves, and how humans and machines collaborate.

LLMs Simplified is your guide to understanding and applying this transformative technology. This book is built to help you decode the essence of LLMs—how they are trained, how they learn, how they reason, and how they can be embedded into real-world systems. But beyond that, it's a framework for responsible innovation in a world that increasingly depends on AI for decision-making, personalization, and automation.

The journey begins with language itself—its structure, its ambiguity, and why it remains one of the most difficult problems in AI. We will walk through the milestones that brought us here: from early rule-based systems and probabilistic models to the revolutionary architecture of Transformers and today's agentic AI systems, capable of autonomous planning and multi-modal reasoning.

But this is not just a technical exploration. LLMs are embedded in society, and their impact stretches beyond code. With great power comes the urgent responsibility to address questions of bias, safety, alignment, and transparency. Throughout this book, you will find not just practical strategies for deploying LLMs, but also ethical frameworks for guiding their use in high-stakes environments—from healthcare to finance, education to governance.

Whether you're building enterprise solutions, shaping product strategy, or simply trying to stay ahead of the curve, this book is for you. Each chapter is designed to deepen your understanding and equip you with actionable insights for building AI-native systems that are intelligent, adaptive, and human-aligned.

The age of agentic AI has begun. We are moving beyond models that answer questions to systems that take initiative, collaborate with humans, and continuously learn from their environment. This next chapter of AI is not about replacing human intelligence—it's about expanding it.

Thank you for joining this exploration. The terrain is vast, the pace is accelerating, and the opportunities are extraordinary. Let's navigate the world of LLMs together—with clarity, purpose, and imagination.

CHAPTER ONE

The Language of Intelligence

Why Language Matters in AI

Language is more than just a medium of communication — it is the connective tissue of human cognition, collaboration, and civilization. It encodes not only facts and instructions but also emotion, nuance, belief systems, and shared cultural memories. From legal contracts to lullabies, from code comments to customer complaints, language is the infrastructure of thought and human interaction. It is how we reason, negotiate, educate, express, and build.

Given this centrality, any serious attempt at building artificial intelligence that can assist — or eventually collaborate — with humans must first address one foundational challenge: understanding language.

The Human Edge: Language as Cognition

Unlike other signals such as images or numbers, language is abstract, recursive, and deeply contextual. It allows us to:

- Represent complex ideas through sequences of arbitrary symbols (words).
- Convey implicit meaning through tone, structure, and word choice.
- Adapt messages based on audience, intention, and feedback.
- Share knowledge across generations and geographies.

Language, in short, is not just how we communicate. It is how we *think*. This makes natural language not just an interface for AI but a window into human reasoning itself. As such, language modeling isn't simply a technical feat; it's a cognitive milestone.

The Role of Language in Artificial Intelligence

For decades, artificial intelligence was largely symbolic — rules, logic, and structured data. These systems could play chess, calculate routes, or automate factory lines, but they couldn't hold a conversation or summarize a legal document. The emergence of **natural language processing (NLP)** as a frontier within AI changed that.

Today, language models can:

- Read and understand legal, medical, financial, and technical documents.
- Generate fluent text indistinguishable from human writing.
- Answer questions, translate languages, summarize content, and even write poetry.
- Interact with users through voice and text in customer service, education, healthcare, and more.

Language has transformed from a barrier into a bridge — enabling machines to operate across unstructured data, provide intelligent responses, and interface with humans naturally.

Language as a Universal Interface

In enterprise settings, language is present in every process:

- **Customer support:** Chat, voice, email.
- **Sales and marketing:** Campaigns, feedback, personalization.
- **Operations:** Logs, alerts, service tickets.
- **Compliance:** Regulations, audits, documentation.
- **Knowledge management:** Reports, manuals, internal wikis.

LLMs enable AI systems to act on this linguistic layer — reading it, understanding it, reasoning about it, and even generating new content — without requiring rigid data formats or custom programming.

This unlocks a powerful proposition: instead of training people to talk to machines (through software, dashboards, interfaces), we are now training machines to understand people — in their language, their tone, and their context.

The Shift from Data-Centric to Language-Centric AI

Previous generations of AI required well-labeled datasets, formal inputs, and domain-specific models. But with the rise of large language models trained on vast, diverse corpora, the paradigm is shifting:

- **Language is now the interface.** You can "program" a model with instructions in plain English (or any major language).
- **Context is king.** Through prompts, LLMs can be adapted to new tasks without retraining.
- **Knowledge is emergent.** LLMs capture facts, patterns, and heuristics from the data they ingest — a kind of synthetic common sense.

This transition makes LLMs far more accessible and flexible for enterprises across the globe — even those without massive labeled datasets or AI engineering teams.

Language Models as Intelligent Systems

Large language models do more than generate text. They *model* the probability space of human language. This means they can:

- Predict what comes next in a sentence (completion).
- Fill in missing information (inference).
- Rephrase or translate ideas (transformation).
- Classify, cluster, or rank information (decisioning).
- Simulate dialogues and even personalities (agentic behavior).

This predictive ability, when layered with tools like memory, planning, and APIs, creates the foundation for **agentic AI** — systems that can reason, act, and learn across time and context.

Why It Matters for the Future

Language models are becoming the backbone of human-AI collaboration. Their applications are not just futuristic — they're immediate and impactful:

- **Doctors** can summarize patient notes and medical histories instantly.
- **Lawyers** can draft and review contracts with AI copilots.
- **Teachers** can personalize feedback and generate lesson plans.
- **Business leaders** can extract insights from unstructured reports and customer feedback.
- **Developers** can build conversational apps using natural prompts instead of formal programming.

As models become multimodal — understanding not just language, but images, audio, video, and code — the potential expands exponentially.

But with this power comes responsibility. The way language models interpret, generate, and replicate language can shape public discourse, influence decisions, and impact lives. Which is why ethics, transparency, and inclusion are not optional add-ons, but fundamental design principles.

Final Thoughts: Language Is the Foundation

If artificial intelligence is to serve humanity, it must understand humanity — and that begins with language. From the earliest words we speak as children to the most complex contracts we sign as adults, language is how we encode and enact intelligence.

Large language models are not just tools for writing better emails or automating support tickets. They are part of a broader shift: toward systems that reason with us, assist us, and augment our intelligence.

Understanding why language matters in AI is the first step in unlocking what these systems can do — and how we can build them to serve the best in us.

What Are Language Models?

At their core, **language models** are mathematical systems trained to understand and generate human language. But their simplicity in definition belies their sophistication in capability. To grasp what language models are — and why they're so transformative — we need to unpack both their foundational principles and their evolving role in artificial intelligence.

A Simple Idea with Profound Implications

The fundamental job of a language model is to determine the likelihood of a sequence of words. Given a sequence of text, a language model estimates how probable a certain word or phrase is in that context. This allows it to complete sentences, suggest corrections, generate responses, or summarize content — all by learning patterns from data, not from hard-coded rules.

For example, if you start a sentence with "The capital of France is...", a well-trained language model will predict that "Paris" is the most likely next word — not because it knows geography in the human sense, but because it has seen enough examples of similar phrasing in its training data.

In this sense, a language model doesn't "know" in the way we do. Instead, it captures **statistical associations** between words, phrases, and structures — an immense and nuanced pattern recognition engine that reflects how language is used across billions of texts.

From Patterns to Meaning

While early models focused purely on word-level predictions, modern language models go far beyond surface-level patterns. They capture deeper linguistic and semantic structures, including:

- **Grammar and syntax:** The rules governing sentence construction.
- **Semantics:** The meanings of words in different contexts.
- **Pragmatics:** The implied or situational meaning behind words.
- **Discourse coherence:** How different parts of a text relate to one another.
- **World knowledge:** Facts and general reasoning embedded in the data.

This enables them to perform not just completion tasks, but also comprehension, summarization, translation, question answering, and reasoning. A model that begins by predicting "what comes next" eventually learns enough structure to respond meaningfully to complex instructions.

Training Language Models: Learning from Data at Scale

Language models are trained using a method called **self-supervised learning** — meaning they learn directly from the text without requiring manual labels. During training, parts of the input are hidden (masked or truncated), and the model learns to predict the missing elements.

To do this effectively, language models are exposed to vast amounts of diverse, unstructured text: books, websites, conversations, news articles, code, technical documentation, and more. The training process involves adjusting billions (or even trillions) of internal parameters so that the model becomes better at predicting the correct next word in any given context.

The more data a model sees, and the more parameters it has to capture patterns, the better it can generalize to new language tasks. This gives rise to the term **"large" language models** — where scale in both training data and computational capacity plays a crucial role in performance.

A Shift from Rule-Based to Data-Driven Intelligence

Traditionally, natural language processing relied on handcrafted rules — systems designed by linguists and engineers to handle grammar, tokenization, or parsing. These systems were brittle, language-specific, and required constant updates to handle edge cases or new usage trends.

Language models changed this paradigm. Instead of explicitly programming the rules of language, we now let models **discover** those rules by analyzing massive datasets. This data-driven approach enables:

- **Greater adaptability:** Models can generalize to new topics, domains, or dialects without manual reprogramming.
- **Multilingual capability:** The same model can understand and generate multiple languages.
- **Emergent behavior:** Models can learn surprising abilities (e.g., basic arithmetic, code synthesis, analogical reasoning) without being explicitly trained for them.

This transition from symbolic rules to statistical learning marks one of the most important shifts in the history of artificial intelligence.

Language Models as a Foundation for AI Systems

A language model, in its raw form, is a probabilistic engine that predicts word sequences. But when paired with additional components — memory, retrieval systems, tools, or APIs — it becomes a foundation for intelligent behavior.

For example:

- In a chatbot, a language model powers the natural dialogue.
- In a search engine, it helps rank and summarize documents.
- In a legal AI system, it may analyze contracts or generate clauses.
- In agentic AI, it enables multi-step reasoning, decision-making, and planning.

The modularity of language models makes them highly composable — they can be plugged into various pipelines, workflows, or user experiences to deliver intelligent, context-aware behavior.

Why They Matter Now

While language models have existed in some form for decades, the explosion in their capability — marked by models like OpenAI's GPT series, Google's PaLM, Anthropic's Claude, and Meta's LLaMA — is a recent phenomenon. The convergence of four key trends made this possible:

1. **Massive data availability:** The internet provided a rich, multilingual, ever-growing corpus.
2. **Advances in compute infrastructure:** Modern GPUs and TPUs enabled large-scale training.
3. **Breakthroughs in model architecture:** Especially the Transformer, which replaced recurrent and convolutional methods.
4. **Emergence of generalization:** Models began excelling not just on specific benchmarks but across many tasks, often without task-specific tuning.

The result is a family of models that can write, converse, code, translate, plan, and even reason — all using the same underlying principle: modeling the structure of language.

More Than Just Text: Language as the API for Everything

In the age of LLMs, language is not just a medium — it's the **interface** for interacting with software, services, and even other agents. You can instruct a model to:

- Book a meeting.
- Generate SQL queries.
- Summarize legal risk.
- Draft an email campaign.
- Identify sentiment in customer feedback.

This creates a profound shift for developers, enterprises, and users alike. Instead of clicking through UIs or coding against rigid APIs, users can describe their intent in natural language — and the system responds appropriately.

Language becomes the API. And the model becomes the intelligent middleware between humans and digital systems.

The Foundation of Agentic AI

As we move toward agentic systems — autonomous AI agents that can operate over time, reason about goals, and interact with tools — language models are the heart of their cognition. These agents use language models to:

- Parse goals from user input.
- Break down tasks into subtasks.
- Retrieve relevant knowledge.
- Generate actions, responses, or even code.
- Reflect, learn, and improve over time.

In this sense, language modeling is no longer a niche capability; it is the cognitive substrate on which next-generation digital agents are being built.

From Words to Meaning: How LLMs Understand Language

At first glance, language may appear to be a simple sequence of words arranged in logical order. But the true power of language lies in its ability to carry **meaning** — meaning that often transcends the literal, depends on context, and shifts with nuance, tone, or even silence. For machines to be useful partners in human-centric tasks, they must go beyond recognizing words. They must learn to **understand** them.

Large Language Models (LLMs) are designed to do exactly this — to move from surface-level pattern recognition to a form of **semantic understanding**. But how is this possible, given that these models are trained not with real-world experience, emotions, or intent, but with text?

Let's demystify how LLMs, built entirely on mathematical foundations, manage to create an illusion — and increasingly, a reality — of understanding.

Language as Data: A Statistical View of Meaning

At their core, LLMs treat language as data. Every word, sentence, paragraph, or document is converted into numerical form — specifically, into a sequence of **tokens**, which represent fragments of text. These tokens are mapped to high-dimensional **vectors**, allowing models to manipulate language mathematically.

From this perspective, LLMs do not "understand" words as humans do. Instead, they develop a **probabilistic intuition** about language by observing vast quantities of examples. They learn which words tend to appear together, which structures are typical in certain contexts, and what kinds of responses are expected after specific prompts.

Crucially, the model does not memorize language — it **generalizes** from it. Just as a child learns that "apple" and "fruit" often belong in similar conversations, a model learns that words and phrases exist in **semantic neighborhoods**, each tied to different probabilities, meanings, and uses.

Context: The Invisible Force Behind Meaning

If there's one superpower that distinguishes LLMs from earlier AI systems, it's their ability to model **context**. Older systems relied heavily on predefined grammar rules or keyword spotting. But meaning in human language is highly dependent on *where* and *how* a word is used.

Consider the sentence:
"The bank raised the interest rate."
The word "bank" here refers to a financial institution.

Now compare:
"The fisherman sat on the bank and cast his line."
Here, "bank" means the edge of a river.

LLMs handle this effortlessly — not because they've been explicitly taught definitions, but because they've seen millions of examples where "bank" co-occurs with words like "raised" and "interest" in financial contexts, or "fisherman" and "cast" in environmental ones. The model uses **contextual embeddings** — representations of words that change based on surrounding words — to infer intended meaning.

This ability to represent words **dynamically**, not statically, is one of the key breakthroughs of modern language models.

Layers of Abstraction: From Syntax to Semantics

Understanding language involves multiple layers:

- **Surface level (syntax):** The grammar, punctuation, and structure.
- **Intermediate level (semantics):** What the sentence actually means.
- **Deeper level (pragmatics):** What the speaker intends, and what the listener infers.

LLMs, especially those based on **Transformer architectures**, use multiple layers of neural computation to capture these levels. The lower layers might recognize grammar and sentence construction. The middle layers start capturing meaning — for example, identifying whether a sentence is a question, a command, or an observation. The higher layers begin to tease out **intent**, **tone**, and **implication** — learning not just what is said, but what is *meant*.

This multi-layered representation is what allows LLMs to perform diverse tasks such as:

- Summarizing long documents,
- Answering ambiguous questions,
- Translating across languages and cultures,
- Rewriting text to match tone or audience,

- Generating emotionally appropriate or stylistically consistent outputs.

Emergent Understanding: Beyond Explicit Training

One of the most intriguing phenomena with LLMs is **emergence** — the spontaneous development of capabilities that were not explicitly programmed into the model. For example, a model trained on predicting the next word in a sentence might unexpectedly learn:

- Arithmetic reasoning,
- Code generation,
- Question answering,
- Logical deduction.

This happens because language itself contains latent structure. By training on large corpora that include Wikipedia, books, research papers, conversations, codebases, and more, the model learns **general-purpose representations** that mirror human knowledge and reasoning. In effect, the model begins to **approximate understanding** — not in a conscious way, but in a functional one.

This is why LLMs can write essays, reason about causes and effects, detect contradictions, or even offer philosophical musings. They are not conscious, but they are **coherent**. They echo the reasoning encoded in the data they've seen, stitched together by billions of learned parameters.

Meaning Without Grounding? The Ongoing Debate

Critics often raise a fair question: *Can a model truly "understand" if it doesn't experience the world?*

This touches on a long-standing debate in linguistics and AI — the **symbol grounding problem**. Human meaning is tied to embodiment: we know what "cold" means because we've felt it. We understand "fear" not just as a word, but as a visceral state.

LLMs, by contrast, are disembodied. Their "understanding" is based entirely on patterns in language, not on lived experience.

And yet, in practice, LLMs demonstrate a remarkable **functional grasp** of meaning. In many contexts — from summarizing articles to answering medical questions — their outputs are useful, relevant, and precise. Whether or not this constitutes true understanding is philosophical; what matters for enterprise and application is that the model behaves as if it understands — reliably, transparently, and safely.

Why This Matters for Enterprise and Agentic AI

In enterprise settings, most critical data is unstructured — hidden in text, emails, reports, contracts, chats, and logs. Traditional software struggles to make sense of this. But LLMs excel precisely in this domain. By converting raw language into structured, actionable insight, they unlock:

- Automated document processing and contract analysis,
- Semantic search and discovery across millions of records,
- Intelligent agents that understand user intent and respond appropriately,
- Context-aware assistants that help employees with planning, research, and communication.

When these capabilities are paired with tools, memory, feedback loops, and goals — the building blocks of **agentic AI** — the result is a new kind of digital collaborator. One that doesn't just respond, but reasons. One that adapts to each user, each use case, and each evolving need.

Conclusion: The New Language of Intelligence

LLMs don't "understand" language the way we do — but they **model** it in a way that captures much of its depth, structure, and nuance. By learning from data, modeling context, and reasoning probabilistically, they turn raw text into meaningful, contextually rich outputs.

The journey from words to meaning is not about replicating the human mind — it's about **augmenting human capabilities**. It's about building systems that can read, write, explain, summarize, translate, and converse — in ways that feel intelligent because they are grounded in the structure of language itself.

As we build more advanced models and wrap them in agentic frameworks, the ability to understand language will become not just a feature, but a foundation — for how machines collaborate with humans, in every domain, across every language, and with increasingly powerful results.

Pattern Recognition and Prediction

At the heart of every language model lies a deceptively simple idea: **language follows patterns** — and machines can learn to recognize and predict those patterns. From the rhythm of poetry to the structure of contracts, from informal chats to scientific abstracts, human language, though vast and varied, is not random. It carries statistical regularities, syntactic rules, semantic cues, and pragmatic signals. These patterns, when learned at scale, empower machines to anticipate meaning, generate coherent text, and perform reasoning tasks with surprising fluency.

From Chaos to Structure

To a machine, raw language is just a stream of symbols. Unlike numbers in a spreadsheet, words carry no inherent numerical value. Yet, when exposed to billions of examples, patterns begin to emerge:

- Certain words frequently co-occur ("artificial intelligence", "climate change").
- Word order reflects grammar ("She eats" is valid; "eats she" is not).
- Context shifts meaning ("bank" in finance vs. riverbank).
- Sentence structure mirrors intention (questions, commands, narratives).

Language models, especially LLMs, do not memorize the world. Instead, they encode **probabilistic expectations**. They learn that in a given context, certain words or phrases are more likely than others — and that these probabilities evolve as context deepens.

This is where prediction begins.

Prediction as a Form of Understanding

While it may sound narrow, prediction is a powerful proxy for understanding. When a language model predicts the next word in a sentence, it is not merely guessing; it is integrating context, modeling syntax, estimating intent, and surfacing relevant knowledge. For example:

- Given “The capital of France is...”, it predicts “Paris” — not because it has memorized trivia, but because millions of contexts have reinforced this association.
- Given “She walked into the room, saw the broken glass, and felt a surge of...”, it may predict “fear” or “anger”, inferring emotion from narrative.
- Given code comments, it can anticipate the next function or logic block in programming languages.

This ability to *complete*, *correct*, or *continue* sequences makes LLMs not only linguistically competent but also functionally useful in real-world applications.

Recognizing Deep Patterns Across Domains

Crucially, pattern recognition in language is not limited to grammar or vocabulary. Modern LLMs learn high-dimensional representations of meaning — abstractions that connect seemingly unrelated domains:

- They detect analogies and metaphors (e.g., “data is the new oil”).
- They align narratives (e.g., mapping customer complaints to product faults).
- They identify causal relationships in text (e.g., “due to supply chain issues, shipments were delayed”).
- They match questions to answers, problems to solutions, and tasks to tools.

In doing so, LLMs are not just recognizing surface-level patterns, but **semantic structures** — the architecture of meaning. This is what enables them to generalize to new tasks, adapt to new domains, and even exhibit emergent capabilities (e.g., reasoning, summarization, code synthesis) not explicitly trained into them.

The Enterprise Lens: Patterns in Business Language

In an enterprise context, pattern recognition takes on enormous value:

- **Customer service:** Detect recurring complaints, sentiment shifts, or service gaps.

- **Fraud detection:** Identify suspicious linguistic patterns in calls, messages, or claims.
- **Risk management:** Flag anomalies in compliance language or legal contracts.
- **Market intelligence:** Extract insights from earnings calls, analyst reports, or social media chatter.

These are not isolated use cases — they represent a new kind of intelligence infrastructure. One where every email, chat, report, or transaction becomes a potential input for analysis and action.

With LLMs, businesses can finally scale the human capacity for pattern recognition to millions of documents and signals — without needing to predefine every rule or keyword.

From Static Models to Adaptive Agents

Traditional language models recognize and predict patterns in static settings — given a prompt, they produce an output. But with the rise of agentic AI, these capabilities become **interactive and iterative**:

- Agents can observe changes in patterns over time — spotting trends, anomalies, or drifts in user behavior.
- They can update internal knowledge through retrieval, feedback, or planning — refining predictions dynamically.
- They can simulate hypotheses, run experiments, and make data-informed decisions.

In this context, prediction is no longer just about finishing a sentence — it's about **forecasting needs**, **adapting responses**, and **orchestrating actions** based on anticipated outcomes.

This is where the boundary between language model and intelligent agent begins to blur.

Limits and Challenges in Prediction

Of course, pattern recognition is not understanding in a human sense. LLMs do not possess consciousness, self-awareness, or grounded knowledge of the physical world. Their predictions are based on correlations, not causation. This leads to:

- **Hallucinations:** Plausible-sounding but false outputs.
- **Bias amplification:** Learning patterns of prejudice embedded in data.
- **Overconfidence:** Fluent language masking uncertainty or gaps in reasoning.

Recognizing patterns is powerful — but without guardrails, it can also reproduce and reinforce existing flaws in language, culture, or decision-making systems. That's why interpretability, robustness, and responsible design must evolve alongside scale.

Why This Matters Now

As LLMs become core to business workflows, consumer applications, and societal infrastructure, their ability to recognize and predict patterns is not just a technical asset — it is a strategic advantage. Enterprises that can harness this capacity will be able to:

- Understand their customers in real time.
- Make faster, smarter decisions based on unstructured inputs.
- Automate knowledge work while maintaining nuance and quality.
- Build AI-native systems that adapt, learn, and scale.

In a world awash with information, the true value lies not just in storing or searching data, but in **interpreting it through patterns**, predicting what matters next, and acting meaningfully.

This is the promise of language intelligence — and it begins with the machine learning to see what we often overlook: the structure within the noise, the signal in the stream, the pattern behind the words.

Completing, Translating, Summarizing, and Conversing

The Core Competencies of Modern Language Models

As large language models (LLMs) evolve, their most immediately recognizable capabilities lie in four key linguistic tasks: **completion**, **translation**, **summarization**, and **conversation**. These are not merely features—they are the building blocks of language intelligence. They reveal the model's capacity to understand syntax and semantics, retain and adapt context, and generate coherent, goal-directed output.

These tasks are the new literacy of intelligent systems, enabling a machine not just to parse or process language, but to participate in it meaningfully.

Text Completion: The Engine of Prediction

At the heart of every large language model is a deceptively simple idea: given a sequence of words, what is the most probable word (or token) to come next?

Text completion is where this predictive capacity first reveals its power. Whether finishing a sentence, writing a paragraph, or continuing a thought, LLMs can generate coherent and contextually relevant language that aligns with human expectations.

This isn't guesswork—it's statistical foresight powered by billions of patterns observed during pretraining. The model learns to associate sequences with likely continuations across a diverse range of domains, from casual conversation to legal argumentation.

In practical terms, this manifests in real-world tools such as:

- Autocompleting search queries or code blocks.
- Drafting email replies or legal clauses.
- Generating story continuations or creative content.

What's remarkable is not just that models complete text, but that they can maintain logical consistency, adopt a specific tone or persona, and even reflect implicit goals (e.g., persuasive vs. factual completion) based solely on input context.

This ability is what makes LLMs inherently flexible—they don't just answer questions; they extend thought.

Translation: Bridging Languages and Cultures

Language models are fundamentally multilingual. Trained on large corpora that span dozens of languages, they learn structural correspondences and semantic parallels between linguistic systems.

Unlike traditional translation models that were trained pairwise between languages, LLMs take a more holistic view: they understand language as a latent space, where meaning can be encoded and re-expressed in any compatible linguistic system. This allows them to perform zero-shot or few-shot translation with surprising fluency.

For example:

- An LLM can translate a technical manual from Japanese to Spanish without ever being explicitly trained on that pair.
- It can preserve idiomatic expressions, grammatical tense, and stylistic cues that are often lost in rigid rule-based systems.
- It can also adapt to domain-specific language—like translating legal terminology, product documentation, or poetic verse—based on context and examples.

But the implications of this go far beyond convenience. Language translation unlocks:

- Cross-border customer support.
- Real-time diplomatic or humanitarian communication.
- Education and knowledge-sharing across linguistic divides.

In a globalized world, the ability to translate is the ability to connect—and LLMs are emerging as universal translators that respect nuance, not just words.

Summarization: Distilling Meaning from Information Overload

We live in a world drowning in text: emails, reports, policies, chat transcripts, articles, and documentation. Summarization—the act of extracting essential meaning from verbose input—is an indispensable skill for both humans and machines.

LLMs perform two broad types of summarization:

1. **Extractive Summarization**, which selects key sentences or phrases directly from the input.

2. **Abstractive Summarization**, which paraphrases and condenses the content using new language.

The latter is where LLMs shine. They can understand not just what was said, but what was *meant*—grasping core arguments, emotional undertones, and even implications.

Examples include:

- Summarizing a complex research paper into a single paragraph.
- Creating executive summaries from financial reports.
- Generating bullet points from customer feedback or survey results.

This capability is particularly transformative in enterprise and governance contexts, where decisions often rely on comprehending vast textual datasets in minimal time. LLMs augment cognitive capacity by offering distilled, human-readable insights at scale.

Importantly, LLMs can summarize across modalities too—combining inputs from text, images, and metadata—to generate rich overviews that humans would struggle to produce without significant effort.

Conversing: The Emergence of Natural Dialogue

Perhaps the most visible face of language models is their ability to engage in **conversation**.

Conversational ability requires more than generating grammatically correct sentences. It involves:

- **Context awareness**: Remembering and building upon previous turns in dialogue.
- **Intent inference**: Understanding the user's goals, even when not explicitly stated.
- **Tone control**: Matching the emotional register or professional context.
- **Turn-taking**: Knowing when to respond, ask clarifying questions, or remain silent.

Early chatbots operated through rules or decision trees—shallow simulations of conversation. LLMs, by contrast, offer dynamic, improvisational dialogue that feels authentic and personalized.

This evolution has enabled:

- Virtual assistants capable of multi-turn task completion.
- Therapy bots and mental health companions that offer empathetic engagement.
- Customer support agents that understand nuance and resolve issues without escalating.
- Educational tutors that adjust explanations based on student understanding.

In agentic systems, this conversational layer becomes the primary interface—allowing users to delegate tasks, query knowledge bases, or orchestrate workflows using natural language instead of menus and code.

As these systems become multimodal, the dialogue itself evolves into a richer form—combining voice, visual cues, gestures, and memory into seamless human-AI interaction.

A Unified Capability Stack

Though completion, translation, summarization, and conversation may seem like distinct tasks, they are all manifestations of the same core engine: a probabilistic understanding of language in context.

These capabilities reinforce one another:

- Summarization enhances conversation by helping the model recall key points.
- Translation enables global dialogue by bridging language gaps.
- Completion powers both summarization and conversation by generating relevant, coherent text.

Together, they form the foundation of any agentic AI system that hopes to assist or collaborate meaningfully with humans.

Language as Interface: Emotion, Empathy, and Context

Language is not just a conduit for conveying facts or instructions; it is also a bridge that carries the subtleties of human emotion, empathy, and context. These elements—often intangible yet deeply influential—shape how we understand each other and, consequently, how we interact with the world around us. In the realm of artificial intelligence, particularly large language models (LLMs), replicating this deeply human aspect of language is one of the greatest challenges and most exciting frontiers.

As we delve into how language functions as an interface between humans and AI, we encounter three essential layers: emotion, empathy, and context. These layers form the cornerstone of effective communication and, when integrated into AI systems, enable machines to move beyond rote answers and into nuanced, human-like interaction.

Emotion: The Subtle Undercurrent of Communication

In every conversation, emotion plays a foundational role, even if it's not overtly expressed. When we speak, we do more than just deliver information—we convey how we feel about what we're saying. This emotional subtext is often conveyed through word choice, tone, rhythm, and body language, but in text-based communication, much of it is embedded in the words themselves.

Imagine receiving a customer service response: "I understand you're upset. Let's resolve this issue together." The words themselves contain an implicit promise of understanding, care, and collaboration. They do more than just acknowledge the problem; they convey emotional support.

For an AI system to truly interact with humans, it must understand emotion at a deep level. Large language models, with their vast capacity to process and generate text, are now beginning to understand emotional nuance. Through techniques like **sentiment analysis**, LLMs can identify whether a piece of text carries a positive, negative, or neutral sentiment. But this is just the surface. True emotional understanding requires the model to go beyond recognizing words like "happy" or "sad." It demands an awareness of emotional tone in context. For instance, the sentence "I'm fine" could convey genuine contentment, a subtle plea for attention, or even sarcasm, depending on the surrounding context.

Advances in LLMs have enabled them to better interpret emotional cues in text, making them more adept at engaging with humans in emotionally intelligent ways. Whether in customer service, therapy chatbots, or personal assistants, the ability to read, respond to, and even simulate emotion is vital for creating meaningful, supportive interactions.

Empathy: Bridging the Gap Between Machine and Human

Empathy is often regarded as the ability to understand and share the feelings of others. It's a concept central to human relationships, fostering trust, connection, and communication. In the context of AI, empathy transcends the mechanical interpretation of language—it's about creating an illusion, or perhaps even a reality, of understanding.

For LLMs, empathy goes beyond sentiment analysis. It's about the model recognizing the human element in a situation and responding accordingly. This involves not only detecting emotion in text but also interpreting the intent behind that emotion. An empathetic AI would not simply recognize that a customer is frustrated—it would adapt its responses to help alleviate that frustration in an appropriate way, offering solutions, reassurance, or a calming tone.

Imagine an AI in a healthcare scenario: when a patient expresses anxiety about an upcoming procedure, an empathetic system would not just acknowledge the fear but would provide comforting and relevant information to ease the patient's mind. It could even offer emotional support by recognizing the tone of the patient's language and responding with appropriate care.

LLMs are increasingly trained on vast datasets that include diverse human emotions, experiences, and reactions, allowing them to recognize patterns that suggest underlying feelings. This allows AI to generate responses that feel more human, not just in factual content but in emotional engagement as well. However, true empathy—especially in complex, deeply personal situations—remains a challenge. While AI can simulate empathy by mimicking patterns seen in emotional responses, the deeply nuanced, human experience of empathy, with its layers of intuition, experience, and judgment, is a frontier that LLMs are still working toward understanding.

Context: The Key to Meaningful Interaction

Context is the key that unlocks meaning in language. Without context, words are just sounds or symbols with no inherent value. Take the word "bank"—it could refer to a financial institution, the side of a river, or a place to store resources. It's only through context that we understand which "bank" is being referred to.

In AI, context plays an even more significant role, particularly when dealing with language. LLMs, especially those built on the Transformer architecture, excel in contextual understanding. Their ability to process large swathes of text allows them to capture intricate details about what is being discussed, who is speaking, and what the goals of the conversation are. By keeping track of prior conversation turns, understanding linguistic patterns, and analyzing word placement, LLMs can generate highly relevant and contextually aware responses.

Context also extends beyond the text itself. In a multimodal AI system, context includes non-verbal signals like tone of voice, facial expressions, and body language, which enrich the overall interpretation of the interaction. In this way, AI is beginning to learn how to navigate conversations not just from a linguistic perspective but from a deeply human, holistic one.

In enterprises, context is essential for applying LLMs in meaningful ways. In customer service, for example, LLMs need to not only recognize the immediate request of a customer but also recall past interactions, preferences, and behavior. This enables systems to deliver personalized, efficient responses—making the customer feel heard and understood.

Emotion, Empathy, and Context: The Future of Human-AI Collaboration

The integration of emotion, empathy, and context into LLMs doesn't just improve the AI's conversational abilities—it enables a new dimension of interaction that feels genuinely human. Imagine a future where AI systems act as empathetic collaborators in our daily lives. Whether you're drafting an email, troubleshooting a problem, seeking advice, or learning a new concept, your AI assistant would be more than just a tool; it would be an understanding, responsive partner.

These human-like interactions bring significant implications for the workplace, healthcare, education, customer service, and beyond. Empathetic AI systems could lead to more effective and personalized healthcare, where virtual assistants provide emotional support alongside medical guidance. In education, they could offer tailored learning experiences that adjust to the emotional state and cognitive needs of students.

However, with this power comes a responsibility to ensure that AI systems are not just technically proficient but also ethically designed. The way AI interprets and responds to human emotion and context must be transparent, fair, and inclusive, ensuring that these systems respect privacy, avoid harmful biases, and operate with integrity.

Conclusion: The Art of Communication in AI

As LLMs evolve, the ability to replicate emotional intelligence, empathy, and contextual understanding will play a pivotal role in how we interact with machines. Language is not simply a tool for relaying facts; it is the very fabric through which we experience and interpret the world. By embedding these elements into AI systems, we can create technologies that feel more like trusted companions than impersonal tools—technologies that can genuinely enhance the way we live, work, and relate to one another.

A New Learning Paradigm

The field of artificial intelligence has undergone a monumental transformation over the past few years, largely driven by the shift from traditional rule-based systems to learning-based models. This shift is perhaps best exemplified by the emergence of **large language models (LLMs)** and their underlying **deep learning** architecture, which represent a radical departure from earlier approaches to machine learning and AI.

The Traditional Learning Model: Rules and Heuristics

In the early days of AI, systems were built upon a **knowledge-based** or **symbolic approach**. These systems relied on pre-defined rules, logic, and structured input. The development process was painstakingly manual: experts encoded knowledge in the form of rules, and the machine would execute them to produce output. While this method could work in narrowly defined tasks like playing chess or solving mathematical equations, it faltered in understanding human language, reasoning in complex contexts, or adapting to new, unforeseen situations.

Such rule-based systems were highly deterministic. They followed explicitly defined paths, with little to no ability to generalize or adapt beyond their narrow parameters. When confronted with ambiguity, variation, or new data, these systems would struggle.

The Rise of Statistical and Machine Learning Models

As AI researchers sought more flexible and adaptive solutions, they turned to **machine learning** — a paradigm where models "learn" patterns from data, rather than being explicitly programmed. The key distinction here is that **machine learning** doesn't rely on fixed rules but instead learns from examples.

Early machine learning models, such as **decision trees**, **support vector machines**, and **logistic regression**, could handle tasks like classification, regression, and basic pattern recognition. But even these models faced limitations when dealing with complex, high-dimensional data — particularly language. The sheer variability, nuance, and context embedded in natural language made it challenging for traditional machine learning methods to grasp its full complexity.

The Shift to Deep Learning: Learning from Layers

Enter **deep learning**, a breakthrough technology that brought about a new way of learning. Deep learning models, particularly **neural networks**, attempt to mimic the human brain's structure through layers of interconnected "neurons." These models have an inherent advantage in processing large amounts of data and recognizing patterns in complex inputs.

The shift to deep learning in the mid-2000s marked the beginning of a new learning paradigm in AI. Rather than relying on shallow, hand-crafted features, deep learning allowed systems to automatically extract features and learn hierarchical representations of data. Early successes in computer vision and speech recognition demonstrated the immense power of this approach.

Yet, despite its impressive capabilities, deep learning on its own still struggled with one of the most challenging tasks in AI: understanding and generating natural language in a coherent, context-aware manner.

Transformers: The Game Changer

The true leap in the evolution of language models came with the **Transformer architecture**, introduced in the 2017 paper *"Attention is All You Need."* The Transformer was a significant innovation because it moved away from the recurrent and sequential structure of previous models (like **RNNs** and **LSTMs**) and instead utilized **self-attention** mechanisms to process entire sequences of data at once.

In essence, Transformers allow models to simultaneously consider all parts of an input sequence (e.g., a sentence) at every step, capturing long-range dependencies and contextual information more effectively. This new architecture enabled the development of **unsupervised learning** techniques, where models could pre-train on massive amounts of text data without explicit labels.

The ability to learn from vast amounts of unstructured text — coupled with powerful **transfer learning** capabilities — marked the dawn of a new era in AI: one where models could generalize across a wide array of tasks without being explicitly retrained for each one.

Unsupervised Learning: Scaling Up Language Models

What makes LLMs particularly groundbreaking is their ability to learn in an **unsupervised** manner. Unlike traditional machine learning models that rely heavily on labeled data (i.e., data annotated with the correct answer), LLMs are trained on vast amounts of **raw text** pulled from diverse sources like books, articles, websites, and even social media. This allows them to internalize the structures, patterns, and relationships inherent in human language without needing explicit annotations.

This form of unsupervised learning allows these models to scale at an unprecedented level. As they are exposed to more and more data, LLMs "learn" the intricate nuances of language, culture, context, idiomatic expressions, and even world knowledge. This ability to process and generate text based on the patterns learned from the data opens up remarkable opportunities in a variety of domains — from content creation to legal analysis to customer support.

Pre-training and Fine-tuning: Tailoring Knowledge to Tasks

The pre-training phase is just one part of this new learning paradigm. Once LLMs have been pre-trained on large datasets, they undergo **fine-tuning**, a process where the model is adapted to specific tasks or domains. Fine-tuning allows LLMs to specialize in particular areas, such as medical diagnostics, financial forecasting, or customer service, by training them on more targeted datasets.

This fine-tuning process relies heavily on the **transfer learning** capability of LLMs. The pre-trained knowledge learned during the unsupervised phase can be transferred to a variety of downstream tasks, enabling the models to handle applications they weren't explicitly trained for. In many cases, fine-tuning requires far fewer data points than training the model from scratch, making LLMs not only powerful but also efficient.

Multimodal Learning: Beyond Language Alone

While the traditional paradigm focused primarily on **unimodal** learning (i.e., one type of data at a time, such as text or images), the latest models have begun to embrace **multimodal learning**. Multimodal models, such as **CLIP** (Contrastive Language-Image Pre-training) and **DALL·E**, combine language processing with image and even video understanding, broadening the scope of what AI systems can perceive and interact with.

This multimodal learning approach provides a more holistic, human-like understanding of the world. It enables AI systems to not only process and generate text but also to interpret images, make sense of video content, and draw connections across different types of media. For example, an AI trained in multimodal learning could automatically generate a textual description for a video clip, or translate text into a visual scene, facilitating new applications in content creation, accessibility, and beyond.

The Autonomous Learning Loop

One of the most exciting developments in the new AI learning paradigm is the rise of **agentic AI**. Traditional AI systems are typically reactive — they perform tasks based on predefined rules or learned data patterns. However, with the advent of LLMs and more advanced architectures, AI systems can take a more proactive, **autonomous** approach. These systems can now take actions in real-time based on their understanding of the environment and continuously learn and improve through interactions.

In agentic AI, models don't just passively respond to prompts or inputs; they actively participate in problem-solving, decision-making, and long-term planning. They can collect feedback, adapt to new information, and optimize their behavior across multiple tasks and domains. This opens up entirely new possibilities for industries where continuous learning and adaptation are critical, such as healthcare, finance, and autonomous vehicles.

A Future of Infinite Possibilities

This new learning paradigm is only the beginning. As models continue to grow in scale, sophistication, and multimodal capabilities, their ability to handle complex, unstructured problems will only improve. We're witnessing the early stages of a revolution where machines no longer simply respond to predefined rules but can reason, generate insights, and even create entirely new forms of knowledge — making the gap between human and artificial intelligence increasingly narrow.

In the next chapters, we will explore how these advancements are driving the evolution of language models, from the advent of deep learning to the transformative capabilities of LLMs in various industries. But first, let's delve deeper into what makes **language models** themselves so powerful and how their design reflects this new era of AI.

The Evolution of Language Models

The development of language models has been a journey of innovation, shifting from rigid rule-based systems to probabilistic approaches, and eventually leading to the emergence of neural networks and the Transformer architecture. This evolution has been marked by key breakthroughs that have propelled natural language processing (NLP) from theoretical concepts to practical, real-world applications capable of transforming industries and human-computer interaction.

From Rules to Probabilities

In the early days of AI, language models were built on rule-based systems. These systems relied on predefined grammatical rules and dictionaries to process language. If a machine was to understand text or speech, programmers would manually code a set of rules about syntax, semantics, and structure. This approach was logical but extremely limited. It could not account for the full richness of language, such as ambiguity, idioms, or the complexities of context. Moreover, these systems struggled to generalize across different domains and languages.

The next leap came with statistical models, which shifted the focus from explicit rules to patterns in language. Instead of relying on hand-coded rules, these models made use of large datasets to calculate probabilities. They analyzed vast amounts of text data to estimate the likelihood of certain sequences of words occurring together.

Statistical language models, such as **n-grams** (which predict the next word in a sequence based on the preceding *n* words), offered an improvement by capturing some of the local structure of language. However, they were still limited in their ability to understand long-range dependencies between words and struggled with rare or unseen word combinations.

This probabilistic approach represented a significant shift away from manual rule-setting, laying the foundation for more sophisticated models. However, the complexity of human language could not be fully captured by these methods alone. A more flexible and powerful approach was required, one that could process vast amounts of data, learn from context, and handle nuanced meanings.

Neural Networks Take the Stage

The arrival of **neural networks** in the mid-2000s marked a new era in AI and language modeling. Neural networks, particularly **recurrent neural networks (RNNs)**, were the first to attempt to model language in a way that approximated how humans process language. Unlike statistical models that consider each word in isolation, RNNs could take previous words in a sequence into account when making predictions about the next word. This allowed RNNs to model some degree of context and long-range dependencies.

However, while RNNs were a step forward, they still faced major challenges. One of the key problems was their difficulty in learning long-term dependencies, especially with sequences that involved hundreds or even thousands of words. To solve this, **Long Short-Term Memory (LSTM)** networks were developed. LSTMs introduced a mechanism to retain information over longer sequences, addressing the vanishing gradient problem and enabling models to better remember and use earlier parts of a sequence. LSTMs powered a variety of NLP applications, including machine translation, speech recognition, and text generation.

Despite their advancements, LSTMs still faced challenges. While they could model the relationships between words in a sequence, they were relatively slow and inefficient when it came to processing large datasets. In addition, LSTMs were designed to process language sequentially, meaning they read text one word at a time. This sequential nature made them less parallelizable and slower compared to newer approaches, particularly in the era of vast computational resources.

The breakthrough that would transform NLP, however, lay in a new architecture that abandoned the sequential nature of language processing altogether — the **Transformer** model.

The Transformer Breakthrough

The introduction of the **Transformer model** in 2017 by Vaswani et al., in the paper *Attention is All You Need*, marked a revolutionary moment in the development of language models. Unlike RNNs and LSTMs, which process data sequentially, the Transformer architecture uses **self-attention** mechanisms to simultaneously process all words in a sentence or sequence. This parallel processing ability makes Transformers not only faster but also much more effective at capturing long-range dependencies.

At the core of the Transformer's power is the **self-attention mechanism**, which allows the model to evaluate the relationships between all words in a sentence, regardless of their position. This means that the Transformer can weigh the importance of each word in relation to the others, even if they are far apart in the sentence. For example, in the sentence "The cat sat on the mat," a Transformer model can understand the relationship between "cat" and "sat" even if other words like "on" and "the" intervene. This ability to focus on the relevant words — the ones that matter most for a given task — is what gives Transformers their remarkable flexibility and efficiency.

The Transformer's parallelism is another key advantage. Instead of processing data word by word, like RNNs, it processes entire sentences or documents in one go, enabling faster training and inference. This is particularly important for scaling models to massive datasets — a critical factor in the rise of large language models (LLMs). With these advancements, the Transformer was able to train on much larger datasets and process more complex language patterns than its predecessors.

The architecture of the Transformer consists of **encoders** and **decoders**, each made up of multiple layers. The encoder reads the input sequence (the text, for example) and generates a representation of it. The decoder uses this representation to generate the output (whether it be translation, summarization, or some other task). Transformers can be trained end-to-end on tasks like translation, summarization, and question answering, where the model learns not only to understand the input text but also to generate meaningful responses.

The impact of the Transformer was immense. It provided the foundation for models like **BERT** (Bidirectional Encoder Representations from Transformers), **GPT** (Generative Pre-trained Transformer), and **T5** (Text-to-Text Transfer Transformer). Each of these models was based on the Transformer architecture and further refined its ability to understand and generate human language.

The **BERT model**, for example, took advantage of bidirectional training, allowing it to better understand the context of words by looking at the entire sequence before and after each word. Meanwhile, **GPT** leveraged a unidirectional approach, making it more suited for text generation. The combination of these innovations led to massive improvements in tasks such as machine translation, summarization, sentiment analysis, and more.

In just a few short years, the Transformer architecture has not only become the foundation of almost all state-of-the-art language models but has also unlocked new possibilities for how AI can understand and interact with human language. The scale at which these models now operate, along with their flexibility and power, has set the stage for the next chapter of AI — **large language models** (LLMs).

From Simple Tasks to Generalized Intelligence

While early language models could perform specific tasks — like answering questions or translating sentences — the arrival of models like **GPT-3** signaled a shift towards **generalized intelligence**. These models, with billions of parameters, could perform a wide range of tasks without requiring task-specific training. By simply prompting them with the right input, they could generate poetry, summarize complex articles, write code, and much more. This shift to generalized intelligence is one of the hallmarks of modern LLMs, and it represents a significant step forward in AI's ability to mimic human-like flexibility and creativity.

The **evolution of language models** from rule-based systems to the powerful, data-driven neural networks we see today illustrates the accelerating pace of innovation in AI. The Transformer architecture, in particular, has catalyzed a new era, enabling models to scale to levels of complexity and generalization that were once thought impossible. These advancements have not only transformed NLP but also reshaped the landscape of artificial intelligence as a whole, opening up new possibilities for AI-human collaboration, automation, and innovation.

The Rise of LLMs: GPT-1 to GPT-4 and Beyond

The story of large language models (LLMs) is one of exponential growth in both scale and sophistication. Just a few years ago, natural language processing (NLP) was largely dominated by smaller, domain-specific models that were capable of handling tasks like named entity recognition or simple question answering. But with the advent of **GPT-1** in 2018, a new era of AI was born. Since then, the field of LLMs has progressed at an unprecedented pace, fundamentally altering how machines understand and generate language.

GPT-1: The First Leap

The first major milestone in the rise of LLMs came with the release of **GPT-1** (Generative Pre-trained Transformer 1) by OpenAI in 2018. This model was based on the Transformer architecture, a breakthrough in deep learning that had revolutionized NLP by allowing models to process and understand long-range dependencies in text more effectively than previous models like RNNs or LSTMs.

GPT-1's breakthrough lay in its **unsupervised learning** approach. It was pre-trained on a massive corpus of text data, using a method known as **language modeling** — where the model learns to predict the next word in a sequence. This training was done without human annotations or task-specific data. Once pre-trained, GPT-1 could then be fine-tuned for specific downstream tasks, such as translation, summarization, or question answering, by exposing it to labeled examples. This approach represented a significant shift away from the task-specific architectures of the past, offering a more generalized model that could excel at a wide range of tasks with minimal adjustments.

While GPT-1 was groundbreaking in its design, it was relatively small by today's standards, with only 117 million parameters. However, its success laid the groundwork for future iterations, demonstrating that large, pre-trained models could achieve state-of-the-art performance on a variety of NLP tasks.

GPT-2: Scaling Up

In 2019, OpenAI released **GPT-2**, which took the core principles of GPT-1 and scaled them up significantly. GPT-2 was a much larger model, with 1.5 billion parameters — more than ten times the size of its predecessor. This increase in scale resulted in a marked improvement in performance, with GPT-2 producing more coherent and contextually relevant text than GPT-1.

One of the most significant features of GPT-2 was its ability to generate text that was remarkably fluent and human-like. It could write essays, generate stories, and even complete unfinished sentences with surprising accuracy. The model also showed an ability to generalize to new tasks with little to no fine-tuning, simply by being prompted with a task description in natural language. This shift in how models could be used — from task-specific training to general-purpose text generation — captured the imagination of the AI community and the public.

However, the release of GPT-2 was not without controversy. Due to concerns about the potential for misuse — such as generating misleading or harmful content — OpenAI initially withheld the full release of the model. This decision sparked debates about the ethics of AI development, and about how much control should be maintained over powerful models.

GPT-3: The Explosion of Potential

The true breakthrough came in 2020 with **GPT-3**, which boasted a staggering 175 billion parameters. This scale allowed GPT-3 to produce text that was not only human-like but often indistinguishable from text written by humans. GPT-3 was able to answer questions, write essays, generate creative content, and even code in multiple programming languages, all based on a simple text prompt.

GPT-3's power came from its scale, which enabled it to learn an immense variety of linguistic patterns and contextual cues from the vast amount of data it had been trained on. It was not just a language model, but a multi-purpose tool capable of performing a wide range of tasks without requiring task-specific training or fine-tuning.

But GPT-3 also revealed the limitations of large language models. While the model could generate impressive results, it was often inconsistent, sometimes producing irrelevant or nonsensical answers. It was also prone to biases and could amplify harmful stereotypes or produce factually incorrect information. These issues highlighted the need for better methods of controlling and fine-tuning LLMs, as well as the importance of addressing ethical concerns around their deployment.

Despite these challenges, GPT-3 marked a turning point in AI development, with its capabilities pushing the boundaries of what was considered possible in natural language understanding and generation.

GPT-4: Refining the Model

In 2023, OpenAI released **GPT-4**, further advancing the capabilities of large language models. GPT-4 built upon the lessons learned from previous iterations, with an even larger parameter count and enhanced fine-tuning techniques that allowed it to generate more accurate, coherent, and context-aware text.

GPT-4's improvements were particularly evident in its ability to handle more complex tasks, such as nuanced reasoning, maintaining context over longer conversations, and answering questions with greater factual accuracy. It also demonstrated improved handling of multiple languages and could generate high-quality content across a variety of formats, from technical writing to creative storytelling.

One of the key innovations in GPT-4 was its multimodal capabilities. Unlike its predecessors, which were purely text-based, GPT-4 could process not only text but also images, allowing it to understand and generate content across different types of media. This multimodal functionality opened the door to even more powerful applications in fields like education, healthcare, content creation, and beyond.

GPT-4 and Beyond: The Future of LLMs

As impressive as GPT-4 is, it is just the beginning of the next chapter in the evolution of LLMs. Researchers are already working on even larger and more sophisticated models, such as **GPT-5**, which will likely push the boundaries of general-purpose intelligence even further. These models will continue to improve in areas like factual accuracy, contextual understanding, and ethical considerations, and will likely introduce new capabilities, such as enhanced reasoning, emotional intelligence, and more effective human-machine collaboration.

However, with the increasing scale and complexity of LLMs comes an even greater responsibility to ensure that these technologies are developed and deployed in a way that benefits society. The risks associated with these models — including misinformation, bias, and misuse — will require thoughtful regulation, transparency, and ethical frameworks to guide their use.

Open Source Models and Global Alternatives

While OpenAI's GPT models have garnered significant attention, they are not the only players in the rapidly expanding world of LLMs. Over the past few years, the rise of **open-source models** has created an ecosystem of alternatives that are accessible to researchers, developers, and enterprises alike. These models allow for greater transparency, control, and flexibility in AI development, and they have become a major force in shaping the future of language technology.

Claude: A Challenger to GPT

One of the most prominent open-source alternatives to OpenAI's GPT models is **Claude**, developed by Anthropic. Named after Claude Shannon, the father of information theory, Claude was designed with a focus on safety and alignment. Anthropic aimed to build a model that could understand and generate language while minimizing the risks of harmful outputs, such as misinformation or biased content.

Claude's architecture is similar to GPT-3 and GPT-4, but with an emphasis on ethical considerations and safe deployment. It has quickly gained attention for its ability to generate high-quality text while adhering to stricter safety protocols.

Gemini: A Multi-Modal Approach

Gemini is another example of a cutting-edge LLM developed by **Google DeepMind**. Unlike GPT-4, which is largely focused on language, Gemini takes a more multimodal approach, incorporating both text and visual understanding. This allows Gemini to perform tasks that involve both language and images, such as interpreting diagrams, answering questions about pictures, and even generating images based on text prompts. The ability to seamlessly switch between multiple modalities positions Gemini as a major competitor in the LLM space, with applications ranging from content creation to healthcare and beyond.

Mistral: Efficiency and Open Access

One of the most exciting open-source models in recent years is **Mistral**, an innovative LLM developed by a community of researchers with a focus on efficiency and scalability. Unlike other large models, Mistral is designed to operate with fewer parameters, while still delivering impressive performance on language tasks. This makes it an attractive option for enterprises that require powerful language models without the computational overhead of massive models like GPT-4.

Mistral's open-source nature has also led to widespread adoption in academic and research communities, allowing for greater collaboration and innovation in AI development.

The Global Landscape: Beyond the West

While the U.S. and Europe have dominated the LLM landscape in recent years, there is a growing movement of models emerging from other parts of the world. **Baidu's Ernie**, **Huawei's PanGu**, and **Alibaba's Tongyi Qianwen** are all examples of LLMs developed by major Chinese tech companies, and they are making significant strides in their respective markets.

These global alternatives are important not only because they offer additional options for enterprises but also because they introduce different cultural, linguistic, and ethical perspectives into the development of LLMs. As AI continues to globalize, it is essential that the field incorporates a diverse range of voices and perspectives, ensuring that the technology is accessible, inclusive, and aligned with global values.

The Future of Open-Source LLMs

As the demand for customizable, transparent, and safe AI grows, open-source LLMs are poised to become even more important. They provide a way for developers and organizations to experiment with new ideas, fine-tune models for specific use cases, and ensure that AI is being built with accountability and ethical considerations in mind. The open-source movement is shaping the future of AI, making it more accessible to all while pushing the boundaries of innovation.

The rise of open-source models and global alternatives also signals the diversification of the LLM landscape. With a wider range of models to choose from, organizations and developers will be able to select models that best fit their needs — whether that's maximizing performance, ensuring safety, or promoting ethical practices.

Agentic AI: From Chat to Action

As artificial intelligence continues to evolve, a new paradigm is emerging — one that moves beyond static, reactive systems to intelligent agents capable of decision-making, action, and learning in real-time. This is the promise of **Agentic AI**, a concept that transforms traditional machine learning models into dynamic, autonomous entities. Rather than simply responding to inputs, agentic AI can take action, adapt to changing environments, and even initiate tasks based on its understanding of context, goals, and interactions.

What Is Agentic AI?

At its core, agentic AI refers to systems that can make decisions, plan actions, and carry out tasks autonomously or semi-autonomously. These systems go beyond just processing inputs and generating outputs (such as chat responses or text summaries) — they can interact with the world, influence outcomes, and evolve based on feedback.

The term "agentic" is rooted in the idea of an **agent** — a system that can act with purpose toward achieving specific goals. Unlike traditional models, which are often confined to specific, pre-defined tasks, agentic AI is capable of making decisions, learning from interactions, and adapting its behavior based on its environment and experience.

In the context of language models, agentic AI takes on a unique dimension. While large language models (LLMs) like GPT-4 can generate human-like text and respond intelligently to queries, agentic AI systems built on these models can move beyond passive conversation. They can *take actions* based on the conversation — making decisions, influencing other systems, or even initiating workflows in response to a user's needs.

From Chat to Action: The Evolution of Interactivity

Historically, AI systems have been used primarily for tasks like classification, prediction, or simple recommendation. They were powerful, but passive. The shift to agentic AI introduces a dynamic layer where systems are not just waiting for user inputs, but actively engaging with their environment, anticipating needs, and taking the next logical steps.

For instance, imagine a virtual assistant embedded within a corporate environment. Instead of merely answering questions or setting reminders, an agentic AI can initiate actions like drafting emails, scheduling meetings, handling customer inquiries, and even updating data in response to changing business metrics. It is no longer simply a tool for interaction; it becomes an active participant in the ongoing operations of the business.

The key to this shift lies in how agentic AI models are trained and structured. They are designed to not only process inputs but to interpret context, recognize goals, and take steps toward fulfilling those goals. This requires the integration of multiple AI components, such as:

- **Decision-making frameworks**: These allow the system to assess the best course of action based on available data.
- **Task-planning capabilities**: Enabling the AI to break down complex goals into actionable steps and to prioritize tasks accordingly.
- **Memory and learning algorithms**: Allowing the AI to retain prior interactions, learn from them, and adjust its behavior for improved performance over time.
- **Environmental sensing**: In some cases, agentic AI can interface with other systems, sensors, or APIs to gather real-time data that influences decision-making.

Practical Examples of Agentic AI

To understand the power of agentic AI, consider its application in various domains:

1. **Customer Support**: Traditional chatbots can only respond to customer queries with predefined responses. However, an agentic AI system can analyze customer complaints, suggest product improvements, initiate service requests, and even escalate issues to human agents when needed. Beyond just answering questions, it actively contributes to resolving

issues and improving the customer experience.

2. **Personal Assistants**: Virtual assistants like Siri or Alexa are examples of early-stage agentic AI, able to execute simple commands and provide responses based on user requests. However, the next wave of agentic assistants will take things further. These AI assistants could manage workflows, anticipate needs (such as setting up meetings based on prior conversations), handle multi-step tasks (like scheduling, drafting, and sending emails), and even negotiate or mediate on behalf of users.
3. **Healthcare**: In medical environments, agentic AI could be trained to interpret patient data (e.g., through electronic health records or wearables), suggest treatments, schedule follow-ups, and even alert medical personnel to anomalies. Beyond just offering suggestions, it can directly influence the care process, assisting doctors with decision-making or streamlining administrative tasks.
4. **Business Process Automation (BPA)**: In the business world, agentic AI could transform the automation landscape. Imagine an AI that doesn't just execute a series of instructions but actively manages and optimizes workflows. It can review reports, suggest efficiency improvements, make financial projections, and even alter business strategies based on real-time data. This goes far beyond traditional automation, creating a level of interactivity and adaptability that drives continuous improvement.
5. **Autonomous Vehicles**: Perhaps one of the most discussed examples of agentic AI is found in autonomous vehicles. These cars need to interact with their environment in real-time, making complex decisions based on sensor data, road conditions, and even social cues (like the behavior of pedestrians and other drivers). The ability of these vehicles to *act* — navigating, adjusting speed, and reacting to dynamic environments — is a direct consequence of agentic AI systems at work.

How Language Models Empower Agentic AI

Large language models like GPT-4 or specialized models trained for specific tasks form the backbone of agentic AI systems, particularly in how these systems understand and interact with human language. Language models provide the natural interface through which users interact with agentic systems. Here's how they play a crucial role:

- **Natural Communication**: Language models allow agentic AI to communicate with humans in natural language, making the interaction fluid and intuitive. Instead of needing specialized programming or commands, users can simply speak or type their instructions in everyday language.
- **Contextual Understanding**: By incorporating the vast contextual understanding that LLMs offer, agentic AI can grasp nuances in conversation, interpret ambiguous or incomplete instructions, and tailor its actions to the specific needs of the user.
- **Adaptive Learning**: With the ability to learn and adjust responses based on previous interactions, language models help agentic AI evolve, making it smarter and more capable over time. This adaptation enables these systems to handle increasingly complex scenarios and deliver more effective outcomes.

Challenges and Considerations

While the promise of agentic AI is immense, its development raises several challenges:

- **Complexity**: The integration of multiple AI components (decision-making, planning, learning, etc.) in a seamless way is a complex task. Agentic systems must balance flexibility with reliability, making the technology inherently difficult to design and deploy.
- **Ethical Concerns**: With greater autonomy comes greater responsibility. Agentic AI systems must be designed with ethical considerations in mind, ensuring that decisions made by AI align with societal values, fairness, and accountability.
- **Transparency**: As agentic AI systems grow more capable, they must remain transparent in their decision-making processes. Users should be able to understand why an AI made a particular choice or took a specific action — something that is challenging when working with highly complex models.
- **Safety**: Ensuring that agentic AI systems operate within safe bounds is critical. Systems that can take action autonomously need to be safeguarded against unintended consequences, errors, or malicious manipulation.

The Road Ahead for Agentic AI

The future of agentic AI is incredibly promising. As models continue to improve, and as more industries integrate these systems into their operations, we are likely to see an explosion in capabilities, ranging from highly interactive virtual assistants to fully autonomous systems that can make and execute decisions in real-world environments.

In the coming years, agentic AI will not only handle more sophisticated tasks but also develop richer, more personalized interactions with users. These systems will collaborate across industries, enhance human creativity, and solve some of the world's most pressing challenges. However, as we move from "chat" to "action," it will be critical to ensure that these systems remain aligned with human values, are transparent in their operations, and are developed with accountability and oversight.

Ethical and Societal Reflections

As the capabilities of large language models (LLMs) evolve, so too does the responsibility that comes with developing and deploying such powerful technologies. These advancements present incredible opportunities for enhancing human productivity, creativity, and decision-making. However, they also raise complex ethical and societal questions that must be addressed thoughtfully. The very nature of LLMs — their ability to process and generate human-like language — places them at the heart of some of the most pressing issues in technology today.

At their core, LLMs are reflections of the data they are trained on. They learn from vast datasets that encompass not only factual knowledge but also societal biases, historical prejudices, and cultural norms. While these models can be seen as tools for enhancing human capabilities, they also carry the potential to amplify existing inequalities, perpetuate misinformation, and erode privacy. The ethical implications of LLMs touch every corner of society, from business to healthcare, education to law, and even personal interactions.

Bias and Fairness

One of the most significant ethical concerns surrounding LLMs is their tendency to perpetuate biases present in the data they are trained on. Machine learning models, including language models, learn patterns from historical data, which can often reflect societal biases — whether intentional or not. These biases can manifest in subtle but impactful ways, such as when a language model inadvertently associates certain professions with a particular gender, or when it generates harmful stereotypes about specific social or ethnic groups.

For instance, a language model trained on a dataset containing biased or unrepresentative examples could generate content that reinforces negative stereotypes or exhibits discriminatory language. This could result in unintended harm, such as reinforcing existing power dynamics or marginalizing vulnerable groups. As LLMs become more deeply integrated into decision-making systems, such as hiring, law enforcement, or healthcare, the potential consequences of these biases are significant. A hiring algorithm that inadvertently favors one demographic over another could exacerbate inequalities in the workforce. Similarly, biased decision-making in healthcare could affect the quality of care provided to diverse populations.

To address these issues, it is crucial to implement strategies that reduce bias in training data, such as using more diverse and representative datasets, and to develop techniques for auditing and correcting biases in language models. Moreover, efforts to ensure fairness in AI must go beyond mere technical solutions; they require a broader societal commitment to understanding and addressing the root causes of inequality.

Privacy and Data Security

As LLMs are deployed in a wide range of applications, privacy concerns become more pressing. Language models are trained on vast amounts of publicly available and proprietary data, much of which may contain sensitive information. While many organizations implement safeguards to anonymize data during the training process, there is still a risk that models could inadvertently generate or infer private details.

For example, a language model trained on large datasets of medical records, conversations, or legal documents could unintentionally reveal confidential information. Moreover, the ability of LLMs to synthesize and generate human-like text raises concerns about the potential for misuse.

Malicious actors could use language models to create convincing fake news, deepfakes, or misinformation campaigns, all of which could have real-world consequences for individuals, organizations, and even governments.

Privacy issues also extend to the way LLMs interact with users. For instance, virtual assistants or chatbots powered by LLMs may collect and process personal information during interactions. Without clear transparency about data collection practices and robust privacy protections, users may unknowingly expose sensitive information, putting them at risk of exploitation or manipulation. This underscores the need for strong regulatory frameworks and industry best practices to protect privacy and ensure responsible data use.

Transparency and Accountability

As LLMs become more integrated into business operations, government services, and everyday life, the question of transparency becomes critical. How do we know that an AI system is making decisions in a fair, unbiased, and accountable manner? Language models are often seen as "black boxes" — their internal workings are complex, and it can be difficult to understand how they arrive at specific outputs. This opacity can be especially troubling in high-stakes areas such as criminal justice, healthcare, and finance, where AI-driven decisions can have life-altering consequences.

To address this, there is a growing demand for "explainable AI" (XAI), which seeks to make machine learning models more interpretable and understandable to humans. For LLMs, this could mean developing techniques that allow users to trace how a model arrived at a particular recommendation or decision. Such transparency not only helps build trust in AI systems but also allows for greater oversight, enabling stakeholders to identify and correct potential errors or biases.

However, transparency alone is not enough. Accountability mechanisms are equally important. When an LLM makes a mistake or causes harm, who is responsible? Should the developers of the model be held accountable for its outputs, or should the organizations that deploy the model bear responsibility? These questions are especially pertinent as LLMs become increasingly autonomous, capable of making decisions without direct human input. Clear guidelines for accountability, as well as robust mechanisms for recourse, are essential to ensuring that AI systems are used ethically and responsibly.

Misinformation and Manipulation

LLMs, with their ability to generate human-like text, present both opportunities and risks in the context of misinformation. While these models can be used to generate useful content, such as educational materials, news summaries, or even creative writing, they can also be exploited to produce deceptive or harmful content. For example, LLMs can be used to generate fake news articles, deepfake transcripts, or fraudulent emails that are indistinguishable from real communications.

The ease with which LLMs can produce realistic-sounding text raises concerns about their potential for misuse in spreading disinformation. In political campaigns, for example, bad actors could use LLMs to create misleading narratives or amplify divisive messages. Similarly, social media platforms could be flooded with AI-generated content designed to manipulate public opinion or incite conflict. Addressing this challenge requires both technological solutions, such as detecting AI-generated content, and regulatory measures that hold platforms accountable for the content they host.

Social Impacts: The Digital Divide

While the benefits of LLMs are vast, there is also the risk of exacerbating the digital divide. Access to advanced AI technologies, including LLMs, is not evenly distributed. Large corporations and well-funded research institutions are at the forefront of developing these systems, while smaller businesses, developing countries, and marginalized communities may not have the resources to take advantage of them.

This divide could lead to greater inequalities in education, healthcare, and economic opportunity. For example, organizations that have access to powerful language models can automate tasks, improve decision-making, and innovate in ways that others cannot. If AI technologies like LLMs are not made accessible and affordable to a broader range of people, it could further concentrate power in the hands of a few, deepening existing societal divides.

Efforts must be made to democratize access to LLMs and ensure that their benefits are distributed equitably. This could involve making open-source models available, investing in AI education and training for underrepresented groups, and ensuring that the deployment of LLMs is done in a way that benefits society as a whole, not just the privileged few.

The Future of Ethical AI

The ethical and societal implications of LLMs are not static; they will evolve as the technology itself continues to advance. New questions will arise about the role of AI in shaping public discourse, influencing elections, or automating key aspects of human decision-making. As we look to the future, it is essential that ethical considerations remain at the forefront of AI development.

The ongoing research into fairness, accountability, transparency, and privacy will be crucial in shaping the trajectory of LLMs and AI as a whole. Collaboration between technologists, ethicists, policymakers, and the public will be essential to ensure that the development of AI is aligned with the broader goals of society — goals that include justice, equality, human dignity, and well-being.

In conclusion, while LLMs represent an incredible leap forward in artificial intelligence, they come with significant ethical and societal challenges that must be addressed. As we continue to harness the power of these models, we must do so with a deep commitment to fairness, responsibility, and transparency, ensuring that the benefits of AI are realized without sacrificing the values that define our humanity.

What Lies Ahead?

As we stand at the threshold of an era defined by artificial intelligence, one thing is clear: the journey of language models and AI is far from over. In fact, it is just beginning. The rapid pace of technological advancements in AI, particularly in natural language processing (NLP) and large language models (LLMs), promises to reshape not only the way businesses operate but also how we interact with technology on a daily basis. But with this promise comes an array of challenges, opportunities, and unanswered questions about the future.

The Next Frontier: Beyond Text Generation

The current capabilities of large language models—such as generating text, answering questions, translating languages, and summarizing documents—are nothing short of remarkable. However, what we have seen so far is only the tip of the iceberg. As the underlying architectures evolve, we can expect LLMs to move beyond their text-based origins into new, more dynamic applications.

One of the most exciting frontiers is **multimodal AI**, where models not only process text but also understand and generate across different types of data—images, videos, audio, and even haptic feedback. By integrating multiple modalities, AI systems will be able to interpret the world in ways that mirror human perception. For example, a multimodal LLM could analyze a scene in an image, interpret the associated text, and even respond with voice or generate new visual content based on a given prompt. This could revolutionize fields ranging from creative industries (such as film and design) to healthcare (with models able to interpret medical imaging alongside patient notes).

Another significant avenue for growth is **personalized language models**. Today, LLMs can be fine-tuned for specific tasks, but they are still relatively generic in their ability to tailor responses to individual users' preferences, experiences, and cultural contexts. In the future, we will see more adaptive systems that continuously learn and evolve based on user interactions, providing highly personalized assistance. These models could integrate personal knowledge about preferences, styles of communication, and past interactions to create experiences that are uniquely tailored to each user, all while maintaining a strong emphasis on privacy and data security.

Moving Towards Autonomous Agents

One of the most intriguing aspects of the future of LLMs lies in their potential to evolve into fully **autonomous agents**. Today, language models like GPT-4 can generate text and answer questions with high accuracy, but they still lack a deeper understanding of the world or the ability to carry out tasks beyond what they've been trained on. However, as models become more sophisticated, they may develop the ability to not only engage in conversations but also perform tasks with minimal human intervention.

For instance, autonomous agents could be employed to automate complex business processes, such as customer service, content moderation, or even strategic decision-making. Imagine an AI system that reads through vast amounts of market data, identifies patterns, and provides executives with actionable insights — all without human oversight. These agents would act not just as tools, but as collaborators, making decisions, learning from outcomes, and optimizing strategies over time.

While we are still far from fully autonomous AI systems, the groundwork is being laid. As agentic AI continues to develop, it will bring with it new ethical dilemmas and challenges around trust, accountability, and decision-making. How do we ensure these systems make fair, ethical decisions? How do we maintain transparency and accountability in AI-driven choices? These are questions that must be addressed as AI moves towards greater autonomy.

Ethics and the Road Ahead

With every new leap in AI's capabilities, ethical considerations become increasingly critical. The deployment of large language models has already brought to light concerns regarding **bias**, **privacy**, and the **potential for misuse**. In the near future, as LLMs are incorporated into more sensitive sectors such as healthcare, finance, law, and even policing, the stakes will only get higher.

Bias is one of the most pervasive challenges in AI. Because large language models are trained on vast datasets scraped from the internet, they inevitably absorb and amplify societal biases, including gender, racial, and cultural prejudices. Even with the most careful curations, it's impossible to fully eliminate all biases, and the consequences of biased models in critical areas such as hiring, lending, and legal judgment could be profound. Therefore, ongoing efforts to create fairer, more transparent models must remain a top priority.

Privacy concerns also loom large. As LLMs gain the ability to personalize responses and interact with users more intimately, there is a growing need to ensure that sensitive data is protected. AI models must be designed to safeguard users' personal information, especially as the technology becomes integrated into applications like healthcare diagnostics, financial advising, and legal consultation.

The potential for **misuse** of AI is another pressing issue. While LLMs hold immense promise, they can also be weaponized. Misinformation, deepfakes, and automated scams are all becoming more prevalent as generative models evolve. The challenge, therefore, is not just about improving the capabilities of AI, but also about ensuring that these systems are used responsibly and for the benefit of society.

Cross-Domain Innovation

The impact of LLMs will not be confined to a single industry or application. We are entering an era of **cross-domain innovation**, where the integration of AI models across various fields will lead to new, unforeseen breakthroughs. Whether it's combining LLMs with robotics to create intelligent assistants capable of performing physical tasks or merging them with IoT (Internet of Things) to optimize industrial operations, the possibilities are vast.

For example, in the field of **healthcare**, LLMs will continue to evolve to interpret and summarize clinical data, provide personalized treatment recommendations, and even act as intelligent assistants to healthcare providers. But as AI is further integrated into the diagnostic process, questions will arise regarding accountability. Will a doctor's decision be considered valid if it was influenced by an AI's recommendation? How do we ensure the accuracy and ethical considerations of such decisions?

Similarly, in **education**, AI's role will become more profound, allowing for personalized learning experiences, real-time feedback, and curriculum development. LLMs could analyze a student's learning habits, strengths, and weaknesses to provide tailored educational content, transforming how we think about pedagogy. However, this also raises concerns around privacy and data security for minors and young adults.

AI and Human Collaboration: The Future of Work

Ultimately, the most transformative impact of LLMs will not be about replacing humans but enhancing human capabilities. **Human-AI collaboration** will define the future of work. Rather than viewing AI as a threat to jobs, businesses will increasingly see it as a tool to augment human potential.

This collaboration could take many forms: automated writing assistants that enhance content creation, AI-driven research assistants that help scientists and engineers explore new ideas, or virtual advisors that assist executives in making data-driven decisions. The key will be in designing systems that complement human strengths, such as creativity, empathy, and ethical judgment, while leaving the heavy lifting — the processing of vast amounts of data, analysis, and repetitive tasks — to AI.

As AI systems become more adept at understanding human language, they will also become better at interacting with people in a way that feels natural and intuitive. The relationship between humans and machines will no longer be adversarial or transactional. Instead, it will be collaborative, with each side contributing its unique strengths.

Looking to the Horizon

As we look ahead, the landscape of language models is rich with potential. We stand at the cusp of an era where AI will no longer just assist but collaborate with us to solve some of humanity's most pressing problems. The question is not if, but how we will build AI systems that are not only powerful but also ethical, fair, and transparent.

The road ahead is filled with excitement, uncertainty, and responsibility. As AI continues to evolve, it is up to all of us — researchers, developers, policymakers, and everyday citizens — to ensure that the language models of the future are developed in a way that benefits all of humanity.

The journey is just beginning, and the best is yet to come. The language of intelligence is here, and it is poised to change everything.

CHAPTER TWO

FOUNDATIONS — STATISTICAL LANGUAGE MODELS

What Are Statistical Language Models?

At the core of many artificial intelligence systems, particularly those dealing with text and language, lies the concept of a **language model**. A language model is essentially a probabilistic model that helps predict the likelihood of a sequence of words or tokens occurring in a sentence. Its primary task is to assign a probability distribution over sequences of words, enabling it to predict what comes next in a sequence given the previous words or to generate coherent and contextually relevant text.

Statistical language models represent the early and foundational approach to building such systems. They rely on statistical methods to analyze and predict the structure of language based on the frequency of word sequences in large corpora of text. Unlike earlier rule-based systems, statistical models learn from data by calculating the likelihood of word sequences occurring naturally within a given language. These models, while relatively simple compared to modern deep learning models, were instrumental in advancing the field of natural language processing (NLP).

How Statistical Language Models Work

Statistical language models operate by calculating the probability of a word or a sequence of words based on historical data. The basic idea is to estimate how likely a particular word (or series of words) is to follow a given context. This probability estimation is generally based on the occurrence of word patterns in a large corpus, often referred to as a "training corpus."

The simplest form of a statistical language model is the **unigram model**, where the probability of a word appearing is independent of the preceding words. More advanced models, however, capture dependencies between words, which leads to the use of **n-grams** and higher-order models.

1. **N-gram Models:**
   One of the most common types of statistical language models is the **n-gram model**, where "n" refers to the number of words taken into account for predicting the next word in the sequence. An **n-gram** model looks at a sequence of *n* consecutive words and estimates the probability of the next word occurring based on the preceding *n-1* words. For example:

   - In a **bigram** model (n=2), the probability of the next word depends on just the previous word:
     $P(w_n | w_{(n-1)})$
   - In a **trigram** model (n=3), the probability of the next word depends on the previous two words:
     $P(w_n | w_{(n-2)}, w_{(n-1)})$

The more context you include (i.e., the larger the value of n), the more accurately the model can predict the next word in a sentence. However, there are trade-offs: as n increases, the model requires exponentially more data to estimate probabilities accurately.

1. **Estimating Probabilities:**
   In statistical language models, probabilities are typically estimated using the frequency of word occurrences in the training corpus. For example, in a bigram model, the probability of the word "**dog**" following "**the**" is estimated as the relative frequency of the bigram "**the dog**" in the training data:

P(dog | the)=Count(the dog)Count(the)P(\text{dog} | \text{the}) = \frac{\text{Count(the dog)}}{\text{Count(the)}}P(dog | the)=Count(the)Count(the dog)

If a particular word combination does not appear in the training corpus, many models use **smoothing techniques** to adjust the probability estimation. One common approach is **Laplace smoothing**, which ensures that no word combination has zero probability, even if it never appeared in the training data.

The Importance of Context

While simple unigram models treat words as independent, real-world language is inherently contextual. Words rarely appear in isolation, and their meaning often depends on the surrounding words. This is where **higher-order n-gram models** come into play. They are more sophisticated than unigram models because they account for the relationships between words in context.

For example, the probability of the word "**bank**" will depend on whether the preceding context suggests the meaning of a financial institution or a riverbank. In a statistical model, this dependency is captured by n-grams, where the occurrence of specific word sequences provides insight into the most likely meaning of ambiguous terms.

Statistical language models can capture short-range dependencies between words, but they struggle with long-range dependencies or maintaining coherent context over longer stretches of text. This is one of the primary limitations of n-gram models.

Limitations of Statistical Language Models

While n-gram models made significant progress in language modeling, they have some notable limitations:

1. **Sparsity Problem:**
   As n increases, the number of possible word combinations grows exponentially. Even with large corpora, many word combinations will never appear in the training data. This leads to **sparsity** — an issue where the model cannot estimate probabilities for all possible word combinations. Smoothing methods help alleviate this to some extent, but they do not entirely solve the problem.

2. **Contextual Limitation:**
   Statistical models based on n-grams can only account for short-term context (the immediate surrounding words). However, language often requires understanding of longer dependencies. For instance, grammatical agreement, metaphors, or even the subject of a sentence can span several words or even sentences, which traditional statistical models may fail to capture.
3. **Memory Usage:**
   Storing all n-grams in memory for higher-order models (especially for very large corpora) becomes computationally expensive. As the value of n increases, so does the memory and computational complexity required to estimate probabilities. This presents a scalability problem when applying these models to large datasets or real-time applications.
4. **Inability to Handle Rare Words:**
   N-gram models struggle when dealing with rare or unseen words, which is a common problem in NLP tasks. Even with smoothing techniques, the model might fail to generalize well to new vocabulary, especially in domains that involve jargon, slang, or emerging terminology.

Applications of Statistical Language Models

Despite their limitations, statistical language models have been crucial in laying the groundwork for more advanced natural language processing techniques. They have been used in a variety of applications, including:

- **Speech recognition:** Predicting the most likely sequence of words given an audio signal.
- **Text generation:** Producing coherent text, for instance, completing a sentence or generating a paragraph based on an initial prompt.
- **Machine translation:** Translating text from one language to another by leveraging the statistical probabilities of word sequences in both languages.
- **Information retrieval:** Ranking search results based on the likelihood of the search query matching documents in a corpus.

While newer, more complex models — such as neural networks and large language models — have surpassed statistical language models in many tasks, these models are still valuable for simpler, less resource-intensive applications, and they provide a foundational understanding of how language models operate.

Conclusion

Statistical language models represent a key milestone in the evolution of natural language processing. They demonstrated that by analyzing word frequencies and patterns, machines could approximate human understanding of language. However, as NLP progressed, these models revealed their limitations, particularly when it came to handling long-term dependencies and large-scale contextual understanding. They paved the way for the development of more sophisticated techniques, such as neural networks and deep learning-based models, which are now the backbone of modern AI systems.

Predictive Power Through Probability

At the core of all language models, whether statistical or neural, lies a fundamental idea: **probability**. Language, by nature, is a system of patterns and structures, and predicting what comes next in a sequence of words — or what a word means in a particular context — boils down to understanding these patterns. Statistical language models harness the power of probability theory to capture and predict these patterns based on data.

In its most basic form, a **statistical language model** attempts to estimate the likelihood of a given word or sequence of words occurring in a particular context. This prediction is based on the frequency of occurrences in large corpora of text and relies heavily on the statistical properties of language. By analyzing these frequencies and patterns, the model can generate plausible text, predict the next word in a sentence, or estimate the likelihood of a sentence being grammatically correct.

The Essence of Probability in Language Modeling

Language modeling is, essentially, the task of assigning probabilities to sequences of words. For example, if you were given the sentence "The cat sat on the ___," a statistical language model would assign a higher probability to words like "mat" or "floor" than to less probable completions like "moon" or "cloud." This is because, based on the vast amount of text data the model has learned from, it recognizes that certain word combinations are more frequent and natural in our language.

The core idea behind statistical language models is rooted in **Markov Chains**, a mathematical framework where the probability of an event (in this case, the next word in a sequence) depends only on the current state (the preceding word or words). In language, this means that the probability of the next word depends on the words that have come before it, though often in a limited context (the last word, a few words, or an entire phrase).

However, language isn't as simple as just looking at the immediately preceding word. The challenge of modeling language involves capturing longer-range dependencies and nuanced contexts — something that basic models like **n-grams** can handle to a limited extent, but which more advanced models like **Hidden Markov Models (HMMs)** and **Conditional Random Fields (CRFs)** attempt to address with greater sophistication.

N-Gram Models: The Building Blocks of Statistical Language Models

N-gram models are one of the earliest and most common types of statistical language models. In an n-gram model, the idea is simple: the probability of a word depends on the previous **n-1** words. For example, in a **bigram model** (where n = 2), the probability of a word is conditioned on the immediately preceding word, as in:

- P(w_n | w_{n-1}) = probability of word n given word n-1.

Similarly, in a **trigram model** (where n = 3), the probability of the next word is conditioned on the two preceding words, and so on for higher-order n-gram models. The key advantage of n-grams is their simplicity and ability to quickly estimate the probability distribution of word sequences.

However, n-gram models are not without limitations. As n increases, the model captures more context, but it also becomes exponentially larger and more sparse, requiring vast amounts of data to remain effective. Moreover, they struggle with capturing long-term dependencies, as their memory is restricted to a fixed window of words.

Hidden Markov Models (HMMs): Adding Structure and Context

To address the limitations of n-grams, **Hidden Markov Models (HMMs)** introduce a more sophisticated structure. HMMs assume that the sequence of words in a sentence is governed by a set of hidden states, and that each state generates an observable output (in this case, a word). Unlike n-grams, which treat words as independent and equally likely based on the immediate context, HMMs add a layer of structure by modeling sequences of words as part of a larger probabilistic process.

HMMs are particularly useful for tasks like **part-of-speech tagging**, **speech recognition**, and **named entity recognition**, where the model needs to consider both the current word and its potential role in a larger sentence structure. The hidden states in an HMM can represent grammatical categories (such as noun, verb, adjective) or other abstract concepts, allowing the model to better capture the syntactic and semantic relationships between words.

Conditional Random Fields (CRFs): Further Enhancing Context

To refine the contextual understanding further, **Conditional Random Fields (CRFs)** extend the idea of HMMs by considering not only the current state but also the entire sequence of words in the context of the surrounding words. In a CRF, the probability of a word sequence is conditioned on the full sequence of previous words, rather than just a small window or hidden states. This allows CRFs to more accurately capture long-range dependencies in language, making them effective for tasks such as **information extraction**, **sequence labeling**, and **image segmentation**.

CRFs are particularly powerful because they can incorporate both structured input features (e.g., word morphology, part-of-speech tags, syntactic trees) and unstructured input (e.g., raw text) to generate more accurate predictions. By considering the broader context, CRFs can overcome the limitations of n-grams and HMMs in tasks where the relationship between distant words matters.

Word Embeddings: Capturing Meaning Beyond Surface Form

While traditional statistical models like n-grams, HMMs, and CRFs focus on word sequences and probabilities, **word embeddings** offer a powerful enhancement by modeling the meaning of words. Instead of relying purely on frequency counts, word embeddings map words to continuous vector spaces where semantically similar words are closer together.

One of the most popular techniques for generating word embeddings is **Word2Vec**, which uses a shallow neural network to learn a dense vector representation of each word based on its surrounding words in a large corpus. Another widely-used approach is **GloVe** (Global Vectors for Word Representation), which also creates vector embeddings but does so by factoring in the global co-occurrence statistics of words in the corpus.

Word embeddings have revolutionized statistical language modeling by providing richer, more nuanced representations of words that go beyond their surface forms. This allows models to better understand synonyms, antonyms, and contextual variations of meaning — something n-grams alone cannot easily capture.

Limitations and Challenges of Statistical Language Models

Despite their success in many applications, statistical language models have inherent limitations:

1. **Sparsity**: As the size of the corpus grows and the model needs to capture higher-order n-grams or more complex dependencies, the required data grows exponentially. This can lead to sparse data issues, especially for lower-frequency word combinations.
2. **Lack of Long-Term Memory**: Even more advanced models like CRFs are still limited by their inability to fully capture long-range dependencies, which can be crucial for tasks that require deep contextual understanding.
3. **Fixed Context Window**: While n-grams can capture local context, they fail to consider the broader context in which words appear. Statistical models also struggle with ambiguity, where the meaning of a word changes depending on the broader sentence or conversation.

4. **Lack of Generalization**: Traditional statistical models heavily rely on the specific dataset on which they were trained, which means they may struggle to generalize to new or unseen data.

The Future of Statistical Language Models

While newer models, especially neural network-based architectures like the Transformer, have begun to take center stage, statistical language models are far from obsolete. They remain foundational for understanding the early principles of language modeling, and their simplicity, efficiency, and interpretability make them valuable tools in certain domains.

Moreover, they offer important lessons in probability and pattern recognition that continue to inform the development of more advanced models. In fact, statistical methods are often used in tandem with deep learning techniques to enhance model accuracy and efficiency.

In the future, we can expect further advances in statistical language models, potentially incorporating hybrid architectures that combine the power of **neural embeddings** with **traditional statistical approaches** to enhance both their flexibility and predictive power.

Conclusion

Statistical language models have paved the way for the current era of advanced AI, providing essential tools for understanding and predicting human language. By leveraging the predictive power of probability, these models have helped shape the field of natural language processing and continue to influence modern AI systems. However, as the complexity of language and the need for context grows, new techniques — particularly those based on deep learning — are extending the boundaries of what language models can achieve. Understanding the foundation laid by statistical models is crucial as we continue to build more intelligent, context-aware systems capable of collaborating with humans on a deeper level.

N-Grams and the Simplicity of Sequence

Before the dawn of neural networks and deep learning, statistical methods were at the forefront of language modeling. These early models laid the groundwork for the complex algorithms that power modern large language models (LLMs) today. The N-Gram model, one of the simplest and most intuitive statistical approaches, remains a key concept in understanding how machines can model language.

At its core, an **N-Gram** model is based on the idea that the probability of a word occurring in a given context can be estimated by looking at the preceding words — or **n-1 words** — in a sequence. In simple terms, it is a method that assumes that language is predictable based on the immediate history of words. This assumption is the foundation for predicting the next word in a sentence, given the previous ones.

What is an N-Gram?

An N-Gram is a contiguous sequence of *n* items (words, characters, or other linguistic units) in a given text or speech sample. In language modeling, these "items" are typically words, though they could also be characters or subword units depending on the granularity of the model. The value of *n* determines the size of the context window that the model uses to make predictions.

Here's how it works:

- **Unigram (1-Gram):** The model only looks at individual words, ignoring the context of other words. It assumes that each word is independent of the others.
- **Bigram (2-Gram):** The model considers the previous word to predict the next. For example, in the sentence "I love programming," a bigram model would look at the pair "I love" to predict "programming."
- **Trigram (3-Gram):** The model looks at the previous two words to predict the next one, making it more contextually aware than bigrams.

The larger the value of *n*, the more context the model uses. A trigram model looks at the last two words before predicting the next word, while a four-gram model would consider the last three. This means a higher *n* captures richer contextual information, but it also increases the computational complexity.

The Simplicity of Sequence

The appeal of N-Gram models lies in their simplicity and their ability to capture local dependencies — the relationship between words that appear near each other. For instance, in English, the word "dog" is often followed by words like "barked" or "chased," but rarely by words like "runway" or "watermelon." By analyzing the sequence of words in this way, N-Gram models can learn useful patterns that help predict the next word based on what came before it.

However, N-Grams rely on the fundamental assumption that **language can be adequately modeled as a sequence of adjacent words**, with no long-range dependencies or deep understanding of the structure of sentences. This assumption simplifies the modeling process, but it also limits the model's capacity to capture more complex linguistic structures, such as:

- **Ambiguity:** The same word can have different meanings depending on its context (e.g., "bark" as in "dog bark" versus "tree bark").
- **Long-distance dependencies:** Some words or phrases have meanings that depend on other parts of the sentence, often separated by several words (e.g., subject-verb agreement or resolving pronouns like "she" referring to "Mary").

The Probabilistic Nature of N-Grams

N-Gram models are based on the idea of **probability theory**, specifically conditional probabilities. The goal is to estimate the likelihood of a word occurring given the previous *n-1* words in a sequence.

In a Bigram model, for instance, the model calculates the probability of a word wiw_iwi given the preceding word wi−1w_{i-1}wi−1, denoted as:

P(wi ∣ wi−1)=Count(wi−1,wi)Count(wi−1)P(w_i | w_{i-1}) = \frac{\text{Count}(w_{i-1}, w_i)}{\text{Count}(w_{i-1})}P(wi ∣ wi−1)=Count(wi−1)Count(wi−1,wi)

This formula essentially tells us the probability of word wiw_iwi following wi−1w_{i-1}wi−1, based on how frequently the pair appears in the training data. If the pair is very common (like "I am"), the model will predict it with a high probability. Conversely, rare pairs (like "elephant apple") will have a low probability.

For **larger N-Grams**, this probability formula extends to include the preceding *n-1* words. A Trigram model, for example, calculates the probability of a word wiw_iwi given the previous two words wi−2w_{i-2}wi−2 and wi−1w_{i-1}wi−1:

P(wi ∣ wi−2,wi−1)=Count(wi−2,wi−1,wi)Count(wi−2,wi−1)P(w_i | w_{i-2}, w_{i-1}) = \frac{\text{Count}(w_{i-2}, w_{i-1}, w_i)}{\text{Count}(w_{i-2}, w_{i-1})}P(wi ∣ wi−2,wi−1)=Count(wi−2,wi−1)Count(wi−2,wi−1,wi)

The key challenge in N-Gram models is ensuring that these probabilities are estimated from sufficient data. **Sparsity** is a common issue: for any given sequence, there may be many possible word combinations that never appear in the training set, resulting in zero probabilities for certain combinations. To address this, smoothing techniques like **Laplace smoothing** or **Good-Turing smoothing** are used to adjust the probabilities of unseen sequences.

Limitations of N-Grams

While N-Gram models are a cornerstone of statistical language modeling, they come with a set of inherent limitations:

- **Context limitation:** The model's ability to predict the next word is constrained by the fixed-size window of prior words. It doesn't account for long-range dependencies or broader linguistic structures. For instance, in a sentence like "She put the book on the table," an N-Gram model may struggle to correctly predict "table" based on just "put the book on."
- **Data inefficiency:** As *n* grows larger, the number of possible sequences grows exponentially, leading to increased data requirements. For instance, a trigram model requires more data than a bigram model to capture sufficient context, and a 4-gram model requires even more.
- **Fixed context size:** N-Grams do not adapt based on the structure of the sentence. A bigram model doesn't "understand" that some sequences of words are more contextually relevant than others.

Despite these challenges, N-Gram models were a huge step forward in the evolution of language processing. They provided a **statistical** approach to modeling language that enabled machines to begin making predictions based on prior context, even though the models themselves lacked deep understanding of the language.

From N-Grams to Neural Networks

While N-Grams laid the foundation, they are far from the most powerful tools available today. The simplicity of N-Gram models — their reliance on relatively short, fixed contexts — limits their applicability to more complex language tasks. With the advent of **neural networks** and **deep learning**, the landscape of language modeling underwent a dramatic transformation, enabling models to capture much more complex relationships and dependencies across words and sentences.

However, understanding N-Grams remains crucial. They serve as the **building blocks** from which many of the most sophisticated language models are constructed, and they continue to provide a useful, interpretable baseline in certain applications, such as in **speech recognition**, **spell checking**, and **machine translation**.

Conclusion

The N-Gram model stands as a simple, yet powerful, method for predicting language sequences based on probability. By focusing on local word relationships, it demonstrated that language could be modeled statistically, setting the stage for more sophisticated approaches. However, as we will explore in later chapters, the limitations of N-Grams — particularly their inability to capture long-range dependencies and complex contextual information — led to the development of more advanced models that would revolutionize how machines understand and generate human language.

Hidden Markov Models and Sequence Learning

Hidden Markov Models (HMMs) were once one of the fundamental approaches to sequence learning, particularly in the realm of language processing. While they have been somewhat superseded by more sophisticated models like neural networks and transformers, they remain an important part of the history of natural language processing (NLP) and continue to offer insights into how sequential data can be modeled probabilistically.

The Basics of Hidden Markov Models (HMMs)

At their core, Hidden Markov Models are a statistical tool used to model systems that evolve over time, where the system's true state is hidden, but we can observe outputs that provide information about these states. The "Markov" aspect refers to the property of the model that assumes the future state depends only on the current state, not on the sequence of events that preceded it. This is known as the **Markov property**.

In an HMM, there are two key elements:

- **States**: These are the hidden aspects of the system. In the case of language, these could represent different parts of speech (e.g., noun, verb, adjective) or grammatical structures (e.g., subject, object, predicate).
- **Observations**: These are the observable outputs, which are typically words or tokens in a sentence. The system's observable state is assumed to provide some probabilistic evidence about the underlying hidden state.

The process of learning in an HMM involves estimating both the hidden states and the likelihood of transitions between these states, based on observed sequences. For instance, in speech recognition, the sequence of spoken words (observable data) can be modeled as a sequence of underlying phonetic states (hidden states).

Components of a Hidden Markov Model

1. **States**: These are the unobservable components that represent the "true" configuration of the system at any given time. For example, in part-of-speech tagging, the states could represent categories like "noun," "verb," or "adjective."
2. **Transitions**: These are the probabilities that describe how the system moves from one hidden state to another. The probability of transitioning from one state to the next is governed by a **transition matrix**, which contains the likelihoods of moving from one state to another at each time step.

3. **Observations**: Each hidden state produces an observable output, typically referred to as an observation. For example, if the hidden state is "noun," the observable output might be a word like "dog" or "car." The observations are governed by an **emission matrix**, which defines the probability of observing a particular word given the hidden state.
4. **Initial States**: At the beginning of a sequence, there is a probability distribution over the possible initial states. For example, in language modeling, this could represent the likelihood of starting with a noun, verb, or some other part of speech.

How HMMs Work

HMMs work by applying the **Markov assumption**, which states that the future state depends only on the current state and not on the sequence of events that came before it. Given this assumption, the HMM can compute the probability of a sequence of observations by considering:

- The probability of starting in each initial state.
- The probability of transitioning from one hidden state to another.
- The likelihood of observing the observed word given the current hidden state.

In language processing, this might look like modeling the probability of a sequence of words based on their corresponding part-of-speech tags. If we know the first word in a sentence is likely to be a noun, and the second word is more likely to be a verb, HMMs can compute the probability of the sequence based on these hidden states.

Training an HMM

Training an HMM involves estimating the parameters that govern the model — namely, the **transition probabilities** between hidden states and the **emission probabilities** between hidden states and observations. The parameters are typically learned from a corpus of labeled data using techniques like the **Baum-Welch algorithm**, which is a special case of the **Expectation-Maximization (EM)** algorithm.

Sequence Learning with HMMs

One of the defining features of HMMs is their ability to handle **sequential data**. Sequences are inherently important in language, as the meaning of words often depends on the order in which they appear. For example, in the sentence "The cat sat on the mat," the sequence of words plays a crucial role in determining the overall meaning.

Sequence learning refers to the ability of a model to learn from ordered data, where each element is influenced by the ones that came before it. In the case of language, this means that the meaning of one word often depends on its position relative to others. This type of learning can be applied in many NLP tasks, such as:

- **Part-of-speech tagging**: Identifying whether a word is a noun, verb, adjective, etc.
- **Named entity recognition (NER)**: Identifying entities like person names, locations, or dates.
- **Speech recognition**: Mapping sequences of spoken sounds (phonemes) to words.

In these tasks, sequence learning via HMMs helps to understand how the preceding elements in the sequence constrain the interpretation of the current element.

Challenges of HMMs in Sequence Learning

While HMMs were an important step in sequence modeling, they have several limitations:

- **Limited to linear dependencies**: The Markov assumption implies that the current state depends only on the previous state, which can be a limitation when long-term dependencies exist between words or phrases. For example, the relationship between "The cat" and "sat" might be obscured by intervening words, yet these dependencies are crucial for understanding sentence meaning.
- **Fixed structure**: HMMs require a predefined number of states, which makes them less flexible in handling the vast variability in language. For example, in more complex tasks like machine translation, the number of

possible "states" is essentially infinite.
- **Difficulty with context**: HMMs do not handle context well when it stretches beyond local windows of observation. This issue becomes especially noticeable in tasks like sentiment analysis, where broader context (e.g., the entire paragraph) might be necessary to accurately interpret a statement.

Despite these limitations, HMMs were a key advancement and paved the way for more sophisticated methods in sequence modeling, like **Recurrent Neural Networks (RNNs)**, which can capture longer dependencies and handle variable-length sequences.

HMMs in the Context of Language Models

In the broader context of language modeling, HMMs served as a stepping stone. They are based on the idea that language can be modeled as a sequence of states and observations, and they helped lay the foundation for more complex models that handle language more naturally.

- **N-gram models** and **HMMs** both aim to predict the likelihood of sequences of words, but HMMs bring a probabilistic structure to this task, focusing on the hidden states that govern transitions between word categories or grammatical roles.
- While modern language models, such as transformers, have far surpassed HMMs in handling complex dependencies, HMMs are still instructive for understanding how probabilistic sequence models work at a fundamental level.

Conclusion: The Legacy of HMMs in Sequence Learning

Hidden Markov Models represent a pivotal development in the history of NLP. They were among the first tools that allowed us to model language as a probabilistic sequence, where the flow of information is determined by the hidden states governing word transitions. While they have been eclipsed by more sophisticated models in many applications, the principles they established continue to inform the development of modern language models, especially in areas where sequence learning is critical.

Conditional Random Fields for Structured Output

In the evolving landscape of natural language processing (NLP), machine learning techniques are often employed to extract structured information from unstructured text. While simpler models, such as hidden Markov models (HMMs) or n-gram models, offer some initial insights into sequential data, they often fall short when tasked with handling complex, context-dependent outputs. This is where **Conditional Random Fields (CRFs)** come into play, providing a robust framework for predicting structured output — an essential requirement in many real-world NLP tasks, such as named entity recognition (NER), part-of-speech tagging, and syntactic parsing.

What Are Conditional Random Fields?

Conditional Random Fields are a type of discriminative probabilistic model designed to predict a sequence of outputs given a sequence of inputs. Unlike generative models (such as HMMs), which model the joint distribution of both the inputs and the outputs, CRFs focus solely on modeling the conditional probability of the output sequence given the input sequence. This distinction allows CRFs to avoid the assumptions that generative models make about the input distribution, which can lead to errors in real-world applications where inputs are noisy or have complex dependencies.

In essence, CRFs are used for sequence labeling tasks, where the goal is to predict a sequence of labels (or tags) for a sequence of observed data points, ensuring that the labels follow a coherent structure. This structure is especially valuable in NLP tasks where the output is not independent from one element to another but must satisfy specific dependencies.

The Mathematical Formulation of CRFs

The core idea behind CRFs is to define a conditional probability distribution over a set of output labels given a sequence of input features. In formal terms, given a sequence of observed inputs X={x1,x2,...,xT}X = \{x_1, x_2, ..., x_T\}X={x1,x2,...,xT} (such as a sequence of words) and a corresponding sequence of labels Y={y1,y2,...,yT}Y = \{y_1, y_2, ..., y_T\}Y={y1,y2,...,yT} (such as part-of-speech tags), a CRF computes the conditional probability P(Y | X)P(Y | X)P(Y | X).

This probability is modeled as:

P(Y | X)=1Z(X)exp (∑t=1T∑kλkfk(yt,yt−1,xt))P(Y | X) = \frac{1}{Z(X)} \exp \left(\sum_{t=1}^T \sum_{k} \lambda_k f_k(y_t, y_{t-1}, x_t) \right)P(Y | X)=Z(X)1exp(t=1∑Tk∑λkfk(yt,yt−1,xt))

Here:

- fk(yt,yt−1,xt)f_k(y_t, y_{t-1}, x_t)fk(yt,yt−1,xt) represents a feature function that captures relevant information at time ttt, such as the transition between labels yt−1y_{t-1}yt−1 and yty_tyt, or the observed input xtx_txt.
- λk\lambda_kλk is the weight of the feature function, which is learned during the training process.
- Z(X)Z(X)Z(X) is the normalization factor (also called the partition function) that ensures the sum of probabilities across all possible label sequences equals 1.

This formulation captures the dependency between adjacent labels in the sequence, making it well-suited for tasks where label dependencies are critical, such as sequential tagging or labeling tasks in NLP.

Why CRFs Are Effective for Structured Output

One of the key advantages of CRFs is their ability to capture dependencies between output labels, which is essential for structured prediction tasks. In many NLP applications, the output is not independent but must follow certain constraints or patterns. For example, in named entity recognition (NER), the likelihood of one word being part of an organization name often depends on the surrounding words (e.g., "Google" and "Inc." are more likely to occur together as part of the same entity).

Traditional models like HMMs or n-grams struggle with these dependencies because they treat each output label independently. CRFs, on the other hand, model the relationship between adjacent labels, allowing them to incorporate contextual information and ensure consistency in the output.

For instance, in part-of-speech tagging, a CRF can recognize that certain words are more likely to follow specific tags. The word "quick" is more likely to follow a determiner (e.g., "The quick brown fox") than a verb (e.g.,

"She quick ran"). CRFs effectively capture such contextual dependencies by modeling the relationship between adjacent tags.

Feature Functions in CRFs

A powerful aspect of CRFs is their flexibility in defining feature functions. These functions can encode a wide range of information that is useful for making predictions. Feature functions can include:

- **State-based features:** These functions depend only on the current word and its assigned label. For example, in named entity recognition, a feature might check whether a word is capitalized or matches a specific dictionary of entity types (e.g., "Google" or "Microsoft").
- **Transition-based features:** These functions capture the relationship between consecutive labels. For example, in part-of-speech tagging, a transition feature might capture the probability that a verb is followed by a noun.
- **Contextual features:** These features consider the surrounding words in a sequence, such as looking at the previous two or three words to infer the most likely part-of-speech tag.

These features can be designed to reflect the specific needs of the task at hand, allowing CRFs to adapt to a wide variety of structured prediction problems.

Training Conditional Random Fields

Training a CRF involves learning the optimal weights for the feature functions, λk\lambda_kλk, that maximize the likelihood of the observed data. This is typically done using **maximum likelihood estimation (MLE)**, which aims to find the weights that make the training data most probable. However, since the normalization factor Z(X)Z(X)Z(X) involves summing over all possible label sequences, computing the exact likelihood can be computationally expensive.

To address this, the **gradient descent** method is commonly used, along with **the forward-backward algorithm** for efficient calculation of the likelihood. Optimization techniques such as **stochastic gradient descent (SGD)** or **limited-memory BFGS** are frequently applied to iteratively adjust the weights of the model.

Applications of CRFs in NLP

CRFs have been successfully applied to many NLP tasks that require structured output. Some common applications include:

- **Named Entity Recognition (NER):** CRFs are used to identify and classify entities in text, such as names of people, organizations, dates, and locations.
- **Part-of-Speech Tagging (POS):** In this task, CRFs assign grammatical labels (such as noun, verb, or adjective) to each word in a sentence, taking into account the context of neighboring words.
- **Syntactic Parsing:** CRFs are used in dependency parsing, where the goal is to find the syntactic structure of a sentence, determining how words are related to each other.
- **Bioinformatics:** In bioinformatics, CRFs are applied to sequence labeling tasks, such as identifying genes, proteins, and other biological entities from genomic sequences.

Challenges and Limitations

Despite their power, CRFs come with some challenges:

- **Computational Complexity:** The training process can be slow for large datasets, particularly due to the normalization factor, which requires summing over all possible label sequences. This can be mitigated through approximations and optimization techniques.
- **Feature Engineering:** While CRFs are flexible in incorporating features, effective feature design remains a crucial aspect of model performance. The quality of the features can significantly influence the model's ability to generalize to unseen data.
- **Dependence on Labeled Data:** Like many supervised models, CRFs require a large amount of labeled training data to achieve optimal performance, which can be expensive and time-consuming to obtain.

Conclusion

Conditional Random Fields provide a powerful framework for structured prediction tasks in natural language processing. Their ability to model dependencies between adjacent output labels makes them especially useful in applications where context and sequential relationships matter. By leveraging rich feature functions and discriminative training, CRFs offer a robust approach to tasks such as part-of-speech tagging, named entity recognition, and syntactic parsing.

However, despite their strengths, CRFs are not without challenges. Their computational complexity, need for labeled data, and reliance on careful feature engineering make them difficult to apply at scale without substantial resources. Nevertheless, when used appropriately, CRFs can provide significant improvements over earlier statistical models, and they remain a key tool in the NLP practitioner's toolkit.

As we move toward more advanced models like deep learning-based systems, CRFs may be integrated into hybrid approaches that combine the strengths of both traditional statistical methods and modern neural networks.

Word Embeddings: Word2Vec and CBOW

Word embeddings have revolutionized the way machines understand the meaning of words, marking a shift away from traditional methods that relied heavily on sparse, high-dimensional vectors. In essence, word embeddings represent words in a dense, continuous vector space, capturing semantic relationships between them. This is a critical development in natural language processing (NLP), enabling machines to move beyond treating words as isolated symbols and instead understand them as points in a rich, high-dimensional space where proximity implies similarity.

The concept of word embeddings emerged as a breakthrough to solve one of the most fundamental challenges in language modeling: how to make sense of the relationships between words. Prior to word embeddings, traditional models represented words as **one-hot vectors**, where each word in a vocabulary was represented as a unique vector of length equal to the size of the vocabulary. In this sparse representation, each vector contained a "1" in the position corresponding to the word and "0" in all other positions. While simple, this method failed to capture any meaningful relationships between words. For instance, the words "king" and "queen" might have a high semantic similarity, but in one-hot encoding, they would be represented as entirely different vectors, without any notion of their shared context.

Word embeddings solve this problem by placing semantically similar words closer together in a continuous vector space, using a technique known as **distributional semantics**. The idea is that the meaning of a word is derived from the company it keeps — in other words, words that appear in similar contexts tend to have similar meanings. To represent this idea computationally, word embeddings learn dense vector representations where words with similar meanings are mapped to nearby points in the vector space.

The Birth of Word2Vec

One of the most popular and influential algorithms for learning word embeddings is **Word2Vec**, introduced by **Tomas Mikolov** and his team at Google in 2013. Word2Vec operates on the principle that words that appear in similar contexts should have similar vector representations. This insight is grounded in **distributional hypothesis**, a concept in linguistics stating that words that share similar contexts also share similar meanings.

Word2Vec uses a shallow neural network architecture to map words to vectors in a lower-dimensional space. The model can be trained using two distinct approaches: **Continuous Bag of Words (CBOW)** and **Skip-gram**. Both approaches aim to learn vector representations of words by analyzing their context, but they do so in slightly different ways.

Continuous Bag of Words (CBOW)

The **Continuous Bag of Words (CBOW)** model is one of the two main techniques used in Word2Vec for learning word embeddings. In CBOW, the task is to predict a target word based on its surrounding context words. Given a fixed-size window of words from the input text, CBOW takes the context words as input and tries to predict the word that fits in the middle.

For example, consider the sentence: "The cat sat on the mat." If the target word is "sat," the context window could include the words "the," "cat," "on," and "the." In CBOW, these words would be used as input, and the model would learn to predict the word "sat" from these surrounding words. The idea is that words that appear in similar contexts — like "cat" and "dog," or "sat" and "stood" — should have similar vector representations because they often appear in similar positions relative to other words.

The key innovation of CBOW is that it doesn't treat the context as an ordered sequence (like in a traditional n-gram model), but rather as a **bag of words** — meaning it disregards word order. This makes the model computationally efficient, as it doesn't require the complexity of modeling word order, yet still captures essential semantic relationships.

When the model is trained, the **input words** are mapped to vectors (also called embeddings), and these vectors are averaged to predict the target word. During training, the model learns to adjust these vectors so that the vectors of words that tend to appear together in the same contexts become more similar in the embedding space.

The Training Process in CBOW

Training CBOW involves two primary steps:

1. **Input Representation**: The context words are converted into vectors, and the model learns the weights for these context vectors.
2. **Prediction**: Using these context vectors, the model attempts to predict the target word (the word in the center of the context window).

In terms of the architecture, CBOW consists of an input layer, a hidden layer, and an output layer. The input layer contains a vector for each word in the context. The hidden layer is where the embeddings (the continuous, dense vector representations) are stored. The output layer attempts to predict the target word from the context. Over time, the model adjusts the vector values in the hidden layer so that words in similar contexts are placed closer together in the embedding space.

Strengths of CBOW

- **Efficiency**: Since CBOW predicts the target word from the context, it requires fewer training examples than other methods, making it computationally efficient.

- **Contextual Learning**: CBOW successfully learns the semantic meaning of words based on their surrounding context, enabling it to capture relationships like synonymy and analogy (e.g., "king" and "queen," "man" and "woman").

Limitations of CBOW

- **Word Order Ignorance**: Because CBOW treats context words as a "bag" with no regard for word order, it loses the sequential information that can be important for understanding meaning. For example, in the sentence "the cat chased the dog," word order matters — the meaning of the sentence would be different if we swapped "cat" and "dog." CBOW doesn't account for this nuance, as it treats the context words as unordered.
- **Context Size**: CBOW requires defining a fixed-size context window, and the choice of window size can significantly influence performance. A too-small window may fail to capture meaningful relationships, while a too-large window may introduce noise and irrelevant words into the model.

Word2Vec in Practice: The Power of Embeddings

The embeddings produced by Word2Vec, particularly via CBOW, provide an elegant and highly effective way of representing words. These embeddings can be used in a variety of downstream tasks such as:

- **Semantic search**: By measuring the cosine similarity between word vectors, one can easily find similar words or phrases.
- **Text classification**: Embeddings can serve as inputs to models for tasks like sentiment analysis, topic modeling, and spam detection.
- **Word analogy tasks**: Using simple arithmetic on the embeddings, one can perform word analogies, such as “man” is to “woman” as “king” is to “queen.”

Embedding Space and Relationships

One of the most fascinating aspects of Word2Vec's embeddings is how they capture rich semantic relationships between words. For example, in a well-trained Word2Vec model:

- Words with similar meanings, such as "dog" and "puppy," will lie close to each other in the vector space.
- Words with opposite meanings, such as "hot" and "cold," will be placed far apart.
- Analogies can be formed, such as "king" - "man" + "woman" = "queen." This demonstrates the model's ability to capture not just synonyms but also relationships between words, which is crucial for understanding human language.

Conclusion

Word embeddings like those produced by Word2Vec through the CBOW method have marked a paradigm shift in how machines process and understand language. They enable AI systems to grasp the underlying relationships between words, providing a much richer understanding of meaning than earlier methods based on sparse, one-hot encodings. By using the context in which words appear to learn dense, continuous vector representations, CBOW allows us to capture the subtleties of language and its semantic relationships — making it an indispensable tool in the arsenal of modern NLP.

The development of word embeddings set the stage for more sophisticated models that can understand, generate, and even reason about language. But even as these models grow in complexity, the fundamental idea remains: language is best understood through the relationships between words, and word embeddings like CBOW are one of the most effective ways to capture these relationships.

Contributions and Constraints of Statistical Models

Before the advent of deep learning-based language models, statistical language models (SLMs) were the primary tool for addressing natural language processing (NLP) tasks. These models relied on statistical techniques to understand and generate language by learning patterns from large text corpora. While they are significantly simpler and less powerful than modern deep learning approaches, statistical language models laid the foundation for the development of more complex systems and continue to play a role in certain specialized applications today.

Contributions of Statistical Models

Statistical language models, built primarily on the principles of probability theory, have contributed significantly to the evolution of NLP in several ways:

1. **Simple Yet Effective Representation of Language**
   At their core, statistical language models represent language as a sequence of words or tokens, with the goal of predicting the probability of a word or token occurring given a preceding sequence. This simplicity made them remarkably effective for many early NLP applications, particularly when data was limited or when computational resources were constrained. The use of statistical methods, such as n-grams (i.e., sequences of n words), allowed these models to capture basic linguistic structures and patterns in text.
2. **Introduction of Probabilistic Models**
   The statistical approach introduced a probabilistic view of language, moving away from deterministic methods and enabling models to estimate the likelihood of various linguistic events. By assigning probabilities to different sequences of words, statistical models could handle ambiguity and uncertainty in language, something that earlier symbolic models struggled with. This probabilistic view also helped bridge the gap between human language's inherent ambiguity and the need for machines to make decisions based on incomplete or noisy data.
3. **Handling Large-Scale Text Data**
   Statistical language models are particularly adept at processing large amounts of text data and learning from it. They can identify patterns, distributions, and frequencies within large corpora, which has been crucial for applications such as speech recognition, machine translation, and text generation. By analyzing vast amounts of unstructured text data, statistical models were able to provide meaningful insights and automate

tasks that were previously reliant on human expertise.

4. **Foundation for Future Models**
   Even with the advent of more sophisticated deep learning-based models like transformers, statistical language models laid critical groundwork in understanding how to represent and process text. Many of the techniques and concepts developed during the statistical era, such as tokenization, n-grams, and word frequency counts, have influenced modern NLP systems. For example, while current models like GPT-4 and BERT are based on neural networks, the idea of estimating conditional probabilities over sequences of words persists in the architecture and functioning of these more advanced models.
5. **Applications in Real-World Tasks**
   Despite being somewhat eclipsed by neural models, statistical language models still play an important role in certain domains. For example, n-gram models remain useful in speech recognition systems where speed and simplicity are crucial, or in real-time applications where more sophisticated models may not be practical due to computational constraints. Additionally, statistical models are often used for simpler tasks such as keyword extraction, text classification, and basic predictive text systems, providing a fast and lightweight solution where deep learning models may be overkill.

Constraints of Statistical Models

While statistical language models were groundbreaking in their time, they also have several limitations that prevent them from matching the power and flexibility of modern deep learning-based approaches. Understanding these constraints is crucial for recognizing the strengths and weaknesses of older models in the context of today's AI landscape.

1. **Limited Context Awareness**
   One of the most significant limitations of traditional statistical models is their inability to capture long-range dependencies in language. For example, an n-gram model is limited to a fixed window of n words, meaning it can only capture short-term patterns in the text. This approach fails to account for the broader context, such as the relationship between different sentences or the underlying themes of

a document. As a result, statistical models often struggle with tasks that require a deeper understanding of context, like sentiment analysis, discourse analysis, or generating coherent, contextually appropriate responses in conversation.

2. **Data Sparsity Problem**
   Statistical models heavily rely on large corpora to estimate probabilities. However, even in large datasets, many word combinations may not occur frequently enough to be included in the model's training data. This leads to the **data sparsity problem**, where the model has insufficient information to make accurate predictions about rare or unseen word sequences. Techniques like smoothing have been developed to mitigate this issue, but they cannot entirely solve it, particularly in more complex or domain-specific language tasks where out-of-vocabulary words are common.
3. **Difficulty with Semantics and Meaning**
   While statistical models can effectively capture surface-level patterns and frequencies in text, they struggle with understanding the deeper meaning or semantics behind those patterns. Language is inherently rich in nuance, figurative expressions, and ambiguity, which statistical models are not equipped to handle. For example, the phrase "barking up the wrong tree" is a metaphor, but a statistical model might interpret it literally based on its n-gram patterns, missing the true meaning. This limitation is one of the reasons why deep learning models, particularly those leveraging word embeddings and context-aware mechanisms, have dramatically improved performance in tasks that require an understanding of meaning.
4. **No Capability for Reasoning or Inference**
   Statistical models excel at estimating the probability of the next word or token in a sequence, but they lack the ability to reason, infer, or engage in complex problem-solving. They do not possess a model of the world or an internal knowledge base, and therefore cannot make logical deductions or connect concepts beyond the immediate text. For instance, a statistical model may not be able to make a coherent argument, understand a chain of reasoning, or solve a complex math problem based on a text prompt. This kind of higher-order cognitive processing is beyond the scope of statistical models and requires more sophisticated architectures, such as neural networks with attention mechanisms.

5. **Scalability and Performance Limitations**
   Statistical models tend to require large amounts of handcrafted engineering to scale effectively. As the size of the data grows, the models must account for an exponentially larger number of word combinations, which makes them computationally expensive. While deep learning models have also faced scalability challenges, their ability to learn rich feature representations through embeddings and their ability to leverage distributed training make them much more efficient and scalable when compared to traditional statistical approaches.
6. **Rigid Structure and Lack of Flexibility**
   Statistical models are often rigid in their approach, requiring predefined rules, frameworks, and constraints (such as n-gram sizes or Markov assumptions). While this can make them easier to understand and interpret, it also limits their flexibility and adaptability to diverse language tasks. In contrast, modern language models, such as transformers, can dynamically adjust their attention mechanisms to different parts of the input data, allowing them to better adapt to a variety of tasks without needing task-specific fine-tuning or feature engineering.

Conclusion: The Legacy of Statistical Models

Despite these limitations, statistical language models have played a pivotal role in shaping the field of natural language processing. They introduced the idea of probabilistic reasoning over language and provided valuable tools that continue to influence modern AI systems. However, as AI research and technology have advanced, especially with the introduction of deep learning and large-scale neural models, statistical approaches have been largely overshadowed in many areas.

Nevertheless, statistical models still offer value in scenarios where simplicity, efficiency, and interpretability are paramount. As part of the foundational toolkit in AI, they serve as a stepping stone toward more sophisticated models, providing insights into how language can be represented and processed.

Today, we move forward from statistical models to more complex systems like transformers, which overcome many of the constraints of earlier approaches and unlock the potential for more advanced, context-aware, and intelligent AI systems.

Real-World Use Cases of Statistical Language Models

Before the dawn of deep learning and Transformer-based architectures, statistical language models (SLMs) were the dominant force in natural language processing. Though largely surpassed by more recent innovations, SLMs played a foundational role in shaping early AI systems and still power specific, resource-efficient applications today — particularly in environments where simplicity, interpretability, or low latency matters.

These models, built upon probabilistic principles such as N-grams and Hidden Markov Models, brought structured reasoning to language tasks. Their success lies not in simulating human-level understanding, but in modeling patterns of word sequences and optimizing for likelihoods. Despite their mathematical elegance and computational efficiency, they operated under key assumptions — limited context, fixed vocabulary, and relatively shallow representations of meaning.

Yet, within those constraints, statistical language models were widely deployed — and in some cases, still are. Below are real-world use cases where these models found (and sometimes continue to find) impactful application.

1. Text Autocompletion and Predictive Typing

One of the earliest and most ubiquitous applications of SLMs has been **predictive text input**. In mobile keyboards, email clients, and search engines, statistical models used N-gram probabilities to suggest the next word a user might type. These systems learned from past sequences — for example, the bigram "thank you" made "very much" a likely continuation.

Though now replaced in most cases by Transformer-backed systems like GPT or BERT, predictive typing systems based on SLMs were lightweight, fast, and easily deployable on-device, making them ideal for resource-constrained platforms. In many lower-end devices or applications prioritizing speed and privacy, they still perform well enough for basic suggestions.

2. Spell Checkers and Grammar Correction

Basic spell-checking systems leveraged statistical models to detect unlikely word sequences and recommend corrections. By computing the probability of word combinations, an SLM could identify when a sentence deviated from normal patterns (e.g., “I can has cheese”) and offer alternatives.

Statistical models also helped in correcting *real-word errors* — mistakes that result in valid words, but incorrect meaning (e.g., "their" vs. "there"). By analyzing the probability of surrounding words, the model could infer which homonym fit the sentence better.

While deep learning has since pushed boundaries in grammar checking (e.g., Grammarly's Transformer-based models), statistical methods remain efficient for lightweight, on-the-fly proofreading tools.

3. Information Retrieval and Search Engines

Search engines in their early incarnations used SLMs to enhance **query understanding** and **document ranking**. Language models helped evaluate how likely a query was to have been generated by the language distribution of a particular document — a principle known as **query likelihood modeling**.

For instance, a document with many occurrences of the phrase "climate change policy" would rank higher for that query because the model estimated a higher probability of that sequence appearing. This statistical approach improved over simple keyword matching by incorporating word order and frequency patterns.

Even today, in enterprise environments where domain-specific search engines are needed, statistical methods provide fast and interpretable retrieval pipelines.

4. Speech Recognition Systems

In the early days of **automatic speech recognition (ASR)**, statistical language models were used to constrain the transcription possibilities. When a speech recognition engine converted audio into a sequence of phonemes or word candidates, an N-gram model helped choose the most probable word sequence.

For example, given audio that could correspond to either "recognize speech" or "wreck a nice beach," a statistical language model would favor the more probable phrase based on prior frequency and contextual probability.

This statistical scaffolding was essential to reducing error rates in early ASR systems and is still embedded within hybrid systems where acoustic and language models interact.

5. Machine Translation (Pre-Neural Era)

Before neural machine translation took over, **statistical machine translation (SMT)** was the prevailing paradigm. These systems learned phrase tables and translation probabilities from bilingual corpora. A statistical language model was then used to evaluate and rank the fluency of candidate translations in the target language.

For example, when translating from French to English, the translation model proposed alternatives, while the SLM ensured that the resulting English sentence followed fluent patterns ("I have eaten" over "I eaten have").

Though superseded by neural approaches like Google's Transformer-based translation, SMT with statistical LMs is still relevant for domain-specific, offline, or privacy-sensitive translation tools.

6. Text Classification and Spam Detection

While deep neural classifiers dominate today, early **text classification systems**, especially for **spam filtering**, often relied on Naive Bayes classifiers — a probabilistic model closely tied to statistical language modeling.

By modeling the conditional probability of words given classes (e.g., "free", "win", "money" given spam), systems could infer the likelihood that a new message belonged to a particular category. These models required far less training data and computation than modern systems, making them viable for real-time email filtering even on legacy infrastructure.

In many government, telecom, and embedded systems where simplicity and explainability are required, such statistical models remain in use or are hybridized with modern LLMs.

7. Text Summarization and Content Extraction

Before LLMs could generate fluent abstractive summaries, **extractive summarization** based on statistical language modeling was the norm. These systems selected key sentences or phrases by analyzing term frequency, positional probability, and topic coherence — often relying on language model scores to prioritize content that matched the dominant themes.

While not truly "understanding" content, SLM-based summarizers worked well in news aggregation, document previews, and even legal or academic tools, where verbosity needed trimming but core ideas had to remain intact.

8. Dialogue Systems and Early Chatbots

Statistical language models powered the earliest **chatbots and dialogue agents**, especially those built on rule-based systems augmented with probabilistic transitions. For example, customer service bots could select the next best response based on the likelihood of phrase patterns following specific queries.

While these systems lacked memory or context tracking, they offered deterministic behavior with acceptable coverage for routine interactions — such as answering FAQs, checking account balances, or logging support tickets. These systems laid the groundwork for today's conversational LLMs.

9. Domain-Specific NLP in Low-Resource Settings

In sectors like **agriculture, local governance, and public health** — especially in regions with limited access to cloud infrastructure or training data — SLMs have remained useful due to their:

- **Low computational requirements**
- **Transparency and interpretability**
- **Ease of localization and rule integration**

For example, SMS-based information systems for farmers could use N-gram models to interpret questions about crop prices or weather updates, often in low-bandwidth, multilingual environments.

In global development and humanitarian contexts, statistical models often form the first wave of AI adoption.

10. AI Education and Research Prototyping

Finally, statistical language models remain essential in **AI education** and **research prototyping**. They are easy to build, visualize, and debug — making them ideal for introducing core concepts such as:

- Language distributions and entropy
- Sequence prediction
- Markov assumptions
- Probabilistic reasoning

In classrooms, labs, and textbooks, SLMs are the conceptual scaffolds upon which modern language models are built. They help learners appreciate both the power and limitations of foundational approaches — preparing them to grasp the leap made by deep learning and LLMs.

Conclusion: Legacy and Ongoing Utility

Though overshadowed by today's deep neural networks, statistical language models remain significant — both as historical milestones and as practical tools. Their influence is embedded in the architecture, intuition, and evaluation metrics of modern LLMs. In contexts where data is limited, interpretability is critical, or compute is constrained, these models continue to serve.

In many ways, statistical models taught us the first fundamental lesson of AI and language: that meaning is not encoded in single words, but in *patterns of usage* across time and context. That lesson remains just as true — if not more so — in the age of agentic, generative, and self-improving AI.

The Legacy of Statistical Thinking

Before neural networks, Transformers, or generative AI captured the world's imagination, language modeling was rooted in something far more classical — **statistics**. At the core of the earliest natural language processing (NLP) systems was a simple yet powerful idea: **language is a sequence of events**, and like any sequence of events, it can be modeled probabilistically.

Statistical language models emerged as the first real attempt to teach machines how to "understand" language in a measurable, empirical way. While these models lacked any true semantic understanding or general reasoning capabilities, they laid the crucial groundwork — methodologically, mathematically, and philosophically — for the large language models (LLMs) that define today's AI revolution.

To appreciate the sophistication of modern LLMs, it is essential to understand the legacy they inherit: a lineage of thought that begins with frequency counts, Markov assumptions, and the quiet rigor of probabilistic reasoning.

Language as a Probabilistic System

Statistical language models treat language as a phenomenon that can be quantified. The central task is to compute the **probability of a sequence of words**. For example, how likely is the sentence:

"The cat sat on the mat."

compared to:

"The sat cat mat on the."

While humans can instantly judge the first as grammatical and meaningful, statistical models do so by computing the relative likelihood of each word following the previous ones, based on patterns seen in real-world data.

This probabilistic framing allowed computers to process vast corpora of text and **learn statistical regularities** — such as which words often appear together, how certain phrases are structured, and what word is likely to come next given a history of previous words.

From Counting Words to Modeling Context

The earliest statistical models were based on **word frequencies** — tracking how often individual words or combinations of words occurred in a corpus. This approach matured into **n-gram models**, which estimate the likelihood of a word given a fixed number of previous words. For example, a trigram model might calculate:

P("mat" | "on the")

meaning the probability of "mat" appearing after the sequence "on the."

These models were:

- **Simple** to implement,
- **Efficient** to compute,
- And surprisingly **effective** in many real-world tasks, such as speech recognition, spelling correction, and autocomplete.

However, statistical language models had an Achilles' heel: **data sparsity**. Natural language is incredibly diverse and generative. Even massive corpora rarely include every possible phrase or sentence. As a result, purely statistical models often failed when faced with unfamiliar word combinations or longer dependencies.

To mitigate this, researchers introduced smoothing techniques, backoff models, and interpolation strategies — all designed to handle rare or unseen sequences more gracefully. These were clever engineering solutions, but they were also **symptoms of a deeper limitation**: the lack of any real understanding of the meaning behind the words.

Statistical Thinking in a Rule-Based World

Statistical approaches to language were radical in their time. For decades, linguistics and AI were dominated by **rule-based systems** — handcrafted grammars, logic-based parsers, and expert systems. These were based on formal logic and syntactic rules — clean, deterministic, and human-interpretable.

Statistical models, by contrast, **embraced uncertainty**. They didn't attempt to "understand" language through rigid rules. Instead, they sought to *approximate* it through patterns in data. This represented a shift in paradigm:

- From *explicit knowledge* to *implicit knowledge*,
- From *deterministic logic* to *probabilistic inference*,
- From *manual curation* to *data-driven learning*.

This shift was not always welcomed. Early statistical approaches were sometimes dismissed as "black box" or "brute force." But as data availability increased and computational power grew, the statistical mindset gained traction — and ultimately paved the way for machine learning.

The Bridge to Modern AI

Though simple compared to today's models, statistical language models introduced several foundational ideas that endure in contemporary LLMs:

1. **Tokenization** — Breaking down language into smaller units (words, subwords) that can be modeled mathematically.
2. **Probability distributions** — Estimating the likelihood of different outputs, not as single answers but as ranked possibilities.
3. **Contextual modeling** — Capturing dependencies between words, even if limited to local context.
4. **Evaluation metrics** — Using perplexity and likelihood scores to evaluate how well a model predicts real language use.
5. **Generalization from data** — Learning language patterns from text alone, without predefined knowledge or rules.

In fact, today's most advanced Transformer-based LLMs — such as GPT-4 or Claude — can still be described in probabilistic terms. They are, at their core, **autoregressive models** that predict the next token given prior context — an idea inherited directly from statistical modeling.

The difference is one of **scale, architecture, and depth**: whereas early models worked with sparse counts and fixed windows, modern LLMs learn dense representations and capture long-range dependencies across millions of parameters and billions of words.

Enterprise Lessons from the Statistical Era

The statistical phase of NLP wasn't just a technical milestone — it was a proving ground for applying language models in real-world settings. Many enterprise NLP applications that emerged in the 1990s and early 2000s were powered by statistical models, including:

- Search engines and information retrieval systems.
- Speech recognition software in call centers.
- Spam detection in email systems.
- Machine translation (e.g., early versions of Google Translate).
- Text classification and sentiment analysis in marketing analytics.

Though these systems lacked true "understanding," they demonstrated that **statistical language modeling could deliver measurable business value** — often outperforming rule-based systems in flexibility, scalability, and adaptability.

This has direct relevance today: even as enterprises adopt sophisticated LLMs, the mindset of **quantifying uncertainty, learning from data, and evaluating with metrics** remains central to successful deployment.

The Intellectual Legacy

Statistical language models mark the beginning of AI's journey toward linguistic intelligence. They embody a way of thinking — that **language, though complex, exhibits structure and predictability** that can be captured through data and computation.

They remind us that breakthroughs often come not from perfect understanding, but from **useful approximations**. And they teach us that in language, as in life, probability and context are everything.

This statistical foundation would eventually merge with neural networks, leading to deep learning models that combine pattern recognition with representational depth. But the spirit of statistical thinking — empirical, iterative, grounded in data — lives on in every token predicted by a modern LLM.

CHAPTER THREE

Neural Language Modeling — The Deep Learning Era

Neural Networks: How Machines Learn

Before a machine can understand language at scale, it must first learn *how* to learn — not through hardcoded rules or labeled dictionaries, but through patterns hidden within massive volumes of data. This capability lies at the heart of *neural networks*, the foundational machinery behind modern large language models.

Inspired loosely by the structure and function of the human brain, neural networks have transformed artificial intelligence from a rule-based logic engine into a dynamic system that can perceive, adapt, and generalize. In the context of language, neural networks provide the computational canvas upon which meaning, context, and creativity are painted.

Let us explore how they work — not just in architecture, but in essence.

From Symbols to Signals: The Shift in Intelligence

Traditional language processing systems operated on discrete symbols: words, tokens, tags. These systems relied heavily on manual feature engineering — a process in which human experts defined the rules for how a machine should interpret and process text. This approach was brittle, expensive, and limited by the scope of human foresight.

Neural networks, on the other hand, operate on *continuous representations* of language. Words are no longer treated as isolated units but as multi-dimensional vectors, learned through exposure to vast linguistic corpora. These vectorized inputs are processed through layers of interconnected nodes (or "neurons"), each layer transforming the input into higher levels of abstraction — from raw characters to grammar, semantics, and ultimately intent.

This learning is not symbolic; it is statistical. A neural network learns by adjusting internal parameters — millions, sometimes billions of them — to minimize error in predicting or generating language. Over time, this results in models that can generalize far beyond their training data.

The Building Blocks of Learning

At the core of every neural network is a deceptively simple mechanism: the neuron. Unlike its biological namesake, an artificial neuron is a mathematical function. It receives inputs, applies a weight to each, sums them, passes the result through a non-linear transformation (called an activation function), and sends the output forward. This process is repeated across layers — each layer extracting more abstract features than the last.

Here's how machines learn through this setup:

1. Input Representation

Language is first converted into numerical form — typically using embeddings, which are dense vectors that capture semantic similarity. For example, "king" and "queen" might be closer in this space than "king" and "car." These embeddings form the input layer of the network.

2. Weighted Transformation

Each input is multiplied by a set of weights — parameters that the model learns. Initially, these weights are random. Through training, they are adjusted to reflect how strongly each input contributes to the desired output.

3. Activation and Propagation

The result is passed through a non-linear function — such as ReLU, sigmoid, or tanh — which allows the network to model complex, non-linear relationships. This activated output is passed to the next layer, and the process repeats.

4. Output Generation

Eventually, the data reaches the output layer, which produces a prediction — for example, the next word in a sentence, or the probability of a sentiment being positive.

5. Learning Through Error

Once the prediction is made, the model compares it to the correct answer using a loss function — a mathematical measure of error. This error is then propagated backward through the network using a method called backpropagation. The weights are updated to reduce future errors, and the process repeats over thousands or millions of examples.

This cycle — *forward pass, error computation, backward pass, weight update* — is the essence of learning in neural networks.

What Makes Neural Networks So Effective for Language?

Neural networks shine in natural language tasks for several reasons:

Distributed Representations

Rather than representing a word as a single symbol, neural networks use embeddings that capture multiple dimensions of meaning. This allows them to recognize that "bank" can refer to both a river's edge and a financial institution, depending on context.

Compositionality

Words gain meaning from context. Neural architectures allow for compositional semantics — that is, understanding how meaning emerges not just from words, but from their order and relationships. This is essential for parsing idioms, metaphors, and syntactic nuance.

Generalization from Data

Unlike symbolic systems, which struggle with exceptions or unseen phrases, neural networks can generalize from examples. If they've seen thousands of articles about climate change, they can discuss new developments with credible fluency — even if those specific sentences were never seen before.

Scalability and Transferability

Neural networks can scale with data and hardware. More layers, more parameters, and more training data typically lead to better performance — up to a point. Furthermore, a model trained on one task (say, language modeling) can be fine-tuned for another (like legal summarization) with minimal additional data — a phenomenon known as *transfer learning*.

Limitations and Challenges

While powerful, neural networks are not infallible. They are:

- **Opaque**: Their decisions are often difficult to interpret, leading to concerns around explainability.
- **Data-hungry**: Training requires vast amounts of data and compute, raising concerns of accessibility and environmental impact.
- **Bias-prone**: If training data contains stereotypes or toxic language, the model can reflect and amplify those patterns.
- **Error-tolerant, not error-free**: Neural networks do not "understand" language as humans do. Their fluency is predictive, not cognitive. They can hallucinate facts, misunderstand nuance, and struggle with uncommon scenarios.

These limitations are not reasons to dismiss the technology — rather, they underscore the need for responsible deployment, domain adaptation, and ongoing refinement.

The Evolution Continues

Neural networks laid the groundwork for modern language understanding, but they are not static. Early networks like simple feedforward models gave way to more sophisticated architectures like Recurrent Neural Networks (RNNs), Long Short-Term Memory (LSTM) models, and eventually the **Transformer** — a game-changing architecture that now powers almost every leading LLM.

As we will explore in subsequent chapters, it is this evolution — from neurons to networks, from sequences to self-attention — that enabled the leap from recognizing patterns in language to generating coherent, contextually aware, and creative outputs. These advances are not just technical achievements; they represent a profound shift in how machines interact with knowledge, meaning, and ultimately, us.

RNNs, LSTMs, and GRUs: The Evolution of Memory in Neural Language Models

As language moved from static statistical models to dynamic deep learning systems, a critical challenge emerged: how can machines understand *sequences*?

Language is inherently sequential. The meaning of a sentence depends not just on individual words but on their order and context. "The cat sat on the mat" is very different from "On the mat, the cat sat." Understanding such sequences — where each token depends on those that came before — requires a model architecture capable of remembering and processing prior inputs over time. This is the essence of **sequence modeling** in natural language processing (NLP), and it gave birth to a class of neural architectures that brought a profound shift in AI's ability to handle language: **Recurrent Neural Networks (RNNs)** and their successors, **Long Short-Term Memory networks (LSTMs)** and **Gated Recurrent Units (GRUs)**.

Let's explore their journey — from early promise to widespread adoption — and why they were critical stepping stones toward the large language models we use today.

Recurrent Neural Networks (RNNs): The First Neural Language Modelers

Recurrent Neural Networks were among the first neural architectures designed specifically for sequential data. At their core, RNNs introduced a simple yet powerful idea: instead of processing all inputs independently, the model would **retain a hidden state that is updated step-by-step as it reads through the sequence**.

Imagine a sentence being read one word at a time. At each step, the RNN takes two things as input: the current word (or its vector representation) and a **memory of the past** — the hidden state that summarizes everything it has seen so far. The output at each step is influenced by both.

This allowed RNNs to, in theory, model dependencies between words across a sentence or even longer texts. For example:

- Recognizing that the word "it" refers to "the cat" two sentences earlier.
- Predicting the verb "eat" in "I will ... the apple" by recalling the subject "I."

In natural language tasks such as next-word prediction, sentiment analysis, or speech recognition, RNNs offered early breakthroughs —

outperforming traditional statistical models by learning representations directly from data without manual feature engineering.

However, RNNs soon revealed a fatal flaw.

The Problem of Memory: Vanishing and Exploding Gradients

While RNNs were conceptually elegant, they struggled in practice when trying to model **long-term dependencies** — remembering information from many steps back in a sequence. For example, understanding the relationship between the subject and verb in the sentence, "The committee that was formed after the merger **has** decided...," requires tracking the subject "committee" over a long distance.

In training RNNs using backpropagation through time (BPTT), the model adjusts weights based on gradients. But in deep or long sequences, these gradients either shrink to zero (vanishing gradient) or explode to very large values (exploding gradient). This makes it nearly impossible for the model to learn what it should remember — and for how long.

The result? RNNs often forgot information after just a few steps, making them ill-suited for tasks requiring long-term reasoning or context tracking.

To overcome this, a new architecture emerged that would become the backbone of NLP for nearly a decade: **Long Short-Term Memory networks.**

LSTMs: Memory with a Gatekeeper

Introduced by Hochreiter and Schmidhuber in 1997, Long Short-Term Memory networks (LSTMs) were a game-changing evolution in sequence modeling. They retained the recursive nature of RNNs but added a critical innovation: **gated memory cells.**

At the heart of an LSTM is a memory cell — a persistent structure that allows information to flow across time steps. Unlike the simplistic hidden state in RNNs, this memory can be selectively updated, read, or erased using **gates**:

- The **input gate** controls what new information is added to memory.
- The **forget gate** decides what old information should be discarded.
- The **output gate** determines what part of the memory should be exposed as output at each step.

These gates are learnable mechanisms — meaning the model learns what to remember and what to forget during training. Crucially, this gating structure mitigates the vanishing gradient problem and allows LSTMs to model long-range dependencies far more effectively than traditional RNNs.

For example:

- In a document classification task, the LSTM can retain key theme-related words that appeared hundreds of tokens ago.
- In machine translation, it can remember sentence structure from the source language while generating fluent text in the target language.

Because of this memory fidelity, LSTMs quickly became the go-to architecture for many NLP tasks, powering applications like:

- Speech recognition (used in early versions of Siri and Google Voice).
- Language modeling for predictive text keyboards.
- Named entity recognition, sentiment analysis, and machine translation.

But LSTMs, while powerful, had their own complexities. They were computationally expensive, required careful tuning, and involved multiple gates and internal states. The search for a simpler yet equally powerful architecture led to the rise of **Gated Recurrent Units.**

GRUs: The Lightweight Memory Network

Gated Recurrent Units (GRUs) were introduced in 2014 as a streamlined alternative to LSTMs. They aimed to achieve similar performance with fewer components and lower computational overhead.

GRUs simplify the gating mechanism by combining the input and forget gates into a single **update gate** and using a second **reset gate** to control the flow of past information. This reduced complexity makes GRUs faster to train and easier to implement — particularly in scenarios where computational resources are limited.

Despite their simplicity, GRUs often perform on par with LSTMs on many tasks, especially when datasets are not extremely long or complex. They retain the ability to:

- Model long-term dependencies (though slightly less effectively than LSTMs in some cases).
- Handle noisy or variable-length sequences with robustness.
- Generalize well across domains and languages.

In enterprise settings, GRUs found favor in time-sensitive applications like:

- Real-time text prediction.
- Chatbot engines for customer support.
- Sentiment tracking in social media streams.
- Email sorting and auto-reply systems.

Their efficiency made them well-suited for deployment in edge devices or mobile apps where memory and compute budgets are constrained.

RNNs, LSTMs, and GRUs: A Legacy of Sequential Intelligence

Collectively, RNNs, LSTMs, and GRUs represent the first true wave of **neural language understanding**. They taught AI not just to process language, but to remember it — to model time, sequence, and context in ways that statistical models could never do.

Their importance cannot be overstated. Without them, we would not have had:

- The rapid advances in machine translation pre-Transformer.
- The first generation of smart assistants and voice interfaces.
- The ability to model documents, dialogues, and narratives as living, unfolding sequences rather than static bags of words.

Even though newer architectures like the **Transformer** have largely supplanted them in large-scale language models due to superior scalability and parallelism, RNN-based models still serve as foundational architectures in:

- Educational environments for teaching deep learning.
- Low-latency systems where efficiency trumps complexity.

- Hybrid models that blend symbolic and neural reasoning.

Understanding how RNNs, LSTMs, and GRUs paved the way for today's LLMs offers more than just historical context — it offers insight into the **evolution of memory in AI**, and how each generation of architecture has brought us closer to machines that can think, reason, and respond like humans.

Convolutional Approaches to Language

While convolutional neural networks (CNNs) are most famously associated with computer vision, their application to natural language processing (NLP) marked an important turning point in the evolution of neural language modeling. At first glance, language may seem like an odd domain for convolutional architectures. Text, after all, is sequential and symbolic, not spatial and visual. But as researchers began to explore CNNs for text understanding, a new insight emerged: language, like images, contains local patterns — and CNNs are particularly good at detecting and abstracting such patterns.

Understanding the Intuition Behind CNNs for Language

In computer vision, convolutional layers detect local features such as edges, corners, and textures by scanning small regions (filters) over the image. Similarly, in NLP, these filters can slide over sequences of words or characters to detect useful linguistic patterns such as n-grams, phrases, or syntactic motifs. The model doesn't process the entire sequence in one go. Instead, it processes chunks of text locally, extracts features, and passes them through multiple layers of abstraction to capture higher-level semantic structures.

For example, in a sentence like *"The stock price surged after the earnings report,"* a convolutional model might identify localized patterns like *"stock price"*, *"surged after"*, or *"earnings report"*, and then learn that such patterns are indicative of positive sentiment or economic growth. These fragments, once encoded, can help in downstream tasks like classification, translation, summarization, or question answering.

From Words to Feature Maps

To apply convolutional techniques to language, textual data must first be transformed into a numerical format — typically through word embeddings. These embeddings map each word in a sentence to a fixed-length vector that captures its semantic properties. A sentence thus becomes a sequence of vectors: a matrix where each row represents a word's embedding.

A convolutional layer then applies multiple filters of varying widths across this matrix. Each filter is designed to capture specific patterns across neighboring words — much like how different-sized filters in image recognition capture various levels of detail. A narrow filter might capture simple bi-grams or tri-grams, while wider filters might encapsulate entire clauses.

The output of these filters — known as feature maps — provides a condensed representation of the most relevant local patterns in the text. Pooling operations (such as max-pooling) are often used afterward to downsample the feature maps and retain only the most significant features, ensuring that the model remains computationally efficient.

Key Strengths of CNNs in NLP

Despite their origins in vision, CNNs introduced several compelling strengths for processing language:

1. **Parallelism and Efficiency:**
   Unlike recurrent neural networks (RNNs), which process input sequentially and are inherently slow, CNNs apply filters across the input in parallel. This enables faster training and inference, which is especially beneficial when dealing with long documents or in real-time applications.
2. **Local Invariance and Pattern Detection:**
   CNNs excel at detecting local patterns that are position-invariant. For language tasks such as sentiment analysis, topic classification, or spam detection, the presence of key phrases matters more than their precise position in the text. CNNs naturally account for this.
3. **Hierarchical Representation Learning:**
   As CNNs go deeper, they build a hierarchy of features — from word-level motifs to phrase-level meanings to sentence-level abstractions. This

mirrors how humans interpret language: by stacking layers of interpretation and context.

4. **Low Memory Footprint:**
   CNNs generally have fewer trainable parameters than RNNs, especially when using narrow filters and aggressive pooling. This makes them attractive for deployment in mobile and edge devices, where computational resources are limited.

Applications of CNNs in Language Tasks

Convolutional models have proven effective across a variety of language processing tasks:

- **Text Classification:**
  One of the most successful early uses of CNNs in NLP was for classifying short text snippets, such as news headlines, product reviews, or tweets. CNNs can extract key phrases and assign labels like *positive*, *negative*, *news*, *spam*, or *urgent*.
- **Sentence Matching and Similarity:**
  In tasks like paraphrase detection or question-answer matching, CNNs are used to encode both inputs and measure their similarity via learned vector spaces.
- **Named Entity Recognition (NER):**
  By processing character-level embeddings through CNNs, models can recognize entities such as names, dates, and locations more robustly, even when faced with misspellings or novel variations.
- **Speech and Character-Level Language Modeling:**
  CNNs have been adapted for subword and phoneme-level modeling, particularly in speech recognition systems where local temporal features are crucial.

Limitations and the Path Forward

While convolutional models brought new power and efficiency to NLP, they also had limitations that ultimately led to the rise of transformer-based architectures:

- **Limited Contextual Awareness:**
  CNNs are inherently local. Their filters only span fixed-size windows, which means they struggle to model long-range dependencies unless stacked in deep, complex layers.
- **Rigid Input Structure:**
  Unlike transformers, which can dynamically weigh relationships between any two tokens in a sequence, CNNs rely on static filters. This makes them less adaptable to subtle contextual shifts.
- **Lack of Attention Mechanism:**
  CNNs treat all positions equally unless specifically weighted, whereas transformers use attention to focus on the most relevant parts of the input, improving both accuracy and interpretability.

Despite these constraints, convolutional approaches have not disappeared. They continue to be used as building blocks in hybrid architectures — often in combination with RNNs, attention layers, or transformers. For instance, CNNs are frequently used in the early stages of a model to process raw input like characters or speech signals, before passing the processed signals to more powerful contextual models.

Legacy and Influence on LLMs

CNNs played a critical transitional role in the journey toward large language models. They proved that deep architectures could learn meaningful linguistic features from raw text — without manual engineering of features or linguistic rules. They also demonstrated that sequence modeling could benefit from architectures beyond the traditional RNN.

Many lessons from CNN-based models — such as layer stacking, feature abstraction, and positional invariance — found their way into transformer architectures. Even today, elements like convolutional positional encodings and hybrid CNN-attention modules are being reintroduced into modern LLMs to improve speed and reduce inference costs.

In short, convolutional approaches to language laid the groundwork for the architectural innovation that powers the agentic, multimodal, and context-sensitive LLMs of today.

Attention Mechanisms Before Transformers

Before the Transformer architecture revolutionized natural language processing, attention mechanisms had already begun reshaping how neural networks handled sequences of data — particularly in tasks like machine translation, summarization, and question answering. Though Transformers later placed attention at the center of their architecture, its conceptual foundations were laid during the reign of recurrent neural networks (RNNs) and their variants like LSTMs and GRUs.

To understand the significance of attention, we must first examine the limitations of traditional sequential models and how attention emerged as a solution to their shortcomings.

The Bottleneck of Fixed-Length Contexts

In early neural language models, particularly those based on RNNs and LSTMs, the processing of a sentence or sequence occurred one token at a time. These models built a representation of the input incrementally, passing information forward from one time step to the next.

While RNNs were a major advancement over statistical methods, they suffered from an inherent limitation: the **fixed-length context vector**. When used in encoder-decoder architectures — especially in tasks like machine translation — the encoder would compress an entire input sequence into a single vector. The decoder would then rely on that vector to generate the output sequence.

This approach posed a fundamental problem: how can a single vector, no matter how cleverly designed, encapsulate all the nuanced information of a long sentence, document, or dialogue? In practice, it couldn't. Important details were lost, especially for long-range dependencies where the beginning of the sentence might contain crucial information for decoding the end. The result was degraded performance and limited generalization.

The Emergence of Attention: A Paradigm Shift

The solution came in 2014 with the introduction of the **attention mechanism**, most notably in the context of neural machine translation by Bahdanau, Cho, and Bengio. Their idea was conceptually simple yet profound: instead of encoding the entire input into a single bottleneck vector, why not let the model "look back" at the entire input sequence at every decoding step?

This gave rise to what is now known as **additive attention**, or more generally, **soft attention.**

In this setup:

- The encoder still processes the input sequence and produces a sequence of hidden states (one for each token).
- The decoder, at each step, doesn't rely on a single fixed vector. Instead, it dynamically calculates a **weighted sum** of all the encoder's hidden states.
- These weights represent how much "attention" the decoder should pay to each input token, conditioned on the current decoding state.

This mechanism provided a powerful benefit: the model could now focus on relevant parts of the input sequence when generating each output token. It no longer had to store everything in a single memory — it could attend to what it needed, when it needed it.

Contextual Relevance: Soft Alignment Over Hard Rules

Prior to attention, aligning elements of source and target sequences in translation was a rigid, often handcrafted process. Attention changed that. Now, the model could **learn alignments automatically**.

For example, in translating an English sentence to French, attention could help the model learn that the English word "bank" in the context of a river should be aligned with "rive," not "banque." And that alignment could vary dynamically depending on the sentence.

These attentional weights, often visualized as matrices or heatmaps, made the inner workings of models more interpretable. They showed which parts of the input the model was focusing on at each output step — a crucial step toward explainability in neural systems.

Types of Early Attention Mechanisms

Several variants of attention emerged in the pre-Transformer era, including:

- **Additive Attention (Bahdanau Attention):** Computes the alignment score using a feedforward neural network. It's expressive but computationally heavier.

- **Dot-Product Attention (Luong Attention):** A more efficient version where attention scores are computed using the dot product between hidden states. Simpler and faster but less flexible when sequences vary significantly.
- **Global vs. Local Attention:** Global attention considers all positions in the input sequence for alignment, while local attention restricts focus to a window of positions. This tradeoff balanced accuracy with computational cost.

Each of these innovations improved the quality of generated outputs across tasks and paved the way for more sophisticated mechanisms. But they still operated on top of sequential architectures like RNNs and LSTMs — meaning they inherited their limitations.

Attention's Limitations Within Sequential Models

Despite its success, attention had a ceiling when embedded within RNNs:

- It still processed sequences token by token, step by step.
- Training was slow due to the inherently sequential nature of RNNs.
- Long sequences still posed problems because of memory decay and vanishing gradients, though mitigated somewhat by LSTMs and GRUs.
- Parallelization was limited: each time step depended on the previous one, making it difficult to scale.

These constraints begged a bold question: what if attention weren't an *add-on* to sequential models, but the *core* mechanism of the model itself?

Toward Full Attention: The Precursor to a Breakthrough

By the mid-2010s, researchers began experimenting with architectures that reduced dependence on recurrence. These explorations hinted at a radical new architecture that would abandon recurrence entirely and rely solely on attention to model dependencies.

This set the stage for the 2017 paper titled **"Attention Is All You Need,"** which introduced the **Transformer architecture** — a model that leveraged attention not as a supplement to RNNs, but as a replacement. Transformers removed the constraints of sequence-by-sequence processing and introduced fully parallelizable models capable of capturing complex dependencies across entire texts.

But that's the next chapter.

For now, it's important to recognize that **attention mechanisms before Transformers** were more than an optimization — they were a conceptual turning point. They marked a transition from rigid, position-based representations of language to dynamic, context-aware interpretations. They showed that understanding language is not about treating all words equally, but about **focusing** — paying the right kind of attention to the right information at the right time.

In this, attention mirrored a distinctly human trait: selective focus in a sea of noise.

And in doing so, it brought machines a step closer to real language understanding.

Reinforcement Learning in NLP

While supervised and unsupervised learning have been instrumental in teaching machines to understand language, they are not enough to create intelligent agents that adapt, make decisions, and learn through interaction. This is where **reinforcement learning (RL)** comes in — a powerful paradigm that allows models to learn from experience, trial and error, and dynamic feedback. In the context of natural language processing (NLP), reinforcement learning adds a crucial dimension: **intentionality and interactivity**.

Instead of passively absorbing patterns from static corpora, models trained with reinforcement learning can engage in a goal-driven process — adjusting their behavior based on rewards or penalties received from the environment. This capability forms the bedrock of **agentic AI** — intelligent systems that act autonomously, refine their outputs over time, and optimize for long-term objectives.

What Is Reinforcement Learning? A Quick Primer

At its core, reinforcement learning is inspired by how humans and animals learn through consequences. An agent operates in an environment, takes actions, observes the outcomes (states), and receives rewards based on how favorable those outcomes are. Over time, the agent learns a **policy** — a mapping from states to actions — that maximizes cumulative reward.

Unlike supervised learning, which learns from labeled examples, RL requires no explicit answers. Instead, it optimizes behavior based on feedback loops, making it especially suited for **dynamic, interactive, and sequential decision-making** — all of which are central to conversational AI, dialogue systems, and agentic applications.

Why Reinforcement Learning Matters in NLP

Natural language is inherently sequential and interactive. Conversations unfold one utterance at a time. Writing a good response depends on context, tone, user intent, and even prior interactions. Traditional training methods fall short when the goal is not just to generate fluent text but to achieve a specific **long-term goal** — like keeping a user engaged, solving a query, or adhering to safety norms.

Reinforcement learning allows NLP models to:

- **Adapt dynamically** to user behavior or feedback.
- **Balance trade-offs** between short-term responses and long-term goals (e.g., user satisfaction).
- **Optimize for metrics that are hard to supervise**, such as helpfulness, safety, or persuasiveness.
- **Learn through interaction**, enabling continual improvement over time.

Applications of RL in NLP

1. Dialogue Systems and Conversational Agents

Reinforcement learning enables dialogue agents to learn not just what to say, but how to **sustain meaningful interactions**. These systems are trained to maximize a reward signal — such as conversation length, resolution success, or user satisfaction. Over time, the agent can learn which types of responses lead to productive conversations versus dead ends or frustration.

This is particularly important in customer support, healthcare bots, educational tutors, and personal assistants, where outcomes matter more than linguistic fluency alone.

2. Text Generation with Alignment

One of the most notable breakthroughs in NLP came with **Reinforcement Learning from Human Feedback (RLHF)** — a technique that fine-tunes language models not just for next-token prediction but for *alignment* with human preferences.

In this process:

- Human annotators rank multiple model-generated responses to prompts.
- A reward model is trained to predict which responses are preferred.
- The main language model is then fine-tuned using reinforcement learning (typically with the Proximal Policy Optimization algorithm) to generate outputs that maximize reward according to the trained reward model.

This approach was central to the development of **ChatGPT** and other aligned LLMs. It enables models to be more helpful, harmless, and honest — qualities that are difficult to encode in pretraining data alone.

3. Question Answering and Search Optimization

Reinforcement learning is also used to improve the performance of **retrieval-augmented generation (RAG)** systems and question-answering agents. Here, the reward can be tied to whether the correct answer was retrieved, whether the answer was helpful, or how confidently the user rated the interaction.

Agents can learn **search strategies**, refine their selection of evidence, or even formulate better follow-up queries, leading to more accurate and satisfying results.

4. Personalized Recommendations and Adaptation

In enterprise applications like **content personalization**, **email summarization**, or **adaptive learning platforms**, reinforcement learning allows models to personalize responses based on user feedback — explicit (like ratings or clicks) or implicit (like dwell time or return frequency).

For instance, an enterprise assistant could learn that a certain executive prefers brief summaries over detailed reports, and adapt accordingly over time, even without retraining from scratch.

Challenges in Applying RL to NLP

Despite its potential, reinforcement learning in NLP introduces significant challenges:

- **Sparse and delayed rewards:** Unlike games, where feedback is immediate, NLP tasks often have long sequences before any meaningful feedback is available. This makes learning inefficient and unstable.
- **Exploration vs. exploitation:** Finding the balance between trying new linguistic strategies and sticking to known effective ones is non-trivial — especially when safety and tone matter.
- **Credit assignment:** Determining which part of a generated response led to a positive or negative reward is complex due to the entangled and abstract nature of language.
- **Scalability and compute:** RL-based fine-tuning requires more computational resources than standard supervised training. It's harder to scale and generalize.
- **Reward model bias:** If the human preferences or reward functions are flawed, the model may learn unintended behaviors or exploit reward loopholes.

Looking Ahead: RL as a Core Pillar of Agentic AI

Reinforcement learning is no longer an exotic side track in NLP — it is quickly becoming a foundational layer in building **interactive, agentic, and adaptive language systems**. Future AI agents will not just answer questions; they will:

- Learn from outcomes.
- Adapt to personal or organizational goals.
- Reason over time and across tasks.
- Balance trade-offs between competing objectives (accuracy, speed, safety, engagement).

As the frontier shifts from passive prediction to active assistance, RL will play a central role — enabling language models to move beyond static responses toward dynamic, personalized, goal-driven behaviors.

In enterprise contexts, this will redefine automation and augmentation:

- **Autonomous copilots** that refine their advice based on user corrections.
- **Legal and compliance agents** that navigate complex document workflows with evolving strategies.
- **Customer engagement bots** that learn over time to improve loyalty and reduce churn.

Reinforcement learning will be the differentiator between static AI and **self-improving AI** — a critical stepping stone toward truly intelligent systems.

Ensemble and Hybrid Architectures in Neural Language Modeling

As deep learning continues to advance, no single architecture — whether RNN, CNN, LSTM, or Transformer — is sufficient to tackle the full spectrum of language-related challenges with consistent excellence. Natural language is far too varied, nuanced, and context-dependent. To handle these complexities and maximize performance across diverse tasks, researchers and engineers have increasingly turned to **ensemble** and **hybrid architectures**.

These architectures combine the strengths of multiple models or paradigms, often achieving better generalization, robustness, and accuracy than any single model alone. In many cases, ensemble and hybrid models form the foundation for production-grade systems in enterprises — from fraud detection and legal research to translation engines and conversational AI.

The Rationale for Combining Models

No model is perfect. Each neural architecture excels at certain types of reasoning or representation:

- **Recurrent networks** (like LSTMs and GRUs) model sequential dependencies effectively but struggle with long-term context and parallelism.
- **Convolutional networks** excel at local feature extraction and are computationally efficient but lack global context modeling.

- **Transformer models** capture long-range dependencies through self-attention but may require vast resources and struggle with fine-grained local patterns or noisy data.
- **Statistical models** or rule-based systems, while limited in expressiveness, can still be precise and interpretable in specific domains.

By combining different types of models — or multiple instances of the same model trained differently — ensembles and hybrids harness complementary strengths, reduce individual weaknesses, and build a more stable, intelligent system.

Ensemble Architectures: Multiple Minds Working Together

An **ensemble** in the context of neural language modeling is a collection of independent models whose predictions are aggregated — typically through averaging, voting, or weighted combinations — to produce a final output.

Benefits of Ensemble Models:

1. **Improved Accuracy:** The aggregation of multiple model outputs can smooth out individual errors and improve generalization.
2. **Reduced Variance:** Ensembles are less likely to overfit the training data, especially when component models have different architectures or training data splits.
3. **Robustness:** If one model performs poorly on edge cases or under noisy inputs, others can compensate, leading to more resilient systems.
4. **Domain Adaptation:** Different ensemble members can be tuned to different subdomains, languages, or data types.

Common Ensemble Techniques in NLP:

- **Bagging (Bootstrap Aggregating):** Training multiple instances of the same architecture on different subsets of the data to create a diverse set of models.
- **Model Averaging:** Taking the average of output probabilities from multiple models, often used in classification and translation.

- **Voting Systems:** Each model votes on a classification or decision; the majority vote determines the final output.
- **Mixture of Experts (MoE):** A more dynamic ensemble where only a subset of expert models are activated for each input based on a gating network. Modern large-scale LLMs, such as GShard and Switch Transformers, utilize MoE to manage scale and computation efficiently.

In enterprise deployments, ensembles are commonly used in mission-critical applications such as document classification, fraud detection, multilingual support systems, and question-answering engines where accuracy cannot be compromised.

Hybrid Architectures: Fusing Diverse Modeling Paradigms

Where ensembles run multiple models in parallel or in aggregation, **hybrid architectures** are more integrative. They embed different modeling paradigms *within* a single architecture, often by stacking or interleaving components from different neural network types — or even combining neural and symbolic systems.

Hybrid models can be thought of as **deeply integrated pipelines** that:

- Leverage different learning mechanisms at different stages.
- Combine low-level pattern detection with high-level reasoning.
- Enable multi-scale and multi-modal learning within the same model framework.

Examples of Hybrid Language Models:

1. **CNN + RNN Hybrids:**
   CNNs are used to capture short-range lexical and syntactic features from raw text, and their outputs are passed into RNNs (or LSTMs) for modeling long-range dependencies. These hybrids have been particularly effective in sentence classification and named entity recognition tasks.
2. **RNN + Transformer Hybrids:**
   Some architectures use RNNs to maintain compact, time-dependent

representations while Transformers handle attention across broader context windows. This approach can balance efficiency and depth of context in streaming applications like speech recognition or real-time translation.

3. **Symbolic + Neural Hybrids:**
   Neural networks are fused with rule-based systems or knowledge graphs to inject symbolic reasoning into probabilistic language models. This is especially relevant in domains requiring verifiability or external grounding — such as finance, legal tech, and scientific research.
4. **Neural + Retrieval-Augmented Hybrids:**
   Models like RETRO (Retrieval-Enhanced Transformer) and RAG (Retrieval-Augmented Generation) enhance language models by combining generation with external memory or document search. Instead of storing all factual knowledge in model weights, these systems dynamically retrieve relevant data during inference, improving performance on open-domain question answering and reducing hallucinations.
5. **Multimodal Hybrids:**
   In models like Flamingo, Gemini, or GPT-4V, different neural components process visual, textual, or auditory inputs and then fuse them via cross-attention or shared embedding spaces. These hybrids enable sophisticated capabilities like image captioning, visual QA, and video-language understanding — powering the next generation of human-computer interfaces.

Why Ensemble and Hybrid Models Matter in the LLM Era

As LLMs move from experimental labs to production systems, their architecture must evolve beyond raw scale. Simply increasing model size isn't always the best solution for real-world deployment. Enterprises and developers need:

- **Efficiency:** LLMs that are fast, cost-effective, and require less fine-tuning.
- **Robustness:** Models that perform reliably across tasks, domains, and noisy inputs.

- **Interpretability:** Systems that can provide confidence scores or explanations.
- **Modularity:** Architectures that can incorporate domain-specific knowledge or plug into structured databases.

This is where ensemble and hybrid designs offer compelling advantages. They allow for:

- **Model specialization without rigidity** — different components can be optimized for specific subtasks.
- **Sustainable scaling** — combining smaller models instead of a single massive one.
- **Greater flexibility** — hybrid systems can evolve more gracefully as new modalities or data types are introduced.

A Path Toward Agentic Intelligence

Hybrid and ensemble architectures also lay the groundwork for **agentic AI** — systems that don't just respond to prompts but can plan, remember, reason, and act autonomously. An agentic system may:

- Use a hybrid reasoning core combining LLMs with symbolic logic.
- Consult an ensemble of models for decision calibration or self-correction.
- Retrieve knowledge, update memory, and adapt behavior dynamically.

Such architectures reflect a shift toward *modular intelligence* — not unlike the human brain, where different regions specialize in different types of cognition but work together seamlessly.

Conclusion: Intelligence Through Integration

The evolution of neural language modeling has moved from simple sequence models to deeply layered systems capable of nuanced understanding and generation. But true intelligence — especially the kind required for enterprise-scale AI and agentic systems — demands **integration**.

Ensemble and hybrid architectures represent the intelligence of *diversity*: the ability to leverage different strengths, reconcile different views, and adapt to complex, changing environments. As language models continue to evolve, their ability to reason, collaborate, and serve across domains will depend not only on size or speed, but on how *well they combine* the best of what we know.

Scaling Challenges and Milestones

The success of neural language models over traditional statistical approaches wasn't instantaneous. It was the outcome of persistent innovation, structural breakthroughs, and relentless scaling — in data, model size, and compute. Each major leap in neural language modeling came with its own challenges, and overcoming them marked key milestones in the journey toward today's agentic, self-improving large language models.

The Scaling Imperative

At the heart of the deep learning revolution is a deceptively simple idea: performance scales with size. More parameters, more training data, and more compute power yield better results — often in surprising, nonlinear ways. This observation, formalized in scaling laws for language models, suggested that increasing model size wasn't just beneficial — it was foundational.

But scaling neural models posed enormous technical, architectural, and resource challenges. It required breakthroughs not only in algorithm design but also in systems engineering, distributed computing, and optimization strategies.

Challenge 1: The Compute Wall

One of the first bottlenecks encountered was the sheer computational cost of training large neural models. Early RNNs and LSTMs were already compute-intensive, especially when training on sequences of natural language. These models had to process tokens one at a time due to their sequential architecture, making parallelization difficult.

As the field moved from millions to billions of parameters, training even a single model began to require months of time on thousands of GPUs — with costs stretching into the millions of dollars. These resource demands limited participation to elite research labs and Big Tech companies with deep pockets and cloud-scale infrastructure.

This led to a dual-track development path:

- A race to build larger models (by OpenAI, Google, Meta, and others).
- A parallel effort to improve training efficiency, through methods like gradient checkpointing, mixed-precision arithmetic, and model parallelism.

Challenge 2: Data Curation at Scale

Neural language models rely on massive volumes of text. But simply collecting more data isn't enough — the *quality* and *diversity* of that data matter greatly.

Web text, news articles, books, Wikipedia, and forums became primary sources of training corpora. However, this raised questions:

- How do we filter out low-quality, biased, or duplicated content?
- How do we ensure diversity in languages, dialects, and domains?
- How do we prevent contamination from test sets or sensitive data?

Creating high-quality, multilingual, domain-rich datasets became a critical milestone. Projects like Common Crawl, The Pile, and RedPajama emerged as large-scale open corpora. Yet, much of the highest-quality data remains proprietary — giving certain organizations a lasting data advantage.

Challenge 3: Model Instability and Catastrophic Forgetting

As models grew in size and complexity, training stability became a serious concern. Gradient explosions, vanishing gradients, and optimization failures were common, especially in early deep recurrent models.

In recurrent architectures like RNNs and LSTMs, long-term dependencies were notoriously hard to learn. Despite mechanisms like gating and memory cells, these models struggled with understanding long documents or context spanning multiple paragraphs.

The introduction of the **Transformer** architecture resolved many of these issues by replacing recurrence with attention mechanisms. This not only improved stability but also unlocked massive parallelization — a key enabler for modern LLMs.

Yet, even Transformers introduced their own complexities:

- Training required careful initialization, learning rate schedules, and large batch sizes.
- Fine-tuning sometimes led to catastrophic forgetting, where models lost general capabilities after task-specific updates.
- Managing context length, especially in enterprise applications with long documents, remained an open challenge.

Each of these hurdles required novel training paradigms, such as curriculum learning, adapter layers, retrieval-augmented generation, and memory-augmented networks.

Challenge 4: Generalization vs Specialization

A major milestone in neural modeling was achieving models that not only performed well on training data but could *generalize* to unseen tasks — without needing retraining.

GPT-2 and later GPT-3 showed that large enough models could perform zero-shot and few-shot learning by conditioning on examples in the prompt. This was transformative. It meant a single pretrained model could serve multiple purposes — classification, summarization, question answering — without task-specific retraining.

However, generalization came with tradeoffs. Larger models:

- Required careful prompt engineering for optimal performance.
- Sometimes produced plausible-sounding but factually incorrect outputs.
- Struggled with tasks that demanded structured logic, long reasoning chains, or strict factuality.

To address these, the community moved toward hybrid approaches: foundation models pretrained on diverse data, followed by domain-specific fine-tuning or RLHF (reinforcement learning with human feedback) to align behavior with human preferences and enterprise needs.

Challenge 5: Alignment, Ethics, and Trust

As neural language models became more capable, a new frontier emerged: *alignment*. How do we ensure that models act in ways consistent with human values, legal norms, and safety requirements?

Scaling had introduced new risks:

- Larger models were more likely to amplify biases found in their training data.

- Their outputs, while fluent, could be misleading or toxic.
- Black-box behavior raised concerns about explainability and auditability.

Thus, a key milestone in the field was the development of **instruction-tuned**, **aligned**, and **safety-augmented** models. OpenAI's GPT-3.5 and GPT-4, Google's Gemini, and Anthropic's Claude models incorporated alignment techniques through RLHF, constitutional AI, or supervised fine-tuning on curated datasets of human preferences.

This alignment work was particularly critical for enterprise and public sector applications, where trust, accuracy, and traceability are non-negotiable.

Milestones That Changed the Game

Several key breakthroughs defined the modern era of neural language modeling:

1. **2017 – Transformer Architecture (Attention Is All You Need):**
   Replaced recurrence with attention; enabled massive scaling.
2. **2018 – BERT:**
   Introduced masked language modeling and bidirectional attention for understanding tasks.
3. **2019 – GPT-2:**
   Demonstrated emergent capabilities in text generation and zero-shot learning.
4. **2020 – GPT-3:**
   With 175 billion parameters, showcased few-shot learning, API-based deployment, and LLM-as-a-service models.
5. **2022-2023 – ChatGPT, GPT-4, Claude, Bard:**
   Brought conversational AI to the mainstream, incorporating memory, alignment, and early agentic behavior.
6. **2024–2025 – Agentic LLMs and Multimodal Models:**
   Models like GPT-4.5, Gemini 1.5, and Claude 3 advanced interactivity, multimodality, tool use, and self-correction — edging closer to truly autonomous agents.

Each of these milestones reflected not just architectural shifts, but successful navigation of scaling challenges across data, compute, governance, and trust.

Scaling Forward: Beyond Parameters

Today, the frontier is no longer just about bigger models — it's about **better models**:

- More efficient and greener training.
- Models that adapt to users and remember context over long horizons.
- Agents that can reason, plan, act, and reflect.
- Enterprise-grade tools with privacy, customization, and observability baked in.

The future of neural language modeling will not be won purely by scale — but by how intelligently we scale. The next milestone is not merely technical. It is human-centric: building systems that are collaborative, controllable, and beneficial to all.

CHAPTER FOUR

Decoding the Transformer — The Engine of Modern LLMs

Attention Is All You Need

In 2017, a groundbreaking paper titled *"Attention Is All You Need"* introduced a radically new approach to sequence modeling — the **Transformer architecture**. Unlike previous neural network models that relied on recurrence or convolutions to process sequential data like language, the Transformer model proposed a bold idea: eliminate both.

Instead, it placed the entire burden of understanding, processing, and generating language on a single core mechanism — **attention**.

This deceptively simple concept reshaped the landscape of natural language processing (NLP), catalyzing the development of powerful models like BERT, GPT, T5, and, eventually, the generative large language models (LLMs) powering today's AI revolution.

The Problem with Traditional Sequence Models

To appreciate the Transformer, it helps to first understand what it replaced.

Prior to Transformers, language models typically used **Recurrent Neural Networks (RNNs)** or their more advanced variants like **LSTMs** and **GRUs.**

These models processed language tokens one at a time — maintaining an internal memory of past words as they moved through a sequence.

While conceptually sound, this sequential nature came with drawbacks:

- **Slow training:** Tokens had to be processed one after another, limiting parallelization.
- **Difficulty with long-range dependencies:** RNNs struggled to connect information across long sequences (e.g., relating the subject of a sentence to a verb far away).
- **Vanishing gradients:** As sequences grew longer, gradients became unstable during training, affecting learning.

Enter the Transformer: a fully parallel, position-aware, attention-driven architecture that sidestepped these problems with elegance and scalability.

What Is Attention, and Why Does It Matter?

At the heart of the Transformer is **self-attention**, a mechanism that allows the model to dynamically focus on different parts of the input when processing a token. Unlike traditional approaches that rely on fixed-size windows or step-by-step memory, attention enables the model to "look around" the entire sentence — and even across documents — to determine what matters most at any given point.

Think of it like this: when a human reads a sentence like

"The bird saw the man with the telescope."

— they might pause to ask: *Who has the telescope? The bird or the man?*

Understanding this ambiguity requires weighing relationships across multiple words — not just those nearby. This is what attention does: it computes **relevance scores** between all tokens in a sequence, allowing the model to decide which words to pay more attention to when processing each token.

Self-Attention: A Closer Look

In a self-attention layer, each token (word or subword) is transformed into three vectors:

- **Query (Q)** — what it wants to know.

- **Key (K)** — what it has to offer.
- **Value (V)** — the actual content to retrieve if there's a match.

The model computes a **similarity score** between each token's query and every other token's key — this determines how much attention the token should pay to others. These scores are then used to weight the value vectors, producing a contextualized representation for each token.

In practical terms, self-attention means:

- Every token learns to interpret itself **in the context** of the entire sentence.
- The model can capture **hierarchical, syntactic, and semantic** dependencies — without being constrained by linear order.
- Training can be **fully parallelized** — a dramatic boost in performance over RNNs.

This simple mechanism is recursive and scalable, making it ideal for training on massive datasets with billions of tokens — which is exactly what modern LLMs do.

Multi-Head Attention: Seeing From Many Angles

A single attention mechanism might focus on grammatical structure, while another might focus on coreference, and yet another on semantic relationships.

To allow the model to look at the input from multiple perspectives simultaneously, Transformers use **multi-head attention** — running multiple self-attention operations in parallel, each with its own learned parameters. The outputs from these heads are then combined and passed on for further processing.

This means a single Transformer layer can:

- Attend to subject-verb agreement in one head.
- Track sentiment in another.
- Follow narrative structure in yet another.

By layering these insights across multiple layers, the model builds deep, nuanced representations of language.

Positional Encoding: Knowing the Order Without Recurrence

Since the Transformer processes tokens in parallel — not sequentially — it lacks any inherent sense of token order. To solve this, it injects **positional encodings** into the input embeddings. These encodings help the model understand whether a token appears first, last, or somewhere in between.

These encodings are often implemented as sine and cosine waves of varying frequencies or learned vectors, and they are added to the input embeddings before attention is applied. This small step is what allows Transformers to capture the linear structure of language — essential for tasks like syntax parsing or sentence generation.

The Power and Simplicity of "Attention Only"

The title of the original paper — *Attention Is All You Need* — wasn't just catchy. It was a manifesto.

It proposed that **recurrence and convolution were unnecessary**, that a model could learn everything it needed about language by dynamically attending to context. This bold assertion proved correct.

Since then, the Transformer has:

- **Replaced RNNs and CNNs** as the architecture of choice in NLP.
- **Scaled effortlessly** to billions of parameters.
- **Powered generalist models** that can translate, summarize, code, chat, and more.
- **Become the foundation of agentic AI**, where language models interact with tools, memory, and humans in complex workflows.

Attention alone proved not only sufficient — but superior.

Why This Matters in the Age of LLMs

The success of the Transformer isn't academic. It underpins every modern large language model — including GPT-3, GPT-4, PaLM, Claude, LLaMA, and Gemini. It is the architecture that made agentic AI feasible, scalable, and practical.

In enterprise contexts, this means:

- **Faster model training:** Parallel processing allows efficient use of compute resources.
- **Greater versatility:** One architecture can support multiple language tasks.
- **Improved performance:** Attention leads to richer understanding of domain-specific language.
- **Plug-and-play extensibility:** Transformers are modular — they can be fine-tuned, extended with memory, or integrated with external tools.

From automated legal analysis to personalized marketing copy, from customer service to scientific discovery, the Transformer is the hidden engine behind intelligent systems that speak, think, and adapt.

Final Thoughts: From Mechanism to Movement

"Attention is all you need" wasn't just a research title — it became a turning point in the history of AI. The Transformer proved that language understanding could be reimagined not through mimicry of human memory or rigid rule-based logic, but through flexible, learned focus.

The elegance of attention lies in its simplicity — yet its impact is profound. It turned the art of language into a scalable science, laying the foundation for general-purpose intelligence systems.

As we move into the era of agentic AI — where models don't just complete text but interact, reason, and adapt — attention will remain the cognitive backbone of the machines we build.

Anatomy of the Transformer

To understand how large language models (LLMs) like GPT, Gemini, or Claude work, we must begin by dissecting the architecture at their core: the **Transformer**. Introduced in 2017 by Vaswani et al. in the seminal paper *"Attention is All You Need"*, the Transformer fundamentally redefined how machines process sequential data such as text.

Unlike its predecessors—Recurrent Neural Networks (RNNs) and Long Short-Term Memory (LSTM) networks—which processed text sequentially, Transformers introduced a new paradigm: parallel processing with self-attention. This enabled unparalleled scalability, efficiency, and accuracy in modeling complex language patterns.

Let's now unpack the core components of the Transformer: **embeddings, layers, attention heads, positional encodings**, and the architectural duality of **encoder and decoder**.

Embeddings: Turning Words into Vectors

Before the Transformer can work with language, it must convert human-readable text into machine-readable numerical form. This is where **embeddings** come in.

Words, subwords, or tokens are mapped into high-dimensional continuous vector spaces. These embeddings capture semantic meaning based on usage. For instance, the words "king" and "queen" would occupy nearby spaces in this vector world, reflecting their related meanings.

Transformers typically begin by looking up each token in an **embedding matrix** — a learned representation that evolves during training. The output is a sequence of dense vectors, each encoding the identity and (eventually) the meaning of the input token.

However, these embeddings alone are insufficient — they carry no information about the order in which tokens appear. That's where positional encoding comes in.

Positional Encoding: Injecting Sequence into Structure

Transformers, unlike RNNs, have no inherent sense of sequence. They treat all tokens simultaneously and independently. This boosts parallelism but loses order — a critical property of language.

To address this, the Transformer adds **positional encodings** to the input embeddings. These are specially constructed vectors that indicate a token's position in the sequence.

There are two main approaches:

- **Fixed positional encodings**, such as sinusoidal functions used in the original paper, where the encoding at each position is derived mathematically.
- **Learned positional encodings**, where position vectors are learned like word embeddings.

By adding these encodings to the input embeddings, the model can distinguish between "the cat chased the dog" and "the dog chased the cat" — both made of the same words but entirely different meanings due to word order.

Layers: Stacking Depth for Abstraction

The power of the Transformer lies not just in its individual components, but in how they are **stacked into deep layers.**

Each Transformer layer consists of:

1. **Multi-Head Self-Attention**
2. **Feedforward Neural Network (FFN)**
3. **Residual Connections and Layer Normalization**

These layers are stacked repeatedly (e.g., 12, 24, or 96 times) to create deeper models. Each layer processes the outputs of the one below, gradually building more abstract, contextual representations.

In earlier layers, the model may detect grammar or syntax; in later layers, it grasps logic, relationships, or domain-specific knowledge. This hierarchical abstraction is key to the Transformer's ability to generalize.

Attention Heads: The Heart of the Transformer

The **attention mechanism** is the beating heart of the Transformer, allowing the model to "look around" at other words in the sentence when processing a specific word.

Each attention operation produces a *weighted average* of other token representations based on how relevant they are. These weights are learned during training and allow the model to capture long-range dependencies, relationships, and contextual clues.

Rather than relying on a single attention mechanism, the Transformer uses **multi-head attention** — running several attention operations in parallel, each with its own learnable projection. This allows the model to capture different types of relationships simultaneously.

For instance, one head might learn syntactic dependencies (like subject-verb agreement), while another learns semantic roles (like actor-action-object).

These multiple heads are then concatenated and linearly transformed, fusing multiple perspectives into a richer understanding.

Encoder vs. Decoder: Two Halves, Two Roles

The original Transformer architecture is divided into two halves: the **encoder** and the **decoder**, each designed for different tasks.

Encoder: Understanding the Input

The encoder is responsible for **digesting the input sequence** and converting it into a dense, contextualized representation. It consists of a stack of identical layers, each with:

- Multi-head **self-attention**: where each word can attend to every other word in the input.
- Position-wise feedforward network: to transform and refine the attended information.
- Add & norm layers (residual connections + layer normalization): to stabilize learning and preserve gradients.

Encoders are ideal for **understanding tasks** — such as classification, sentiment analysis, and question answering — where the goal is to interpret a given piece of text.

Decoder: Generating the Output

The decoder, on the other hand, is designed for **generation** — producing output sequences such as translations, summaries, or conversational responses.

It also contains multiple layers, each composed of:

- Masked self-attention: ensuring that the model can only attend to earlier positions in the output (important during training to prevent cheating).
- Encoder-decoder attention: allowing the decoder to focus on relevant parts of the encoded input.
- Feedforward network and add & norm layers, like in the encoder.

Decoders are central to **sequence generation tasks**, where the model generates one token at a time based on the input and the tokens it has already generated.

Unified or Split Architecture

While the original Transformer used an **encoder-decoder** structure (e.g., in **T5**, **BART**, or **MarianMT**), many modern LLMs use a **decoder-only** architecture, like the GPT series. These models discard the encoder entirely and focus on **autoregressive generation**, where each new token is predicted based on previous tokens in the sequence.

Conversely, models like **BERT** use only the encoder and are trained in a **bidirectional** fashion to understand entire sequences for tasks like classification, extraction, or representation learning.

Whether encoder-only, decoder-only, or encoder-decoder, the Transformer remains the universal scaffold on which today's most powerful language models are built.

Closing Thoughts

The Transformer's anatomy — from token embeddings to multi-head attention, from deep layered abstraction to its dual architecture — is the blueprint for nearly every major language model today. Its elegance lies in its modularity: simple components, when combined with scale and data, yield emergent capabilities that rival or exceed human-level language understanding and generation.

Understanding these building blocks isn't just academic. For enterprise leaders, developers, and AI practitioners, it's essential knowledge — enabling you to choose, fine-tune, and deploy LLMs that are aligned with your goals, data, and values.

Transformer-Based Model Families

The Transformer architecture, first introduced in 2017 through the groundbreaking paper *"Attention Is All You Need,"* has become the foundational design behind virtually all large language models today. But the Transformer itself is not a singular model — it is a flexible and extensible neural architecture that has since given rise to an entire ecosystem of specialized models, each with its own purpose, training paradigm, and strengths.

Over time, this architecture has been adapted, refined, and optimized by research labs and AI companies to solve distinct classes of tasks — from understanding language to generating it, from classification to summarization, from multilingual translation to domain-specific reasoning.

This section explores the key Transformer-based model families that have shaped the modern LLM landscape, demystifying their origins, design principles, and roles in real-world AI applications.

BERT: Bidirectional Encoder Representations from Transformers

BERT was a landmark innovation introduced by Google in 2018 that changed the trajectory of natural language understanding (NLU). Prior to BERT, most language models processed text from left to right (unidirectionally), limiting their contextual awareness. BERT, in contrast, introduced a **bidirectional approach**, allowing the model to look at the full context of a word — both the words that come before and after it — during training.

The core training objective for BERT is **Masked Language Modeling (MLM)**: randomly masking words in a sentence and training the model to predict the missing words. This forces the model to understand language deeply, rather than relying on superficial co-occurrence patterns.

BERT became the new standard for tasks like sentiment analysis, question answering (QA), named entity recognition (NER), and more. However, it is **not generative** — it's optimized for understanding, not producing text.

GPT: Generative Pretrained Transformer

In contrast to BERT, GPT was designed from the outset for **generation**. Introduced by OpenAI, the GPT family follows a **unidirectional** or **causal** approach — the model learns to predict the next word in a sequence, given all the previous words. This autoregressive setup makes it ideal for fluent text generation.

The GPT models are trained on vast datasets in an unsupervised manner, then optionally fine-tuned for specific tasks. GPT-2 and GPT-3, in particular, showcased the **emergence** of general-purpose language abilities: from summarization to translation, question answering to storytelling —

without explicit task-specific training.

GPT is a true workhorse of agentic AI: capable of not just completing text but reasoning across complex prompts, synthesizing information, and even simulating dialogue. This makes it foundational for conversational agents, copilots, creative writing tools, and more.

T5: Text-to-Text Transfer Transformer

Developed by Google Research, T5 reimagined all NLP tasks as a **text-to-text problem**. Whether the goal is translation, summarization, classification, or question answering, everything is cast as: "input text → output text."

For example:

- Input: "Translate English to French: The book is on the table."
- Output: "Le livre est sur la table."

This unified framing makes T5 highly versatile and elegant. Trained on a massive multi-task dataset called **C4 (Colossal Clean Crawled Corpus)**, T5 demonstrated strong generalization across many benchmarks.

T5 combines BERT's deep understanding with GPT's generation capabilities — it uses both an **encoder and a decoder**, making it a full **sequence-to-sequence model**, particularly well-suited for complex transformations of text.

RoBERTa: A Robustly Optimized BERT Approach

RoBERTa, also by Facebook AI (Meta), is not a fundamentally new architecture, but rather an optimized reimplementation of BERT with several critical improvements:

- Trained on more data.
- Longer sequences.
- Removed the next sentence prediction task (NSP) which BERT used but proved less helpful.
- Larger mini-batches and more training steps.

The result was a model that significantly outperformed BERT on many standard NLP benchmarks. RoBERTa illustrates a key point in the LLM era: **sometimes better training trumps architectural changes.**

In enterprise environments, RoBERTa is a popular choice for building high-accuracy classifiers, compliance detectors, and QA systems, especially when fine-tuned on in-domain data.

XLNet: Generalized Autoregressive Pretraining

XLNet, created by researchers at Google and Carnegie Mellon, addresses a key limitation of BERT's masked language modeling: the mismatch between pretraining (predicting masked words) and fine-tuning (predicting sequences).

XLNet introduces **permutation-based language modeling** — instead of masking words, it learns to predict tokens in all possible orders of the sequence. This allows it to capture bidirectional context (like BERT) while still being **autoregressive** (like GPT).

XLNet's architecture is also enhanced with components from Transformer-XL, enabling **longer context windows** than traditional Transformers. This makes XLNet especially valuable for tasks requiring understanding of long documents or complex sequences.

DistilBERT: Lighter, Faster, Smaller

While full-sized BERT is powerful, it is computationally expensive. DistilBERT is a **compressed version of BERT**, designed through a process called **knowledge distillation**, where a smaller "student" model learns to mimic the behavior of a larger "teacher" model.

DistilBERT retains 97% of BERT's performance while being 40% smaller and 60% faster. It is ideal for resource-constrained applications — such as mobile devices, real-time inference, or scaled deployments across millions of users.

DistilBERT underscores an emerging trend: **model efficiency is becoming as critical as accuracy**, especially in production.

mBERT: Multilingual BERT

mBERT is a multilingual extension of BERT, trained on over 100 languages simultaneously using Wikipedia data. It learns **shared representations across languages**, allowing it to perform tasks like multilingual QA or zero-shot translation.

Unlike traditional translation models, mBERT does not require explicit alignment between languages — it learns a **language-agnostic embedding space**, where similar ideas map to similar representations regardless of language.

This makes mBERT a powerful tool in global enterprise environments, cross-cultural applications, and international customer support — where language diversity is the norm.

ERNIE: Knowledge-Enhanced Pretraining

ERNIE (Enhanced Representation through Knowledge Integration), developed by Baidu (and later adapted by others), incorporates **structured knowledge** into the Transformer training process.

While models like BERT or GPT learn from raw text, ERNIE augments this with **entity-level and fact-level awareness** — integrating knowledge graphs, semantic roles, and named entities during training. This allows ERNIE to better understand relationships between concepts, and reason beyond surface-level patterns.

ERNIE exemplifies the next frontier in LLMs: **combining statistical learning with symbolic knowledge** to produce models that not only read but understand.

Other Notable Transformer Families

Several additional Transformer-based models have emerged, each targeting specific niches:

- **CamemBERT**: A BERT variant fine-tuned for the French language.
- **ALBERT**: A Lite BERT, which reduces parameter count through cross-layer sharing and factorized embeddings.
- **ELECTRA**: Trains more efficiently by replacing masked language modeling with a "discriminator" task — distinguishing real tokens from fake ones.

- **BioBERT, SciBERT**: Domain-specialized BERT variants for biomedical and scientific text.
- **FLAN-T5 and PaLM**: Google's later models that build on the T5 framework with reinforcement learning and human feedback (RLHF).
- **Phi, Orca, LLaMA**: Open-source model families aimed at compact, aligned, or instruction-tuned LLMs.

Each of these represents an evolutionary response to a specific need — be it speed, accuracy, domain fit, or generalization.

Final Thoughts: A Thriving Ecosystem

The Transformer has catalyzed an explosion of innovation in language modeling. From the generative power of GPT to the language-agnostic reach of mBERT, from the interpretive depth of BERT to the task unification of T5, each model family reflects a deepening understanding of both language and intelligence.

For enterprises, governments, and developers alike, this diversity offers a robust toolkit to match AI capabilities with real-world needs — whether the goal is global scale, domain specificity, ethical alignment, or resource efficiency.

Understanding these model families is more than academic curiosity — it's the key to making informed choices in the AI-first era.

Pretraining, Fine-Tuning, and Transfer Learning

At the heart of modern large language models lies a powerful three-stage learning paradigm: **pretraining, fine-tuning**, and **transfer learning**. These stages form the backbone of how transformers evolve from general-purpose statistical learners to domain-aware, task-specialized assistants that can power a wide range of intelligent applications.

The Power of Pretraining: Learning from the World

Pretraining is the foundational phase in the life cycle of a large language model. It is during this phase that the model is first exposed to the broad and chaotic richness of human language — the messy, unstructured, contradictory, and nuanced text data that spans books, articles, websites, code repositories, transcripts, and more.

Unlike traditional supervised learning, which depends on curated labels, pretraining is largely **self-supervised**. That is, the model learns by predicting parts of the data from other parts — without needing external annotation.

For example, in autoregressive models like GPT, the model is trained to predict the next word in a sequence. Given a fragment like "The sun rises in the...", it must guess what comes next — "east." This simple act, performed billions of times across diverse text, builds a statistical map of language: syntax, semantics, grammar, idioms, world knowledge, and even style.

In contrast, models like BERT use **masked language modeling** — randomly hiding words and forcing the model to infer the missing parts from context on both sides. This bidirectional perspective makes BERT-like models well-suited for understanding the meaning of entire sentences or documents.

Pretraining is **massive** in scale. Models are trained over billions (or trillions) of words, using vast computational resources across hundreds or thousands of GPUs. But the result is a model that develops **general linguistic intelligence**: a high-dimensional, flexible understanding of how words, concepts, and facts relate.

At this stage, the model has not been taught to *do* anything specific — it has merely absorbed the statistical structure of language and knowledge embedded in its training corpus. Think of this as giving the model its *education* — reading all the books in the library, understanding patterns, but not yet specializing in any profession.

Fine-Tuning: Specializing the Generalist

While pretrained models are broadly capable, they are not immediately optimal for specific tasks. A model trained to predict the next word in a novel or news article may not be accurate enough to classify legal documents or answer customer support tickets out-of-the-box.

This is where **fine-tuning** comes in.

Fine-tuning is a **targeted, supervised learning process** that adapts the pretrained model to a specific downstream task using labeled data. For instance:

- A model fine-tuned on customer interactions can become a customer service chatbot.
- One fine-tuned on medical records can assist in diagnosis or summarization.
- Another fine-tuned on legal texts can help with contract review or legal research.

During fine-tuning, the model's parameters are updated — usually to a smaller extent than during pretraining — so it can learn the patterns that matter most for the target task. Crucially, because the model has already learned rich general-purpose language patterns during pretraining, it requires **far less data and time** to adapt compared to training a model from scratch.

Fine-tuning can also include **instruction tuning**, where the model learns to follow human-written instructions in natural language — making it more responsive to queries and more aligned with human expectations. This is essential in building LLMs that can act as assistants, not just text generators.

In many cases, enterprises conduct fine-tuning using proprietary or domain-specific data. For example, a telecom company might fine-tune an LLM on call center logs, complaint resolution emails, and regulatory FAQs to create a multilingual customer assistant.

The key advantage is this: **fine-tuning allows a general model to become expert in your domain**, without needing to build a new model from scratch.

Transfer Learning: Reusing Intelligence

Pretraining and fine-tuning together constitute a broader paradigm called **transfer learning** — a major breakthrough in modern AI.

Transfer learning means that a model trained on one task or dataset can be repurposed and adapted to another, often with minimal data or training. This is a sharp departure from traditional machine learning, where models had to be trained from the ground up for every task, every time.

In the context of transformers and LLMs, transfer learning operates at multiple levels:

1. **From general to specific**: A model pretrained on general internet text is fine-tuned for a legal, medical, or enterprise use case.

2. **From one language to another**: Multilingual models pretrained on dozens of languages can be adapted to local languages with limited data — crucial for inclusion in developing regions.
3. **From one task to another**: A model fine-tuned for question answering can often be adapted to summarization or classification with minimal changes.

Transfer learning reduces the cost of AI adoption dramatically. Enterprises no longer need vast labeled datasets or huge compute budgets to build intelligent systems. They can start from powerful open-source or commercial base models and adapt them incrementally — making high-quality AI feasible for even low-resource contexts, such as low-end smartphones or bandwidth-limited regions.

In fact, in edge use cases — like real-time spam/scam call detection on-device — small, transfer-learned models are often deployed on-device without requiring server connectivity, ensuring privacy, speed, and accessibility for millions of users.

Putting It All Together: The Learning Lifecycle

Let's summarize how these components interact in the development of LLMs:

1. **Pretraining** builds a massive, general-purpose model with linguistic and factual knowledge from large-scale corpora. It's expensive and time-consuming, but done only once (usually by a foundation model provider).
2. **Fine-tuning** adapts this model to specific tasks, domains, or companies using task-specific data — making it practical, relevant, and safe for deployment.
3. **Transfer learning** enables this adaptation efficiently, allowing models to move between tasks, domains, and languages — often without full retraining.

This lifecycle — pretrain, fine-tune, transfer — is not static. With **agentic systems**, the loop can continue indefinitely. Models can self-adapt, observe feedback, improve iteratively, and even retrain on-the-fly. This opens the door to **self-learning systems** that evolve with use, data, and human interaction.

Why This Matters for the Enterprise and the World

In a world increasingly powered by language — documents, conversations, search queries, compliance records, and multilingual chat — the ability to harness language at scale is not a luxury but a necessity.

The pretraining-fine-tuning-transfer paradigm makes this possible:

- **Start with intelligence** that understands the world.
- **Specialize it** to your industry, language, and workflows.
- **Deploy it at scale**, responsibly and cost-effectively.

This is the blueprint not just for building better chatbots or automating workflows — but for creating intelligent assistants, decision-support tools, and agents that learn and grow with you.

Real-World Applications of Transformer Architectures

The introduction of the Transformer architecture in the seminal 2017 paper *"Attention Is All You Need"* fundamentally redefined what was possible in artificial intelligence. Unlike its predecessors — recurrent or convolutional networks — the Transformer was designed for scale, parallelism, and context awareness. This has made it the backbone of nearly every large-scale AI system built since, particularly in the realm of language, vision, code, speech, and beyond.

Transformer models are no longer confined to academic research or benchmark datasets. They are deployed at scale across industries, influencing real-world experiences, accelerating productivity, and driving billions in economic value. What follows is a deep exploration of how Transformer architectures are reshaping the world across sectors, modalities, and workflows.

1. Natural Language Processing: The First Frontier

The earliest and most impactful applications of Transformers emerged in **natural language processing (NLP)**. Transformers can model long-range dependencies, understand contextual relationships between words, and handle polysemy and ambiguity far better than previous architectures.

Real-world NLP applications powered by Transformers include:

- **Text summarization** in news aggregation platforms, legal tech, and enterprise documentation systems.
- **Machine translation** across more than 100 languages, now offering near-human fluency in real-time communication platforms.
- **Text classification** for sentiment analysis, hate speech detection, spam filtering, and intent recognition in customer support.
- **Named entity recognition (NER)** to extract names, places, dates, and monetary amounts from contracts, emails, and reports.
- **Conversational AI**, where Transformers power chatbots, virtual assistants, and dialogue agents that can hold context-rich conversations across turns.

These use cases form the foundation of intelligent enterprise automation, enabling systems to read, write, and understand language at scale.

2. Search, Retrieval, and Recommendation

Transformer-based models such as **BERT**, **T5**, and **ColBERT** have revolutionized search engines by enabling **semantic understanding** rather than just keyword matching.

Real-world impact includes:

- **Enterprise search platforms** that retrieve documents or knowledge base entries based on user intent, not exact word matches.
- **Legal and compliance tools** that surface relevant precedents or policy documents with high contextual alignment.
- **E-commerce recommendation engines** that personalize product suggestions based on natural language queries, reviews, and behavioral embeddings.
- **Healthcare knowledge retrieval** systems that assist clinicians in surfacing research papers, treatment options, and patient insights.

These models dramatically improve relevance, reduce noise, and enable deeper knowledge discovery across fragmented data silos.

3. Intelligent Code Generation and Developer Copilots

Code is a form of language, and Transformers trained on programming languages (e.g., Codex, CodeT5, PolyCoder) have unlocked a new era in **developer productivity**.

Real-world Transformer-powered capabilities include:

- **Autocomplete and code generation** in IDEs, assisting developers with syntax, logic, and best practices.
- **Code translation and refactoring**, converting code between languages or upgrading legacy codebases.
- **Bug detection and resolution**, suggesting patches, test cases, or alternatives based on learned patterns.
- **Documentation generation**, where models write inline comments or API usage summaries.

Enterprise development teams now use Transformers to speed up delivery cycles, reduce technical debt, and onboard junior developers more effectively.

4. Vision-Language Applications and Multimodal Intelligence

Transformers are not limited to text. Vision Transformers (ViTs), multimodal models (like CLIP, Flamingo, and Gemini), and image-captioning systems have extended the architecture's reach into the visual domain.

Key real-world applications include:

- **Image search and tagging**, where models generate rich semantic labels from images.
- **Visual Question Answering (VQA)**, enabling AI to understand charts, dashboards, product manuals, and user-uploaded content.
- **Digital accessibility**, converting images and documents into screen-reader-friendly text.
- **Surveillance and anomaly detection**, where models identify objects, behaviors, or events of interest in real-time video streams.
- **Retail applications**, where shelf monitoring, product discovery, and customer analytics are powered by visual-language fusion.

Transformers allow enterprises to merge structured and unstructured sensory data into unified decision-making pipelines.

5. Real-Time Translation and Cross-Cultural Communication

Multilingual Transformer models like **mBART**, **mT5**, **mBERT**, and **NLLB (No Language Left Behind)** have made it possible to provide accurate, real-time translation in over 200 languages, including under-resourced ones.

Real-world impacts:

- **Global customer support** in native languages without the need for local agents.
- **Cross-border e-commerce**, where product descriptions, reviews, and communications are seamlessly translated.
- **Multilingual education platforms**, delivering content to learners regardless of their linguistic background.
- **Government and humanitarian outreach**, ensuring that critical health, policy, or disaster-related information reaches remote communities.

By reducing the language barrier, Transformers expand inclusivity, access, and participation across global societies.

6. Agentic AI Systems and Autonomous Workflows

With instruction-following models (e.g., GPT-4, Claude, Gemini) and fine-tuned agents like AutoGPT or ReAct-style planners, Transformers are now core to **agentic AI** — systems that can reason, plan, and take action.

These agents, often configured via APIs or tools, are being used to:

- **Automate repetitive workflows** such as meeting note generation, email triage, or HR onboarding.
- **Orchestrate multi-step tasks**, such as compiling market research, generating reports, or booking travel.
- **Simulate domain experts**, providing legal, financial, or medical insights based on context.
- **Integrate with enterprise tools**, reading CRM entries, summarizing call transcripts, and suggesting next steps.

This agentic layer is the future of work — where humans specify goals, and AI systems autonomously execute across tools and data sources.

7. Healthcare and Biomedical Intelligence

Specialized Transformers (e.g., BioBERT, ClinicalBERT, PubMedGPT) have demonstrated strong capabilities in understanding clinical text, research literature, and patient data.

Current applications include:

- **Medical record summarization**, reducing physician burnout while preserving clinical fidelity.
- **Drug discovery and repurposing**, where models mine literature and molecule data for therapeutic insights.

- **Radiology report generation**, converting visual scans into structured summaries using vision-language Transformers.
- **Symptom triage and virtual diagnostics**, through conversational front ends powered by LLMs trained on medical corpora.

These models help bridge the gap between overwhelming medical data and actionable patient care.

8. On-Device and Low-Latency Applications

Thanks to lightweight variants like **DistilBERT**, **TinyBERT**, **MobileBERT**, and **Phi**, Transformer models are now being deployed **on-device**, including on low-end smartphones.

Applications include:

- **Voice call classification and transcription**, where spam/scam/ham detection happens in real-time, without the need for internet connectivity.
- **Privacy-preserving personal assistants**, with models running locally to manage schedules, queries, or messages securely.
- **Offline translation and summarization**, enabling access to critical language services in remote or bandwidth-constrained regions.

This is especially transformative in **developing countries**, where serverless, local intelligence enables inclusive digital access and security at scale.

9. Creative and Generative Applications

Transformers are at the heart of modern creative workflows — from co-writing fiction and generating marketing copy to creating lyrics, scripts, and even jokes.

Examples:

- **Advertising agencies** use GPT-based systems to brainstorm slogans and generate campaign narratives.
- **Filmmakers and content creators** leverage script-writing assistants that understand tone, pacing, and character arcs.
- **Musicians** experiment with lyric generators, chord progressions, and remix suggestions.
- **Journalists** use LLMs for research assistance, headline generation, and automatic summarization.

Here, the Transformer becomes not just a tool for logic, but a collaborator in the artistic process.

10. Strategic Decision Support and Knowledge Reasoning

In corporate boardrooms, regulatory environments, and national security operations, Transformers are assisting in high-stakes, context-rich decision-making.

Applications include:

- **Risk assessment**, drawing insights from legal, financial, and geopolitical narratives.
- **Competitive intelligence**, aggregating public sources, patents, and filings to provide strategy briefs.
- **Regulatory compliance**, scanning policies and laws for relevance, gaps, or updates.
- **Knowledge graphs and memory augmentation**, where models generate and query interconnected facts, entities, and events.

This positions Transformer-based systems not merely as assistants, but as **augmented reasoning engines** for leaders and analysts.

Conclusion: The Transformer as a General Intelligence Substrate

Transformers are no longer just an architecture for NLP. They are a **general substrate** for building intelligent systems that can understand, reason, and interact across text, speech, vision, and code — increasingly with agentic behavior and real-world impact.

From customer support desks in Nairobi to research labs in Boston, from low-end smartphones in Dhaka to cloud-scale APIs in San Francisco — the Transformer is the common engine driving the next wave of AI-native experiences.

Understanding its real-world applications is not just a technical tour — it is a window into how modern civilization is being reshaped, industry by industry, interaction by interaction, word by word.

CHAPTER FIVE

The Age of LLMs — From Foundation Models to Intelligent Agents

The Rise of Foundation Models

Over the last decade, artificial intelligence has transitioned from specialized, narrow applications toward more general-purpose, adaptable, and universal systems. This transformation was neither sudden nor accidental. It was made possible by a class of machine learning systems known as **foundation models** — large-scale models pre-trained on broad and diverse datasets and capable of powering a wide variety of downstream tasks with minimal task-specific tuning.

Foundation models mark a paradigm shift in the way we think about AI development. Instead of building separate models for each task — one for translation, another for summarization, another for sentiment analysis — we now build a single, powerful model that can adapt to all these tasks with little or no additional training. This approach has redefined scale, flexibility, and usability across the AI landscape.

From Task-Specific Models to Generalist Systems

Historically, the AI community relied on task-specific architectures. Each use case — whether it was recognizing faces, detecting spam, or predicting stock prices — required bespoke data pipelines, hand-engineered features, and purpose-built algorithms. These models were often brittle, expensive to maintain, and difficult to transfer across domains.

Foundation models broke away from this paradigm. They are trained on massive, unstructured datasets scraped from the internet — including books, articles, web pages, conversations, and code — encompassing a wide spectrum of human knowledge and expression. The result is a general-purpose model that can perform many tasks without being explicitly trained on each one.

This pretraining phase gives the model a rich internal representation of language, reasoning, and even latent world knowledge — what some describe as *emergent intelligence.* With simple prompting or light fine-tuning, these models can now complete a wide range of tasks: answering questions, summarizing text, generating code, translating languages, and even simulating human behavior.

Why "Foundation" Models?

The term *foundation model* signifies their central role in AI development. Like a foundation beneath a building, these models serve as the base upon which many specialized applications can be constructed. In enterprise settings, a single foundation model can support:

- Chatbots across departments (support, HR, IT).
- Intelligent document processing.
- Legal and compliance automation.
- Personalized marketing content.
- Coding assistants for developers.
- Executive insight summarizers.

Their adaptability makes them not just scalable, but *strategic* — offering a consistent substrate for intelligence across an organization's workflows.

What Makes Foundation Models Different?

Several defining characteristics separate foundation models from traditional AI systems:

1. Scale

Foundation models are massive — often measured in billions or trillions of parameters. This scale is not just for show; it allows them to capture complex patterns, long-range dependencies, and nuanced relationships across language, logic, and semantics. Larger models tend to generalize better, exhibit more robust reasoning, and adapt more easily to novel prompts.

2. Generalization

Unlike earlier models that required task-specific training data and pipelines, foundation models generalize across tasks. With just a few examples (few-shot learning) or even a plain-language instruction (zero-shot learning), they can perform complex operations. This generalization dramatically reduces the need for labeled data and expensive retraining cycles.

3. Transferability

Foundation models exhibit strong transfer learning capabilities. Knowledge learned in one domain (e.g., legal text) can improve performance in another (e.g., contract generation). This makes them highly efficient in multi-domain enterprises and multilingual environments.

4. Modularity

These models can be extended or specialized using techniques like fine-tuning, reinforcement learning, retrieval-augmented generation (RAG), adapters, or prompt engineering. This modularity allows them to serve as a stable core while enabling rapid customization.

5. Emergent Capabilities

As foundation models grow in scale and complexity, they begin to exhibit behaviors not explicitly programmed into them — such as basic arithmetic reasoning, code generation, or chain-of-thought prompting. These emergent properties arise from the sheer volume and diversity of pretraining data and are still an area of active research.

The Strategic Value of Foundation Models for Enterprises

For businesses, foundation models offer a compelling trifecta: **speed, scale, and intelligence**.

- **Speed**: New applications can be deployed in days, not months, since the underlying model already has a generalized understanding of language and knowledge.
- **Scale**: A single model can serve global teams across languages, verticals, and use cases — reducing the need to maintain a fragmented AI stack.
- **Intelligence**: Foundation models can extract, synthesize, and generate content with human-like fluency, enabling automation of previously unreachable tasks (like legal review or creative writing).

This has led many forward-looking enterprises to adopt foundation models not just as point solutions, but as **platforms for AI transformation**. These platforms are being embedded into internal systems, enterprise data lakes, and customer-facing experiences.

Challenges Behind the Hype

Despite their promise, foundation models are not magic wands. They bring a new set of challenges that require careful consideration:

- **Compute Cost**: Training and even inference for large models can be expensive and energy-intensive.
- **Hallucination**: These models sometimes generate plausible but false information, especially when the input is ambiguous or outside their knowledge base.
- **Bias and Fairness**: Foundation models can inadvertently replicate and amplify societal biases present in their training data.
- **Security and Misuse**: The same capabilities that make them powerful also raise concerns about misuse — including misinformation, impersonation, and content generation at scale.
- **Data Privacy**: Since many models are trained on public data, enterprises must tread carefully when integrating proprietary or sensitive content.

Enterprises are increasingly responding to these challenges with hybrid approaches — combining general-purpose foundation models with:

- Private fine-tuning on proprietary data.
- Retrieval mechanisms to ground answers in authoritative sources.
- On-device or edge deployment for privacy-sensitive applications.

- Guardrails and policies to monitor and constrain outputs.

Foundation Models as the Gateway to Intelligent Agents

Perhaps the most exciting evolution is how foundation models are morphing into *agents* — not just responding with text, but taking actions. With memory, planning, goal-setting, and tool use, we are seeing the rise of **agentic AI**: systems that can understand a user's goal, break it into sub-tasks, orchestrate tools or APIs, and refine their strategies based on feedback.

Foundation models are the substrate from which these agents are built. Their deep understanding of language and reasoning enables them to act as planners, decision-makers, and copilots — transforming how we work, build, and interact with software.

The rise of foundation models is not the end point. It is the beginning — a foundation, quite literally — for a new generation of intelligent systems. In the next section, we'll explore how these foundational capabilities are being extended into **agentic architectures**, enabling proactive, dynamic, and autonomous AI assistants that reason, act, and evolve.

From GPT-3 to GPT-4 and Claude to Gemini

The rise of large language models (LLMs) marks a defining moment in the history of artificial intelligence. While earlier generations of AI were domain-specific, rules-driven, and brittle, LLMs offer something radically different: a *general-purpose intelligence layer* that can adapt across languages, domains, and even modalities — all from a single foundation.

The era truly took flight with the release of **GPT-3**, but it didn't stop there. With each generation, these models have evolved not just in size, but in architectural sophistication, reasoning capability, and their potential to act as autonomous agents. Let us trace this arc — from the transformative launch of GPT-3, to the multimodal, memory-augmented promise of GPT-4, and then across parallel innovations from **Anthropic's Claude** to **Google's Gemini**.

GPT-3: The Spark that Lit the Global AI Imagination

Released in 2020 by OpenAI, **GPT-3 (Generative Pretrained Transformer 3)** was a seismic leap. Trained on hundreds of billions of tokens across a diverse swath of internet text, GPT-3's 175 billion parameters enabled it to generate impressively fluent and coherent responses to natural language prompts. It was the first time many people experienced what felt like *conversational intelligence.*

The defining traits of GPT-3 were:

- **Zero- and few-shot learning**: With simple prompting, GPT-3 could perform tasks without task-specific training.
- **Universal adaptability**: It could write poetry, summarize news, generate code, or simulate characters, all in the same model.
- **No fine-tuning required**: Most tasks could be completed with just prompting — an early form of "instruction following".

Yet GPT-3, for all its power, was still a "predictive parrot." It lacked deep reasoning, made factual errors, and could be easily misled by cleverly constructed prompts. It had no memory, no sense of persistent identity, and no awareness of tools or external environments.

Still, it was enough to ignite a global movement — enterprises, startups, and researchers began experimenting at scale, and the term "foundation model" became central to the AI lexicon.

GPT-4: Beyond Language, Toward Thought

By the time **GPT-4** was released in 2023, the bar had been dramatically raised — not just for fluency, but for trustworthiness, multimodality, and reasoning. GPT-4 was not just larger, it was *smarter* — capable of nuanced understanding, more robust factual recall, and less prone to hallucination under pressure.

Key advancements of GPT-4 included:

- **Multimodality**: GPT-4 could accept both text and images as input, enabling it to describe photos, interpret diagrams, or answer questions about charts.
- **Tool use and function calling**: Integrated with tools, plugins, APIs, and code interpreters, GPT-4 could reason *and act*. This laid the groundwork for agentic behavior — not just predicting text, but triggering actions.

- **Higher-order reasoning**: It could solve complex logic puzzles, follow long chains of instructions, and emulate different personas more effectively.
- **Memory infrastructure (in beta)**: For the first time, the model could remember past interactions across sessions — a crucial step toward continuity, personalization, and goal-oriented agents.

GPT-4 marked the transition from general-purpose text generation to **cognitive infrastructure** — models that could serve as assistants, copilots, researchers, analysts, and companions.

The impact on enterprises was immediate. GPT-4 became the foundation for virtual advisors in healthcare, legal research copilots, customer service agents, and data-to-insight pipelines. It also accelerated the move toward **on-device and hybrid inference**, critical for use cases in data-sensitive, low-connectivity, or compute-constrained environments — especially in developing countries.

Claude: Constitutional AI and Safer Reasoning

While OpenAI was pioneering scale and tool integration, **Anthropic** took a different route with its **Claude** family of models. Named after Claude Shannon, the father of information theory, these models emphasized **safety, alignment, and helpfulness** through a framework called **Constitutional AI**.

Claude models, particularly Claude 2 and Claude 3, were trained not only to follow instructions but to *self-regulate*. This meant:

- **Ethical self-awareness**: Claude models used a set of predefined principles ("a constitution") to evaluate and refine their responses.
- **Reduced harmful outputs**: Through iterative reinforcement and preference learning, the models avoided toxicity, bias, or deception more reliably than previous generations.
- **Structured reasoning**: Claude models excelled in breakdown-style answers — step-by-step explanations, context-sensitive summarization, and compositional problem-solving.

Claude's impact lies in demonstrating that **safety and intelligence are not trade-offs**. In enterprise and regulatory environments, where compliance, auditability, and transparency matter as much as performance,

Claude's approach has proven valuable.

Claude is also an important philosophical fork in the AI trajectory — suggesting that general intelligence isn't just about scale, but about governance, values, and introspection.

Gemini: Multimodal Native Intelligence from the Ground Up

Google DeepMind's Gemini, launched in late 2023 and rapidly iterated in 2024, introduced another architectural shift — designing a language model as a *native multimodal system* rather than a text model retrofitted with image or audio capabilities.

While GPT-4 had multimodal abilities, Gemini was **built multimodal from the start**. Its standout features included:

- **Seamless modality integration**: It could move fluidly between text, images, audio, and video — not as separate modules, but as one coherent understanding engine.
- **Scientific and mathematical rigor**: Gemini demonstrated exceptional performance in complex problem solving, scientific reasoning, and programming challenges.
- **Tool orchestration and memory**: Much like GPT-4, Gemini could use tools, access web or code environments, and remember context across tasks — a key ingredient for intelligent agents.

Google positioned Gemini not just as a chatbot or content generator, but as a **cognitive partner for science, education, and research**. Its role in collaborative research, discovery, and productivity applications is expected to grow, especially as enterprises seek AI that can handle diverse modalities and enterprise data formats beyond text.

Convergence: From Models to Agents

Each of these models — GPT-4, Claude, Gemini — reflects a different design philosophy, but all are converging on a shared vision: AI that can understand, reason, adapt, and act in open-ended environments.

This evolution is no longer about generating better paragraphs. It's about **building autonomous, adaptive agents** that:

- Perceive (multimodal understanding),
- Plan (structured reasoning, goal decomposition),
- Act (tool use, function calling, integration with APIs),
- Reflect (memory, self-critique, alignment),
- Learn (fine-tuning, instruction-following, in-context adaptation).

This is the true shift from **foundation models to intelligent agents** — from static predictors to dynamic collaborators.

Implications for Enterprises and Society

For enterprises, these developments are not academic — they are infrastructural. The age of LLMs enables:

- **Language as the new UI** for interacting with data, tools, and systems.
- **Agentic automation** across knowledge work, decision support, customer experience, and cybersecurity.
- **Real-time intelligence** on low-end devices without reliance on cloud APIs — critical for inclusion in emerging markets.
- **Ethically governed AI systems** that align with human values and regulatory frameworks.

For society, it raises deeper questions: How should we design AI that augments rather than replaces human intelligence? Who controls the cognitive substrate of the future? What values, languages, and cultures are embedded in these models?

These are the questions we'll explore further in this book — but first, let's understand how these models learn in the first place, and how we can adapt them for specialized use.

Instruction Tuning, Alignment, and Human Feedback

Large Language Models (LLMs) start life as general-purpose pattern recognizers. After pretraining on massive corpora of text from the internet — books, articles, code repositories, forums, and more — these models develop an impressive ability to predict and generate human-like language. However, in their raw, foundation form, they lack one critical ingredient: alignment with human intent.

Pretrained LLMs don't inherently know how to follow instructions, behave ethically, or interact helpfully with users. They are powerful but ungrounded — capable of producing anything from helpful answers to hallucinated misinformation or toxic outputs. The process of making these models **safe, controllable, and useful** is known as **alignment** — and at the heart of it lies **instruction tuning** and **human feedback**.

The Problem with Raw Pretrained Models

Imagine giving a library of the entire internet to a brilliant but socially unaware mind. It might know every Shakespeare quote and Reddit thread but still not understand when to be concise, how to decline a harmful request, or what kind of tone to use in a sensitive conversation.

Raw LLMs are similar. They:

- Can complete prompts without understanding *what* the user wants.
- May mimic biases and misinformation found in training data.
- Lack grounding in real-world ethics or utility.
- Can be verbose, vague, or misleading in responses.

This unpredictability makes them unsuitable for direct deployment in mission-critical or user-facing applications — especially in enterprise, education, healthcare, finance, and governance. The transition from raw capability to responsible behavior requires careful calibration.

This is where instruction tuning and reinforcement learning from human feedback come in.

Instruction Tuning: Teaching Models to Follow Human Intent

Instruction tuning is the process of fine-tuning a pretrained language model on datasets specifically designed to teach it how to follow **explicit instructions**. This moves the model from "complete this sentence" to "do what I ask."

The process involves:

- Curating datasets of *prompt–response* pairs where the input is a natural language instruction and the output is an ideal, helpful, or task-oriented response.

- Exposing the model to thousands or millions of these examples across diverse domains — summarization, question-answering, reasoning, writing, math, translation, coding, and more.
- Training the model to **understand task intent**, not just mimic surface-level patterns.

For instance, instead of just continuing the sentence "Translate the following to French: Hello," the model learns the task format and adapts to new commands like:

- "Summarize this article in 3 bullet points."
- "Write a polite email declining a meeting request."
- "Find and fix the bug in the following code."

Instruction tuning doesn't require task-specific architecture changes. It simply relies on a well-designed dataset and the model's ability to generalize. This makes it a powerful and scalable approach for aligning foundation models to a wide array of use cases.

The Role of Human Feedback in Fine-Tuning

Even with instruction tuning, LLMs may generate outputs that are technically correct but unhelpful, verbose, evasive, or biased. To refine the model's behavior beyond correctness — toward **helpfulness, harmlessness, and honesty** — we introduce **Reinforcement Learning from Human Feedback (RLHF)**.

This approach adds a human-in-the-loop training phase where the model learns not just *what* to do, but *how* to do it in a way that aligns with human expectations.

The typical RLHF pipeline includes:

1. **Collecting Model Responses**: Multiple completions are generated for a given prompt by the instruction-tuned model.
2. **Human Preference Judgments**: Human annotators (often domain experts) rank these completions based on quality, safety, clarity, tone, and relevance.

3. **Training a Reward Model**: A smaller model is trained to predict the human preference rankings.
4. **Reinforcement Learning**: The original LLM is fine-tuned using reinforcement learning to maximize the predicted human preference score.

This loop — from model output to human judgment to improved behavior — is what transforms LLMs into **helpful assistants**. It is one of the key reasons why models like ChatGPT, Claude, and Gemini feel coherent, context-aware, and polite.

Human feedback serves as a kind of moral and pragmatic compass for the model. It teaches values that the training data can't always encode clearly — like empathy, sensitivity, or professional tone.

Beyond RLHF: Challenges and Evolution

While RLHF has proven incredibly effective, it's not without its limitations:

- **Scalability**: Human labeling is expensive, subjective, and slow.
- **Bias Amplification**: Feedback reflects annotator values, which may be culturally or ideologically narrow.
- **Instruction Ambiguity**: Not all tasks have one "correct" answer. Subjective prompts can lead to inconsistent behavior.
- **Reward Hacking**: The model may over-optimize for the reward function in unintended ways, such as being overly cautious or verbose.

As a result, the field is exploring **alternatives and enhancements** to RLHF, including:

- **Constitutional AI**: Where the model is guided by a predefined set of principles instead of human rankings.
- **Simulated feedback**: Using other AI systems to simulate human critiques and accelerate training.
- **Multi-objective reward tuning**: Balancing trade-offs between helpfulness, conciseness, creativity, and safety.
- **Federated and collective feedback**: Incorporating more diverse global perspectives into model alignment.

These are critical as LLMs enter sensitive domains like law, finance, medicine, and governance, where interpretability, fairness, and accountability are essential.

Why This Matters for Agentic AI

Instruction tuning and human feedback lay the groundwork for **agentic behavior**. Agents are not just stateless text generators. They:

- Understand goals.
- Plan sequences of actions.
- Ask clarifying questions.
- Adapt behavior based on outcomes.

But this requires trust. For an LLM-based agent to book your flight, write your code, summarize your trial records, or analyze your sales pipeline, it must behave predictably, transparently, and ethically.

Alignment ensures that as models gain autonomy, they do not lose guardrails. Instruction tuning gives them clarity of task. Human feedback teaches them the values of cooperation and restraint.

In the enterprise world, these aligned agents:

- Reduce risk in customer service and compliance scenarios.
- Build user trust in AI-enabled workflows.
- Adapt naturally to evolving team goals and policies.

The Future of Alignment: Human-Centric Intelligence

As LLMs scale toward trillion-parameter systems and evolve into multimodal, interactive agents, alignment becomes not just a technical challenge but a **social contract**. The AI systems we build must reflect the values, expectations, and diversity of the people they serve.

Instruction tuning and human feedback are early yet foundational steps in this journey — transforming raw linguistic intelligence into systems that can truly understand, assist, and collaborate with humanity.

The age of foundation models may have begun with self-supervised learning, but the age of intelligent agents begins with **listening to humans**

— not just to what we say, but to what we mean.

Model Distillation and Optimization

As the capabilities of large language models (LLMs) have expanded, so too has their size. Foundation models like GPT-3, PaLM, and LLaMA are composed of hundreds of billions of parameters, requiring vast compute resources to train and deploy. While these behemoths demonstrate remarkable fluency, generalization, and adaptability, they are often impractical for real-world applications that demand speed, efficiency, low latency, and edge deployment. The solution lies in a family of techniques known collectively as **model distillation and optimization.**

These methods aim to retain the intelligence and versatility of large models while drastically reducing their size, energy requirements, and inference cost. In doing so, they pave the way for AI systems that can operate in constrained environments — such as mobile devices, enterprise applications, or even offline edge systems — without sacrificing much in performance. This shift is essential for scaling AI beyond research labs and into everyday life.

What Is Model Distillation?

Model distillation is inspired by the idea that a large, complex model (called the **teacher**) can transfer its knowledge to a smaller, simpler model (called the **student**). The student is trained not directly on the original dataset, but on the outputs — the predictions, probabilities, and intermediate activations — of the teacher. In essence, the student learns *how the teacher thinks.*

This technique was first proposed in the context of classification tasks but has now been adapted for language modeling, question answering, translation, summarization, and more. The goal is to retain the teacher's behavior and accuracy, while drastically reducing the computational burden.

Distillation works because the teacher's outputs often carry more informative structure than the raw labels. For example, in a classification task, the teacher might assign a probability of 0.92 to the correct class, but also 0.05 and 0.03 to plausible alternatives — a signal that guides the student toward a richer internal understanding of the task, beyond just memorizing correct answers.

In the context of LLMs, distillation enables:

- Faster inference on consumer hardware.
- Deployment in latency-sensitive applications.
- Energy-efficient reasoning on edge devices.
- Better compliance with privacy and sovereignty constraints (e.g., on-device AI).

Types of Distillation Techniques in Language Models

Distillation has evolved into a spectrum of strategies tailored to different goals:

1. Logit Distillation
This is the classic form of distillation. The student is trained to match the softmax output of the teacher — i.e., the probability distribution over the next word or token. This soft target is more informative than a one-hot label, allowing the student to learn nuanced semantic gradients.

2. Feature-Based Distillation
Instead of or in addition to matching outputs, the student mimics internal hidden states of the teacher — such as embeddings, attention weights, or intermediate activations. This helps the student internalize the teacher's reasoning patterns and representation learning.

3. Layer-Wise Distillation
In deep transformers, the student can be trained to replicate specific layers of the teacher, or even use a compressed version of each corresponding layer. This enables architectural alignment while reducing depth or width.

4. Sequence-Level Knowledge Transfer
For generative tasks, students are trained not just on word-by-word probabilities but on entire sequences generated by the teacher. This supports better global coherence, helpful in tasks like summarization or story generation.

Beyond Distillation: The Optimization Frontier

While distillation focuses on compressing a pretrained model, **optimization** refers to techniques that improve a model's efficiency during training, inference, or deployment. These include:

1. Quantization

Quantization reduces the precision of model weights and activations from 32-bit floating-point to 16-bit, 8-bit, or even binary formats. Remarkably, many LLMs retain most of their performance even with such compression, especially when fine-tuned post-quantization.

- **Static quantization** applies uniformly post-training.
- **Dynamic quantization** adjusts during inference.
- **Quantization-aware training** incorporates low-precision math during learning, preserving accuracy.

2. Pruning

Pruning eliminates unnecessary weights or neurons from a model. This can be structured (removing entire attention heads or layers) or unstructured (removing individual connections based on their importance scores). Pruning reduces model size and speeds up inference, often with minimal impact on quality.

3. Low-Rank Approximations (LoRA and Friends)

Modern techniques like **Low-Rank Adaptation (LoRA)** approximate weight matrices with smaller low-rank components. This allows for efficient fine-tuning with fewer parameters while retaining the backbone of the original model. LoRA is widely used in instruction tuning, domain adaptation, and edge deployment.

4. Sparse Attention and Efficient Architectures

Researchers are developing architectures like Longformer, BigBird, and Reformer that replace dense self-attention with sparse or locality-sensitive mechanisms. This allows models to scale to longer sequences while reducing compute.

5. Weight Sharing and Parameter Reuse

By sharing weights across layers (e.g., in ALBERT or MobileBERT), models can dramatically reduce parameter count without degrading performance — a useful property when memory is limited.

Enterprise Relevance and Real-World Impact

Distilled and optimized models are not academic curiosities — they are the backbone of scalable AI systems in production. For enterprises, these models offer a powerful balance of intelligence and efficiency:

- **Cost-effective inference** for millions of daily queries without GPU clusters.
- **On-device privacy** where data never leaves the user's phone or facility.
- **Low-latency responses** essential for voice assistants, fraud detection, or customer service bots.
- **Sustainability benefits** from reduced energy and carbon footprint.

A prime example is **DistilBERT**, which achieves 97% of BERT's performance while being 60% faster and 40% smaller. Newer distillation pipelines can compress even larger models like LLaMA-2 or GPT-J into mobile-ready agents with real-time performance.

For edge deployments — such as real-time scam/spam call detection on smartphones — distillation and optimization are not optional. They are fundamental enablers of functionality.

From Distilled Models to Intelligent Agents

Optimized models are also the foundation of **agentic AI** — intelligent systems that can plan, reason, and act autonomously. While foundation models provide general intelligence, agents require:

- Speed to operate in real time.
- Compactness to run locally and privately.
- Flexibility to learn new tasks incrementally.
- Modularity to plug into broader systems (e.g., tools, APIs, databases).

Distilled models can be embedded within agents to power local reasoning while offloading heavy tasks to the cloud when necessary — a hybrid architecture that balances performance, privacy, and cost.

As such, model distillation and optimization are not merely engineering feats. They are design philosophies: *intelligence should be efficient, portable, and human-aligned.*

Closing Thoughts

The age of monolithic, centralized, power-hungry language models is giving way to a more democratic era — one in which compact, distilled, and optimized models serve people wherever they are, across devices, languages, and bandwidth constraints.

Distillation is how we take the towering achievements of LLM research and scale them to the billions who need AI not just in the cloud, but in their hands, pockets, and workflows.

In the journey from raw compute to usable intelligence, **model distillation and optimization are the bridges**. They are how we move from possibility to practicality — from massive general models to agile, agentic AI that actually works for real-world users.

Building Enterprise-Grade LLMs

The real promise of large language models (LLMs) lies not merely in their generative capabilities but in their ability to become embedded, secure, reliable partners in real-world enterprise workflows. However, building *enterprise-grade* LLMs — systems robust enough to be trusted with sensitive decisions, scalable enough to support millions of interactions, and flexible enough to align with specific domains — is a non-trivial undertaking. It requires more than pretraining on public data or wrapping a foundation model with a user interface. It requires engineering, governance, infrastructure, and deep understanding of human-AI collaboration at scale.

The Shift from Prototype to Production

Most enterprises begin their LLM journey with experimentation: prototypes that summarize text, answer questions, or act as copilots for employees. But taking LLMs from prototype to production means addressing five pillars of enterprise readiness:

1. **Security and Privacy**
2. **Accuracy and Alignment**
3. **Latency and Cost Efficiency**
4. **Customization and Domain Adaptation**
5. **Governance, Monitoring, and Control**

Let's explore each in detail.

1. Security and Privacy: Building Trust into the Core

In enterprise environments — especially in sectors like healthcare, finance, telecom, and government — data is confidential, regulated, and high-risk. A model exposed to private user inputs or internal documents must respect strict boundaries.

Building secure LLMs requires:

- **On-Device or On-Prem Deployment:** Especially in geographies with poor connectivity or stringent data localization laws, LLMs must work on edge devices or private clouds — with zero external API dependencies.
- **End-to-End Encryption:** Input/output flows, prompt logs, and internal data should be encrypted at rest and in transit. TLS, secure key vaults, and memory-safe runtime containers are mandatory.
- **No Data Leakage Guarantee:** The model must not "learn" from individual user prompts in ways that persist across sessions unless explicitly permitted. Techniques like differential privacy and fine-tuning isolation play a role.
- **Granular Access Control:** Who can query the model, what kind of data it can access, and how long responses are stored must all be customizable through role-based permissions.

Security is not a bolt-on feature. It is a non-negotiable design principle when LLMs are deployed in the enterprise.

2. Accuracy and Alignment: When Hallucination Is Not an Option

LLMs are probabilistic engines. Their answers are drawn from latent distributions — not always ground truth. In enterprise settings, however, *factuality is sacred.*

To ensure reliability:

- **Retrieval-Augmented Generation (RAG):** Enterprises can "ground" the model by connecting it to trusted internal knowledge bases, ensuring answers reflect current, accurate data rather than relying on frozen weights.
- **Fact-Checking Pipelines:** Generated content can be validated against structured data, rules, or even other models trained to detect inconsistency or hallucination.

- **Custom Guardrails:** Domain-specific constraints (e.g., "never suggest financial products," "always cite regulatory sources") must be enforced with controlled decoding, prompt tuning, or hybrid rule-model frameworks.
- **Alignment with Enterprise Values:** Beyond facts, models must reflect an enterprise's tone, policies, and compliance posture. This involves reinforcement learning with human feedback (RLHF), synthetic feedback loops, and prompt injection testing.

Accuracy isn't just a feature; it's a function of alignment between the model, the context, and the real-world consequences of its outputs.

3. Latency and Cost Efficiency: Real-Time Intelligence at Scale

For models to function as live assistants — especially in high-volume environments like telecom, retail, or customer service — response time and infrastructure cost become critical.

Strategies for performance optimization include:

- **Model Distillation:** Deploy smaller, faster versions of large models using distillation or quantization without significantly compromising quality.
- **On-Device Inference:** Particularly for real-time mobile applications, local inference (e.g., via ONNX, GGML, or Metal acceleration) allows sub-second latency and complete offline functionality.
- **Caching and Reuse:** Frequently asked questions, repeated workflows, or common query patterns can be cached intelligently, avoiding redundant inference.
- **Cost-Aware Routing:** Enterprises can maintain a hierarchy of models — smaller, cheaper models for general tasks and larger, more accurate ones for complex queries — invoked selectively based on need.

An enterprise-grade LLM must be performant under pressure and predictable in cost — not just powerful in a lab.

4. Customization and Domain Adaptation: From Generic to Expert

Foundation models are impressive generalists. But enterprises require experts — models fluent in the language of law, banking, telecom operations, pharmaceutical regulation, or public infrastructure.

Achieving this involves:

- **Fine-Tuning on Proprietary Data:** A model exposed to internal documents, call center transcripts, regulatory filings, or technical logs becomes far more useful than a generic chatbot.
- **Instruction Tuning for Enterprise Use Cases:** Instead of open-ended prompting, enterprise LLMs are trained to follow very specific instructions, workflows, and escalation rules.
- **Function Calling and Tool Use:** LLMs can be augmented with structured capabilities — APIs, database lookups, or robotic process automation (RPA) — so they don't just respond but act.
- **Persona and Brand Alignment:** In customer-facing settings, the LLM must reflect the enterprise's tone of voice, cultural sensitivity, and even regional dialects. This is where prompt engineering meets creative alignment.

A truly enterprise-grade LLM is not a black-box oracle. It is a trained operator — fluent in the organization's knowledge, workflows, and values.

5. Governance, Monitoring, and Control: The Control Plane of AI

As LLMs move into production, visibility and control are critical for responsible operation. Enterprises need dashboards, alerts, audits, and accountability — not just cool demos.

This means:

- **Prompt and Output Logging:** While preserving user privacy, organizations must be able to inspect how prompts evolve, what answers are generated, and whether policy violations occur.
- **Safety and Toxicity Filters:** Real-time filtering of inappropriate, biased, or harmful outputs is essential — especially for consumer-facing deployments.
- **A/B Testing and Feedback Loops:** Iterative improvements are driven by structured evaluation — which responses help users, which don't, and

why.

- **Model Versioning and Reproducibility:** For compliance and debugging, it must be possible to reproduce outputs from any point in time and attribute them to specific model versions.
- **AI Usage Policies and Compliance:** Internal policies on acceptable use, prompt injection resistance, model escalation protocols, and data governance must be enforced consistently.

An enterprise LLM is not a single model — it's a managed system with observability, versioning, feedback, and lifecycle governance.

From LLMs to Intelligent Agents

Enterprise-grade LLMs are not static text generators. They are active agents: aware of context, capable of planning, memory, tool use, and interaction. This transforms them from passive responders into proactive, autonomous problem-solvers.

An LLM that:

- Understands a query,
- Retrieves relevant documents,
- Calls a database,
- Fills out a form,
- Responds in the company's voice,
- And logs its steps for audit

... is no longer just a model. It is an **enterprise agent**.

The journey from foundation models to intelligent agents is already underway. But to fully realize it, enterprises must invest in infrastructure, training, governance, and — above all — trust. Because these systems are not just automating language; they are co-piloting decision-making.

And in high-stakes domains, nothing matters more than intelligent systems you can trust — systems grounded in language, but operating at the speed and scale of enterprise.

Comparing Open vs. Closed Ecosystems

As Large Language Models (LLMs) evolve from static tools into dynamic, intelligent agents, a crucial dichotomy has emerged in their development and deployment: **open ecosystems vs. closed ecosystems**. This divide is not merely technical — it reflects fundamental choices about accessibility, control, innovation, economics, and power distribution in the AI landscape.

Both models — open and closed — have their strengths and trade-offs. Understanding this divide is essential for enterprises, developers, policymakers, and users who must navigate this rapidly evolving terrain to make informed, strategic decisions.

Closed Ecosystems: The Walled Gardens of AI

Closed ecosystems are developed and controlled by a limited number of corporate actors, typically with vast computing, research, and data resources. These include models such as OpenAI's GPT-4, Google's Gemini, Anthropic's Claude, and Amazon's Q, among others. Access to these models is often gated through APIs, paid subscriptions, or proprietary platforms.

Key Characteristics of Closed Ecosystems:

- **Opaque Architecture and Training Data**: Most closed models do not disclose their exact architecture, training data sources, or training methodologies. This opaqueness protects intellectual property but limits transparency.
- **Access via APIs**: These models are primarily offered as a service, where the model runs on the provider's infrastructure. Users send prompts and receive outputs — but cannot modify or inspect the model internals.
- **Rapid Feature Evolution**: Closed models benefit from intense R&D investment and often lead the frontier in terms of performance, capabilities, and agentic extensions (e.g., tools, memory, planning).
- **Integrated Product Ecosystems**: Providers often bundle LLMs into broader cloud platforms, productivity suites, and development tools — reinforcing vendor lock-in but streamlining enterprise integration.
- **Limited Customization**: While fine-tuning and embedding-based retrieval (RAG) are sometimes supported, deep model customization is restricted.

Advantages of Closed Ecosystems:

- **Best-in-Class Performance**: These models frequently top industry benchmarks across reasoning, coding, math, and multimodal tasks.
- **Security and Compliance**: Enterprises can trust robust cloud infrastructure and enterprise-grade SLAs, which are critical in regulated industries.
- **Out-of-the-Box Agentic Capabilities**: Features like tool use, web browsing, memory, and function calling are often bundled, accelerating time to value.
- **Support and Documentation**: Strong customer support, documentation, and integration pathways exist for scaling across business units.

Limitations of Closed Ecosystems:

- **Lack of Transparency**: Enterprises in sensitive domains (e.g., law, healthcare, national security) may be unable to audit how decisions are made.
- **Vendor Lock-In**: Cost structures can scale unpredictably, and reliance on proprietary APIs may inhibit long-term flexibility.
- **Data Sovereignty Concerns**: In jurisdictions with strict data residency laws, sending data to cloud APIs outside national borders can pose compliance risks.
- **Limited Inclusion for the Global South**: Closed ecosystems are often designed for high-resource environments, with minimal support for low-end devices, local languages, or community-specific needs.

Open Ecosystems: Building AI in the Open

Open ecosystems represent a movement toward transparency, collaboration, and decentralization. These include models and initiatives such as Meta's LLaMA, Mistral, Hugging Face's open LLMs, Stability AI, Falcon, and OpenChat. Some of these are fully open (weights, architecture, training data), while others are partially open (e.g., weights are open but data is not).

Key Characteristics of Open Ecosystems:

- **Model Availability**: Model weights and architectures are downloadable, inspectable, and modifiable. This allows anyone to run models on-premise, fine-tune them, or integrate them deeply.
- **Community-Driven Innovation**: Progress is often driven by collaborative, distributed contributors rather than a single corporate entity.
- **Local Deployment**: Open models can run on-device, on local servers, or air-gapped environments — essential for data-sensitive or low-connectivity settings.
- **Interoperable Tools**: Open-source libraries (e.g., LangChain, Transformers, LlamaIndex) foster a composable AI ecosystem.

Advantages of Open Ecosystems:

- **Auditability and Transparency**: Organizations can scrutinize model internals for fairness, bias, and compliance — critical for ethical and regulated deployments.
- **Cost Control and Sovereignty**: Self-hosted models eliminate per-token API fees and reduce dependence on third parties for inference.
- **Fine-Grained Customization**: Fine-tuning, quantization, distillation, and domain adaptation are easier and often community-supported.
- **Inclusion and Innovation**: Open ecosystems support innovation in underrepresented regions — enabling use cases in low-resource languages, edge devices, and constrained settings.

Limitations of Open Ecosystems:

- **Performance Gap at the Frontier**: State-of-the-art closed models may still outperform open models in general capabilities and agent orchestration.

- **Operational Burden**: Running, maintaining, and scaling open models requires engineering skill, infrastructure, and MLOps maturity.
- **Security and Risk Exposure**: Without enterprise-grade guardrails, deploying open models poses risks of misuse, hallucinations, and poor moderation.
- **Fragmentation**: The diversity of tools and forks can result in duplicated effort, inconsistent standards, and integration challenges.

Strategic Implications: Choosing the Right Path

For enterprises, governments, startups, and communities, the open vs. closed decision is not binary — it's contextual.

- **Large Enterprises and Regulated Industries** often gravitate toward closed ecosystems for compliance, security, and support — but are increasingly piloting open models for cost optimization and sovereignty.
- **Startups and Innovators** may adopt open models for flexibility, experimentation, and local deployment — but integrate with closed APIs for high-performance tasks.
- **Developing Countries and the Global South** benefit profoundly from open ecosystems, as they allow local AI capacity-building, inclusion of indigenous languages, and deployment on low-end devices.
- **Governments and Public Institutions** are beginning to fund and promote open LLMs as a matter of national interest and digital independence.

Many organizations are now adopting a **hybrid strategy** — combining open and closed models across different use cases, balancing innovation with risk, and avoiding single-provider lock-in.

Conclusion: A Philosophical and Strategic Choice

The choice between open and closed ecosystems is not just about code, APIs, or infrastructure. It's about **control vs. convenience**, **speed vs. sovereignty**, **opacity vs. auditability**, and ultimately — **centralized power vs. distributed empowerment**.

In the age of intelligent agents and ubiquitous language models, this tension will shape the next decade of technology, policy, and economic development. Open ecosystems offer the promise of democratized AI and local innovation. Closed ecosystems offer refined performance and turnkey deployment.

Both are necessary. But understanding their differences — and aligning them with mission, values, and constraints — will define who leads, who follows, and who gets left behind.

Trends in LLM Evaluation and Benchmarking

As large language models (LLMs) evolve from statistical learners to interactive, goal-directed agents, the way we evaluate them is undergoing a radical transformation. Traditional metrics, once adequate for testing grammar correction or summarization, now fall short when assessing models that can reason, plan, and act autonomously. In this new era, evaluation is no longer just about performance — it's about trust, safety, generalization, alignment, and utility in the wild.

Understanding the shifting landscape of LLM evaluation is crucial for researchers, enterprises, and policymakers alike. It determines not only *what* we measure, but *how* we steer the development of these powerful systems.

From Task-Specific Scores to Capability-Oriented Assessment

Historically, natural language processing (NLP) models were evaluated on narrow benchmarks like sentiment classification (e.g., IMDb), question answering (e.g., SQuAD), or translation (e.g., BLEU score for English-French). These benchmarks were static, curated, and task-specific — and they served their purpose well during the early days of pre-LLM NLP.

However, the emergence of foundation models like GPT, PaLM, LLaMA, Claude, and others — capable of few-shot, zero-shot, and instruction-following behavior — broke the boundaries of those narrow evaluations. These models could generalize across tasks they weren't explicitly trained on. The question shifted from *how well can this model classify tweets?* to *how well can it understand, reason, and interact across domains and modalities?*

Rise of Multitask and Multidomain Benchmarks

To meet this shift, new benchmarks emerged to evaluate broad capabilities:

- **MMLU (Massive Multitask Language Understanding)** tested models across 57 academic subjects from math and history to law and biology — mimicking standardized exams.
- **BIG-bench** introduced tasks from linguistics puzzles to causal reasoning, many of which were previously considered out-of-scope for machines.
- **HELMeval** and **TruthfulQA** focused on hallucination resistance and factual accuracy, recognizing the growing challenge of verifying model output.
- **ARC (AI2 Reasoning Challenge)** and **GSM8K (Grade School Math 8K)** targeted reasoning, especially in multi-step logic and math.

These benchmarks represent a move toward **horizontal evaluation** — assessing breadth — but they still largely assume a passive, response-based interaction.

Evaluating Emergent and Agentic Behaviors

As models are deployed as agents — performing web navigation, executing code, interacting with APIs, conducting multistep research, and autonomously reasoning over long horizons — evaluation must capture **dynamic, procedural, and contextual competence**.

This new class of evaluation requires:

- **Long-context reasoning tests** to assess persistence of understanding over thousands of tokens.
- **Chain-of-thought validation** to ensure internal coherence during step-by-step reasoning.
- **Planning and goal completion benchmarks**, such as those emerging from agent ecosystems like AutoGPT, OpenAgents, and ReAct-style agents.
- **Tool-use assessments**, where the model must reason about which external APIs or plugins to call and when.
- **Meta-prompting scenarios**, where models must update their behavior in response to higher-level instructions or constraints.

Here, success isn't measured by a static answer, but by *whether the model accomplishes a task under real-world constraints* — often with minimal supervision.

From Benchmarks to Behavioral Audits

Another major shift is from *narrow correctness* to *broad alignment* and safety. As LLMs gain influence over workflows, communications, and decisions, it becomes critical to evaluate:

- **Bias** and **stereotyping** in generated content.
- **Toxicity**, **disinformation**, and **manipulability** (e.g., jailbreaks).
- **User alignment**, including helpfulness, harmlessness, and honesty.
- **Value-sensitive behaviors**, especially in culturally diverse or legally sensitive contexts.

This has given rise to **behavioral audits** — a human-centered approach to evaluating LLM behavior in scenarios involving ethics, legality, social norms, or emotional context. Such audits cannot be fully automated and often require human reviewers, scenario design, and interpretation of intent and consequence.

The introduction of red-teaming, adversarial prompting, and community-based evaluation (e.g., model card reviews) reflects a growing recognition: **how a model behaves is as important as what it can do.**

Limitations of Current Evaluation Paradigms

Despite progress, the current landscape faces serious limitations:

- **Static benchmarks age quickly**. Models are trained on web-scale data, and benchmarks can become "leaked" or memorized, leading to inflated scores.
- **Scoring is often ambiguous**. Many tasks (e.g., summarization, explanation, creativity) don't have clear right or wrong answers.
- **LLMs are sensitive to prompts**. Performance can vary widely depending on how a question is phrased, making reproducibility hard.
- **Lack of context awareness**. Many benchmarks do not test models in long or evolving contexts, where real-world deployment scenarios live.

- **Human evaluation is expensive and inconsistent.** Yet for nuanced judgments (e.g., tone, empathy, reasoning clarity), it remains indispensable.

These issues highlight a paradox: the more capable LLMs become, the harder they are to benchmark with traditional AI tools.

The Shift Toward Continuous, In-the-Wild Evaluation

To address these gaps, the field is moving toward **continuous, usage-based evaluation**:

- **User telemetry and feedback loops** from deployed models (e.g., thumbs up/down, rephrasing behavior).
- **Live A/B testing** across prompts, instructions, and system behaviors.
- **Synthetic evaluations** using other LLMs as judges — though this introduces its own biases.
- **Dynamic challenge sets**, where new, evolving prompts are added regularly by communities, researchers, and practitioners.

These approaches treat evaluation not as a static gatekeeping exercise, but as an ongoing dialogue between model developers, users, and systems — more akin to software observability than old-school exam scoring.

Enterprise Needs: Evaluating for Reliability, Adaptability, and Governance

From an enterprise lens, LLM evaluation is deeply practical:

- **Can the model scale across departments with varying jargon and workflows?**
- **Does it produce reproducible results across users and scenarios?**
- **Is it safe, auditable, and policy-compliant under regulatory scrutiny?**
- **Can its performance be monitored and improved continuously without full retraining?**

To answer these, companies are investing in:

- **Domain-specific evaluations** with proprietary data and workflows.
- **Guardrail testing frameworks** that simulate edge cases and stress tests.
- **Governance-ready reporting**, including bias audits and provenance logs.
- **Post-deployment learning loops**, combining user feedback with fine-tuning or prompt engineering.

These priorities signal that **LLM benchmarking is no longer just a research concern — it is a business-critical practice**.

Conclusion: Evaluating Intelligence in the Age of Agents

In the age of large language models, evaluation is no longer a static scoreboard. It is a moving target — as models adapt, tasks evolve, and deployment scenarios diversify. The field is moving toward richer, more nuanced, and behavior-aware evaluations that reflect real-world utility, alignment, and safety.

To build trustworthy, capable, and agentic AI systems, we must rethink not only how we train models — but also how we measure their readiness to serve, support, and collaborate with human users across domains, languages, and cultures.

Evaluation is no longer just a checkpoint. It is the compass by which we navigate the future of machine intelligence.

CHAPTER SIX

Learning at Scale — Pretraining, Fine-Tuning, and Adaptation

What is Pretraining?

Pretraining is the foundational learning phase for large language models (LLMs). It is during this phase that models like GPT, BERT, or Claude first learn the structure, syntax, semantics, and nuances of human language — not by being explicitly taught grammar or vocabulary rules, but by statistically modeling the patterns of language found in vast corpora of real-world text.

At its core, pretraining is the **process of self-supervised learning at massive scale**. The model is exposed to billions — sometimes trillions — of words from books, websites, articles, code repositories, forums, encyclopedias, and more. Through this immersion, it learns to **predict the next token** in a sequence (in causal models like GPT) or **fill in masked words** (in masked language models like BERT). Over time, this prediction task teaches the model a deep and generalized understanding of language and knowledge.

The Mechanics of Pretraining

Pretraining relies on a simple but powerful idea: use the structure of language itself as the learning signal. No labeled data is required. Instead, the model learns from the implicit structure of sentences — their word order, grammar, and logic.

For example:

- In a causal model, given the text fragment "The capital of France is", the model learns to assign a high probability to the word "Paris" as the next token.
- In a masked language model, a sentence like "The [MASK] of France is Paris" teaches the model to recover the missing word "capital" based on surrounding context.

This learning is achieved through gradient-based optimization over billions of training examples. Each time the model incorrectly predicts a word, it adjusts its internal parameters (weights) to better align with the observed data. After hundreds of billions of such updates, the model internalizes complex relationships — not just between words, but between ideas, facts, tone, style, and more.

The Scale of Pretraining

What makes modern LLMs so powerful isn't just the method, but the **scale** at which they are pretrained. This includes:

- **Scale of data:** Pretraining datasets span a wide array of domains and genres — fiction, technical manuals, social media, source code, legal documents, and more. This heterogeneity makes the model general-purpose and highly adaptable.
- **Scale of computation:** Training large models requires vast computing power. Distributed training over hundreds or thousands of GPUs or TPUs across weeks or months is common. This allows for deeper models with more capacity and longer context windows.
- **Scale of parameters:** Models like GPT-4, Claude, or Gemini have hundreds of billions of parameters. These parameters encode the knowledge extracted during pretraining, allowing the model to generalize across tasks and domains.

This immense scale enables **emergent capabilities** — abilities that were not explicitly programmed or expected, such as chain-of-thought reasoning, analogical thinking, few-shot learning, and basic world knowledge.

Why Pretraining Works

Pretraining works because human language is **statistically structured and semantically rich**. Words and phrases follow patterns. Certain ideas tend to co-occur. There are consistent syntactic rules, and there are also rich layers of meaning that can be inferred from context. By being trained to predict parts of language from other parts, LLMs learn to:

- Disentangle syntax from semantics.
- Represent words as dense vectors (embeddings) that capture similarity and context.
- Develop internal representations of abstract concepts.
- Simulate reasoning chains through next-word prediction.
- Store and retrieve factual knowledge implicitly within their parameters.

Pretraining transforms a blank neural network into a general-purpose language understanding engine.

What the Model Learns in Pretraining

During pretraining, the model acquires a wide range of linguistic and conceptual competencies:

- **Lexical and grammatical knowledge**: It learns grammar, word usage, verb conjugations, sentence structures, and punctuation rules across multiple languages.
- **World knowledge**: It absorbs a vast body of general knowledge — historical facts, scientific principles, cultural references, business terminology, and more.
- **Pragmatics and discourse**: It understands context, coherence, topic transitions, and conversational tone.
- **Reasoning patterns**: Through exposure to examples, it picks up logical structures, problem-solving formats, analogies, and argumentation styles.

- **Multilingual understanding**: When trained on multilingual corpora, the model develops cross-lingual alignment — the ability to represent the same concept similarly across languages.
- **Basic programming and domain knowledge**: If source code, legal texts, or medical literature are included, the model gains foundational fluency in those areas.

These capabilities emerge **without supervision** — no human had to label the data, correct the outputs, or define the rules. The model discovers them simply by learning what tends to come next in natural sequences of language.

Limitations of Pretraining Alone

Despite its power, pretraining has limitations:

- **Lack of task-specific behavior**: The model is general-purpose, not tailored to specific use cases like customer support or legal drafting.
- **No grounding in external reality**: The model does not verify facts against live data or the physical world.
- **No understanding of consequences**: It predicts language, not outcomes. This makes it prone to confidently generating plausible but false information (hallucination).
- **Latent bias and toxicity**: Since the training data reflects real-world texts, it can encode social biases, stereotypes, and harmful content.
- **Static snapshot**: Unless continuously updated, pretrained models reflect the state of the world only as it existed at the time of training.

These gaps are precisely why **fine-tuning**, **prompt engineering**, **adapter training**, and **RLHF (Reinforcement Learning from Human Feedback)** have become essential complements to pretraining — shaping a generic model into a safe, task-aligned, and agentic assistant.

Enterprise Perspective: Why Pretraining Matters

For enterprises, pretraining represents an inflection point. Before this era, building language capabilities into software required years of domain-specific data, rule-based engineering, and brittle NLP pipelines. Now, with pretrained models:

- Organizations can achieve high-quality results with minimal data and customization.
- LLMs can be adapted for internal use cases — document search, employee Q&A, customer workflows — with far less effort.
- Even small teams can build intelligent interfaces that previously required massive R&D investments.
- The same foundation model can support dozens of use cases across departments, from finance to HR to product development.

In developing countries or low-resource settings, this opens access to AI-powered tools without needing bespoke data or infrastructure.

Self-Supervised Learning at Scale

The success of modern large language models (LLMs) owes much of its power to a paradigm known as **self-supervised learning.** This learning strategy has radically transformed how AI systems acquire knowledge, moving beyond the limitations of traditional supervised approaches that depend heavily on labeled data. In self-supervised learning, the labels are derived automatically from the data itself — turning raw, unstructured information into a vast training ground for intelligence.

In the context of LLMs, self-supervised learning at scale enables machines to learn language, context, and even abstract reasoning from internet-scale corpora — without requiring manual annotation. It is the engine that powers pretraining, which is the foundation upon which fine-tuning, adaptation, and downstream task performance are built.

From Labeled Learning to Label-less Learning

Traditional supervised machine learning is constrained by the availability and quality of human-labeled data. For tasks like image classification or sentiment analysis, teams must hand-label thousands — sometimes millions — of examples. This approach is not only expensive and time-consuming, but also brittle: models trained this way often perform poorly outside the specific domains or formats they were trained on.

Self-supervised learning flips this paradigm. It creates *pretext tasks* from the structure of the data itself. For example, in language modeling, a self-supervised task could be as simple as predicting the next word in a sentence. Given the input "The sky is...", the model learns to predict likely continuations like "blue" or "clear." No human labeled the phrase — the sentence structure itself provides the learning signal.

This shift from human-supervised to data-supervised learning has unlocked the potential to train models on massive corpora spanning books, websites, codebases, research papers, and dialogues — capturing not just vocabulary and grammar, but also world knowledge, cultural patterns, and domain-specific semantics.

The Mechanics of Self-Supervised Learning in Language Models

In language modeling, self-supervised learning typically involves one of the following prediction tasks:

- **Autoregressive modeling (causal language modeling):** The model is trained to predict the next token (word or subword) given all previous tokens. This is the foundation of models like GPT. The objective is to maximize the likelihood of sequences that resemble natural language.
- **Masked language modeling (MLM):** A certain percentage of the input tokens are randomly masked, and the model learns to predict the original tokens. This approach, used in BERT and its variants, allows the model to develop a bidirectional understanding of language.
- **Denoising or corruption-based tasks:** Here, parts of the input are deliberately corrupted (e.g., removed, shuffled, or altered), and the model must reconstruct the original sequence. This form of learning forces the model to infer global coherence and structure — beyond local token dependencies.
- **Span prediction and infilling:** Instead of predicting just a single missing token, the model is trained to recover entire spans or sequences, enhancing its ability to deal with longer-range dependencies and context synthesis.

What makes these learning objectives "self-supervised" is that no external supervision is required. The data is its own teacher. The model builds a representation of language — its structure, usage, semantics, and even latent relationships — just by solving puzzles embedded in the raw text itself.

Scaling Laws and Emergent Capabilities

Self-supervised learning at scale revealed a profound phenomenon: as models grow in size (parameters), data volume, and training duration, they begin to exhibit *emergent behaviors* — capabilities not present in smaller models, and not explicitly programmed or trained for.

These include:

- **Zero-shot generalization:** The ability to perform tasks never explicitly taught during training.
- **In-context learning:** The model learns to adapt to new tasks simply by seeing examples in the prompt — no gradient updates required.
- **Multilingual fluency:** Understanding and generating text across dozens of languages without specific language supervision.
- **Tool use and reasoning:** Using APIs, calculators, or retrieving knowledge from memory — despite no hardcoding of these skills.

These emergent capabilities are the result of *scale*, *architecture*, and *objective design*. But they are only possible because self-supervised learning makes it feasible to pretrain on unimaginably large and diverse datasets — tens of trillions of tokens — sourced from the open web, books, scientific papers, and more.

Benefits of Self-Supervised Learning at Scale

The appeal of self-supervised learning is not merely academic. It carries significant practical advantages, especially in enterprise and global settings:

1. **Unbounded Knowledge Acquisition:** Models trained this way can ingest knowledge across domains, geographies, languages, and modalities — without handcrafted labeling pipelines.
2. **Reduced Labeling Costs:** Enterprises no longer need to build vast annotated datasets for each new use case. Instead, they can fine-tune or prompt existing models with minimal additional data.

3. **Faster Time to Value:** Once pretrained, these models can be adapted rapidly to downstream tasks — from customer service chatbots to legal document summarization — accelerating deployment timelines.
4. **Cross-Domain Portability:** A model trained on news articles, product reviews, and technical manuals can generalize across sectors, offering flexible intelligence across verticals like finance, healthcare, logistics, and education.
5. **Long-Term Retention and Reuse:** Knowledge gained during self-supervised pretraining forms a reusable substrate for many downstream tasks — reducing redundancy and technical debt in enterprise AI development.

Challenges and Considerations

While powerful, self-supervised learning at scale introduces unique risks and technical challenges:

- **Data quality and contamination:** Since models are trained on vast internet-scale corpora, they may inadvertently learn biases, stereotypes, or misinformation present in the training data.
- **Computational demands:** Pretraining requires massive compute infrastructure, carbon-intensive energy consumption, and careful optimization across hardware and software layers.
- **Interpretability:** Self-supervised models often behave like black boxes. Understanding *why* they make certain predictions or how they represent knowledge remains an open research question.
- **Overfitting to noise:** At scale, even small statistical quirks in the data can be amplified, leading to brittle or unpredictable behaviors in specific contexts.
- **Ethical alignment:** Training on large unfiltered datasets raises questions of consent, copyright, and downstream misuse. Responsible dataset curation and post-training alignment are essential.

The Foundation for Agentic and General AI

Self-supervised learning is not just a more efficient way to train models. It is a necessary precondition for *agentic AI* — systems that can reason, plan, and act across varied environments without being reprogrammed for every new domain.

Because such agents must operate in open-ended, unpredictable scenarios, they cannot rely solely on static, curated datasets. They must learn from raw experience, generalize across tasks, and adapt on the fly. Self-supervised learning is what gives them this capacity. It teaches them to *observe*, *hypothesize*, and *complete*, even in the absence of explicit instruction.

In essence, self-supervised learning enables machines to develop an internal model of the world — not just syntax, but meaning; not just words, but goals and intentions. It is how language becomes a bridge to cognition.

Closing Thoughts

The emergence of LLMs marks a profound shift in how machines acquire, store, and apply knowledge. At the heart of this revolution is self-supervised learning — a method that uses the data's own structure to teach models how to think in language. It has turned the world's text into the world's largest classroom.

As we move toward more capable, multimodal, and agentic systems, self-supervised learning will remain the foundational ingredient. It is the reason these models can scale in knowledge, generalize across tasks, and interface naturally with human beings. In short, it is how machines are learning to learn.

Domain Adaptation and Task-Specific Fine-Tuning

One of the greatest breakthroughs in modern machine learning, particularly in natural language processing, is the decoupling of **pretraining** from **fine-tuning**. Pretraining enables language models to learn the general structure and use of language from vast corpora, while fine-tuning allows them to specialize — to adapt to specific domains, use cases, tasks, and even organizational norms.

This dual-phase learning architecture reflects a core principle of intelligence itself: we first learn broadly from the world, then adapt specifically to situations and goals.

The Need for Specialization in the Real World

While a pretrained large language model (LLM) may demonstrate impressive general fluency across topics — history, science, entertainment, law, and more — real-world applications demand **precision** and **contextual depth.** Enterprises, regulators, educators, healthcare providers, and public agencies all operate within **domain-specific constraints**:

- A legal assistant must understand contractual clauses, precedent, and jurisdictional nuance.
- A medical agent must reason about symptoms, diagnoses, and treatment paths — without hallucination or overconfidence.
- A financial analyst chatbot must parse balance sheets, earnings reports, and macroeconomic signals with accuracy.
- A telecom support assistant must understand industry-specific jargon, troubleshooting flows, and device configurations.

General-purpose models fall short without adaptation. They may misinterpret specialized vocabulary, misprioritize actions, or generate content that's plausible but wrong. That's where **domain adaptation** and **task-specific fine-tuning** come in.

Domain Adaptation: Bridging the Vocabulary and Knowledge Gap

Domain adaptation refers to the process of tailoring a general language model to the linguistic, structural, and conceptual patterns of a specific domain — such as healthcare, law, aviation, telecom, education, or cybersecurity.

1. What Changes in Domain Adaptation?

In domain adaptation, the model retains its general language fluency from pretraining but adjusts:

- **Vocabulary distributions** — to emphasize domain-relevant terms (e.g., "neoplasm" in oncology, "ESG" in finance).
- **Syntax structures** — such as formal academic writing, procedural instructions, or technical diagrams.

- **Conceptual mappings** — how terms relate to one another in the domain (e.g., lab tests and diagnosis codes).
- **Inference patterns** — prioritizing the kinds of reasoning required in the domain (e.g., risk evaluation in insurance).

This doesn't mean retraining the model from scratch. Instead, it involves **continued pretraining** or **lightweight adaptation** on unlabeled or semi-labeled domain-specific data.

2. Strategies for Domain Adaptation

Several techniques have emerged to achieve domain adaptation:

- **Domain-adaptive pretraining (DAPT):** Further training a model on a large corpus of unlabeled domain-specific texts (e.g., medical journals, legal filings, telecom support logs).
- **Adapter modules:** Lightweight, plug-in layers inserted into the model architecture that are trained specifically on domain data, preserving the base model's general knowledge.
- **LoRA (Low-Rank Adaptation):** Efficient fine-tuning technique where only a small subset of parameters are trained, making it ideal for on-device or privacy-preserving scenarios.
- **Prompt tuning and soft prompts:** Instead of modifying the model weights, the system learns prompt embeddings that steer the model behavior for specific domains.

Task-Specific Fine-Tuning: Teaching the Model What to Do

If domain adaptation teaches the model *how to speak the language of a field*, task-specific fine-tuning teaches it *how to perform concrete functions* within that field.

A task could be:

- Classifying SMS messages as spam, scam, or ham.
- Extracting named entities from insurance claims.
- Generating SQL queries from natural language questions.
- Translating voice call transcriptions into structured workflows.
- Summarizing customer complaints into root causes.

Fine-tuning for these tasks typically involves supervised learning — using labeled examples to guide the model toward the desired output pattern.

1. The Fine-Tuning Process

Task-specific fine-tuning involves the following steps:

- **Task definition:** Framing the goal (e.g., text classification, summarization, Q&A, generation).
- **Data collection:** Curating or generating task-relevant examples, ideally high-quality, balanced, and diverse.
- **Model adaptation:** Using backpropagation to slightly adjust the model's weights so it learns to associate inputs with desired outputs.
- **Evaluation and validation:** Testing the model on unseen examples to ensure generalization and robustness.

Fine-tuning is where performance becomes *measurable* — through metrics like accuracy, F1-score, BLEU, ROUGE, or even human evaluation.

2. Multi-Task and Instruction Fine-Tuning

Modern LLMs like GPT-4 and Claude benefit from **multi-task learning** and **instruction tuning** — where models are fine-tuned on a mixture of tasks with natural language instructions.

This creates models that are not just skilled at a single task but capable of **understanding what to do** based on a prompt. For example:

"Summarize this legal contract in plain English."
"Extract all payment terms and highlight potential risks."
"Classify this telecom SMS as scam/spam/ham."

Such models become flexible agents, able to generalize across tasks even with limited task-specific data.

Challenges in Adaptation and Fine-Tuning

Despite their promise, domain and task adaptations bring their own challenges:

- **Data availability:** Many domains have limited labeled datasets or sensitive proprietary data.
- **Catastrophic forgetting:** Overtraining on one domain or task may cause the model to lose general capabilities.

- **Bias reinforcement:** Domain-specific datasets may carry historical, cultural, or legal biases that get amplified.
- **Distributional drift:** Domains evolve. A legal LLM fine-tuned on 2010 regulations may falter on 2025 laws unless continuously updated.
- **Overfitting to shallow cues:** Models may pick up surface patterns instead of deeper reasoning unless care is taken in dataset design.

From Models to Systems: Where Adaptation Becomes Critical

In real-world enterprise and agentic AI scenarios, adaptation is not a "nice-to-have" — it's a **core requirement**. For example:

- In a **telecom fraud detection agent**, you might combine domain-adapted models (trained on industry data), task-specific fine-tuned classifiers (e.g., scam detection from call transcripts), and real-time multimodal inputs.
- In **healthcare**, patient-facing AI agents must adapt not only to medical language but also to privacy norms, local regulations, and individual patient histories.
- In **cross-cultural education**, systems must understand language, pedagogy, and sociocultural sensitivities — adapting across both domain and geography.

Adaptation also supports **on-device intelligence**: a lightweight version of a large model, distilled and fine-tuned to run on smartphones, can deliver powerful results in low-resource settings.

Closing Thoughts

Domain adaptation and task-specific fine-tuning are the twin engines of practical AI deployment. They allow a general-purpose language model to evolve into a specialized assistant, an industry-specific co-pilot, or an intelligent agent that can reason within its environment.

As we move toward more autonomous, agentic AI systems that operate continuously, learn from interaction, and evolve over time, adaptation will not be a one-time activity. It will be an ongoing loop — continuously refined, ethically guided, and organizationally integrated.

In the world of intelligent machines, adaptation is survival. But more than that — it is mastery.

Transfer Learning Across Domains

In traditional machine learning, each new task required its own model, trained from scratch on a task-specific dataset. This approach was not only time-consuming and resource-intensive, but it also failed to capitalize on what the model had already learned in previous tasks. Enter **transfer learning** — a transformative concept that changed the trajectory of modern artificial intelligence.

Transfer learning, at its core, refers to the practice of taking a model trained on one task — typically with large volumes of data — and adapting it to perform a different, often narrower or lower-resource task. With the rise of large language models (LLMs), transfer learning has become a foundational mechanism for building powerful, adaptable, and general-purpose AI systems.

Why Transfer Learning Matters

In real-world scenarios — especially in enterprises — data is often:

- **Sparse** (limited examples for specific use cases),
- **Domain-specific** (legal, financial, medical, telecom),
- **Private or sensitive** (not suited for public model training),
- **Multilingual or stylistically nuanced**.

It's rarely feasible to build massive models from scratch for each of these unique needs. Transfer learning allows us to **leverage the general knowledge embedded in large, pretrained models** and **tailor them to specific domains or tasks**, with far fewer examples and compute requirements.

This concept has made AI more accessible, flexible, and practical — especially in resource-constrained settings or highly specialized fields.

The Mechanics of Cross-Domain Transfer

Large language models, such as GPT, T5, BERT, and others, are typically pretrained on **vast and diverse corpora**. This includes books, websites, encyclopedias, forums, news articles, codebases, and more — enabling them to learn:

- Syntax and grammar,
- Common facts and knowledge structures,
- Reasoning patterns,
- Conversational cues,
- Multilingual signals.

This **pretraining phase** results in a foundation model that is broadly capable of understanding and generating language.

However, when deploying these models to solve domain-specific tasks — say, analyzing telecom service tickets, summarizing legal disclosures, or detecting fraud in transaction logs — we need to **adapt them to the new domain**. This is where **cross-domain transfer learning** becomes essential.

The process usually unfolds in one of three ways:

1. **Feature-Based Transfer**: Extract features from the pretrained model (such as token embeddings or sentence vectors) and use them as inputs to a simpler task-specific model (like a classifier or regressor).
2. **Fine-Tuning**: Further train the entire pretrained model (or a subset of its layers) on labeled data from the target domain, aligning it more closely with the desired behavior and vocabulary.
3. **Prompt-Based or Instruction-Based Tuning**: With instruction-tuned LLMs, instead of training, we guide the model via carefully designed prompts. This is increasingly favored in low-resource or real-time enterprise settings where retraining isn't feasible.

Cross-Domain Generalization vs. Specialization

One of the most powerful traits of LLMs is their **emergent generalization ability**. Even before any fine-tuning, a well-pretrained model can often perform impressively on a new task, thanks to its wide training scope. This zero-shot or few-shot behavior enables LLMs to:

- Translate across languages without being trained on specific language pairs.
- Summarize unfamiliar content formats (e.g., telecom complaint logs or medical case notes).
- Adapt to tone and style (formal, casual, empathetic) with minimal prompting.

However, **true performance parity with domain experts** usually requires further specialization. For example:

- A telecom-focused chatbot needs to understand recharge packs, roaming errors, and network outage phrases.
- A legal summarizer must parse clauses, precedents, and citations.
- A healthcare assistant must interpret symptoms, abbreviations, and ICD-10 codes.

Fine-tuning or continued pretraining on in-domain data allows LLMs to **narrow their attention** and **internalize domain-specific ontologies, jargon, and logic** — without forgetting their general linguistic competence.

Few-Shot and Low-Resource Adaptation

Another key innovation made possible by transfer learning is the rise of **few-shot learning** — where the model is shown a handful of examples (even as few as 5–10) and generalizes behavior effectively.

In practice, this means:

- A legal LLM can summarize a new format of litigation document after seeing a few examples.
- A fraud detection engine can learn new scam tactics from just a few labeled messages.
- A content moderation filter can adjust to platform-specific slang without retraining the full model.

This is especially important in dynamic domains — like fraud detection, cybercrime, social media, or customer experience — where **patterns evolve faster than training pipelines** can adapt. Transfer learning enables **rapid iteration without overhauling the system.**

Challenges in Domain Transfer

While powerful, transfer learning across domains is not trivial. Key challenges include:

- **Domain Shift**: The statistical properties of the target domain may differ drastically from pretraining data. A model trained on Wikipedia and news may struggle with noisy SMS logs or colloquial WhatsApp messages.
- **Catastrophic Forgetting**: Fine-tuning on small, domain-specific datasets can overwrite previously learned knowledge, degrading general performance.
- **Data Scarcity and Labeling Costs**: Many enterprise domains suffer from lack of labeled data, especially for niche tasks or rare event types.
- **Bias Transfer**: Pretrained models may carry forward undesirable biases from the pretraining corpus into the target domain (e.g., reinforcing stereotypes in sensitive areas like healthcare, finance, or hiring).
- **Explainability and Trust**: In regulated domains like law, finance, and healthcare, models must not only perform well but also explain *why* they made a decision — something LLMs are still evolving to do.

Agentic Systems and Transfer Learning

As we transition toward **agentic AI systems** — autonomous agents that observe, reason, act, and adapt — transfer learning becomes even more vital.

These agents operate in **open, unpredictable environments**, across domains, tasks, and modalities. They must learn continually, adapt quickly, and reuse prior knowledge effectively.

For example, a telco AI agent could:

- Understand customer queries in voice or SMS.
- Infer intent (e.g., "network not working" → connectivity issue).
- Pull from previous experience (e.g., "this pattern indicates a regional outage").

- Adapt on-the-fly to evolving customer behavior (e.g., surge in scam complaints).
- Provide regulatory-compliant responses with local context.

All of this requires **layered transfer** — not just across domains (telecom, legal, UX) but also across modalities (text, voice, metadata) and roles (chatbot, summarizer, detector, planner).

The Strategic Advantage

For enterprises, cross-domain transfer learning is more than an engineering trick. It is a **strategic enabler**:

- **Faster time to deployment** for new AI services.
- **Cost-efficient adaptation** in low-data environments.
- **Scalability** across languages, regions, verticals, and regulatory regimes.
- **Continual learning** from edge feedback without centralized retraining.

Organizations that master transfer learning can create AI systems that are not just smarter, but **nimbler, more resilient, and context-aware** — precisely what is needed for real-world impact.

Conclusion

Transfer learning is the bridge that connects general intelligence to specific utility. It turns LLMs from language experts into domain professionals — legal advisors, support agents, fraud analysts, research copilots, and more.

In a world where knowledge is abundant but context is everything, the ability to adapt intelligence across domains is not a luxury — it is the defining capability of enterprise AI.

The next frontier will not be training ever-larger models from scratch. It will be about **crafting intelligent, responsive systems that continuously learn, specialize, and collaborate — grounded in language, and shaped by context.**

Continual and Lifelong Learning

As intelligent systems mature, one limitation of traditional training paradigms becomes increasingly evident: they are inherently static. Once a language model is pretrained and fine-tuned, its knowledge becomes effectively frozen in time. It cannot incorporate new information without retraining, and it cannot adapt its behavior based on new experiences or shifting user needs without manual intervention. In the dynamic environments of the real world — where knowledge evolves, user preferences shift, and contexts change — this rigidity is not just a constraint. It's a flaw.

This is where **continual learning** and its broader vision, **lifelong learning**, come into focus.

The Problem with Static Intelligence

Modern large language models are typically trained in large, discrete phases:

1. **Pretraining** on broad, general-purpose corpora (books, web pages, code, etc.).
2. **Fine-tuning** on more task-specific data (e.g., medical QA, legal summaries).
3. **Deployment** for inference — where the model is used in production to interact with users.

But after deployment, traditional LLMs become "read-only". Any new information they acquire, whether through user interaction or environmental feedback, is external to their learning process. They do not natively evolve. Any improvement requires retraining or updating the model — an expensive, time-consuming process that can introduce **catastrophic forgetting** (where newly learned information erases prior capabilities).

In contrast, human intelligence is **adaptive, incremental, and context-aware**. We learn continuously — every conversation, every mistake, every success informs future actions. We don't need to relearn everything to learn something new. The aspiration in AI is to mirror this: to enable models that can **remember, adapt, refine, and evolve** throughout their operational lives.

What Is Continual Learning?

Continual learning refers to a model's ability to **incrementally learn from new data** or tasks **without forgetting** what it has previously learned. It enables AI systems to:

- **Incorporate new knowledge** without retraining from scratch.
- **Adapt to evolving environments** and changing user needs.
- **Build experience** through interaction, rather than static programming.
- **Retain prior capabilities** while expanding to new domains.

The goal is to allow LLMs to function like intelligent agents that **learn over time**, rather than disposable tools trained once and discarded when obsolete.

What Makes It Difficult?

The core challenge is **catastrophic forgetting** — the tendency of neural networks to overwrite old knowledge when trained on new data. When a model is exposed to new tasks, its parameters adjust to optimize for them, often at the cost of previously learned tasks.

Another complexity is **data privacy and availability**. In many enterprise or edge use-cases, historical data may not be stored indefinitely due to privacy concerns, compliance policies, or storage constraints. This makes it hard for models to revisit earlier training examples, which is how traditional retraining works.

There are also issues of **scaling and efficiency**. Continual learning must happen without exploding compute costs. If every update requires retraining billions of parameters, the solution is not viable — especially for on-device models or low-resource environments like rural smartphones or embedded systems.

Approaches to Continual Learning

Researchers and practitioners have explored various strategies to enable continual learning in LLMs and other deep models. These include:

- **Regularization-based methods**: These penalize changes to parameters deemed important for previous tasks, helping retain old knowledge. Techniques like Elastic Weight Consolidation (EWC) fall into this category.
- **Replay-based methods**: These store a subset of past data (or generate it synthetically) to be replayed alongside new data, ensuring that training doesn't forget earlier tasks. It's akin to human revision.
- **Dynamic architectures**: These expand the model architecture over time, assigning new neurons or layers to new tasks. This avoids interference but can lead to unbounded model growth.
- **Adapter layers and LoRA**: Lightweight modules like adapters or low-rank matrices (LoRA) can be appended to frozen base models and trained incrementally. This enables continual adaptation without changing core weights.
- **Memory-augmented learning**: Some architectures use external memory banks — such as vector databases or long-term caches — to retrieve and incorporate past information at inference time, mimicking episodic memory.
- **Agentic frameworks with feedback loops**: Agent-based systems (e.g., ReAct, AutoGPT, LangGraph agents) can integrate continual learning at the behavioral layer, by adjusting their tool use, planning strategies, and prompting heuristics over time — even if the underlying LLM remains frozen.

Lifelong Learning: The Larger Ambition

Where continual learning focuses on **short- to medium-term adaptation**, **lifelong learning** imagines an intelligence that **never stops evolving**. It's not just about avoiding forgetting — it's about **cumulative, compounding intelligence**.

A lifelong learning model:

- Builds a long-term memory of experiences, tasks, and interactions.
- Learns to learn — identifying patterns across tasks to improve generalization.
- Develops meta-skills like abstraction, planning, reasoning, and tool selection.

- Evolves from passive prediction to active collaboration and decision-making.

In agentic AI, lifelong learning isn't optional — it's essential. An AI assistant for healthcare, law, or enterprise operations must keep up with changing regulations, evolving user preferences, emerging risks, and even the personalities of the humans it assists. Static intelligence cannot meet this bar.

Implications for Enterprises

For organizations deploying LLMs in production — whether for customer support, document processing, fraud detection, or decision augmentation — continual and lifelong learning are vital for:

- **Personalization**: Adapting models to individual users, roles, or departments.
- **Adaptability**: Updating knowledge without constant retraining.
- **Local compliance**: Learning user behavior within specific legal or geographic constraints.
- **Efficiency**: Reducing the need for full retraining cycles and manual reconfiguration.
- **Responsiveness**: Adjusting quickly to new threats (e.g., phishing scams), policies, or data types.

Especially in environments like telco, finance, and public services in developing countries — where infrastructure is limited but contexts are dynamic — continual learning can enable lightweight, on-device models that evolve with use, delivering real-time, context-sensitive intelligence.

The Road Ahead

Lifelong learning is not a solved problem — it is a frontier. But progress is accelerating:

- New architectures (modular LLMs, retrieval-augmented transformers, graph-based agents).
- Hybrid approaches (combining symbolic reasoning with LLMs).

- Online fine-tuning via federated learning or reinforcement learning from user feedback.
- Multi-agent ecosystems where learning is distributed and shared across collaborative AI entities.

The ultimate goal is to create systems that not only process text but **grow with experience** — becoming more aligned, more helpful, and more trustworthy over time.

Just as humans are shaped by what they read, experience, and reflect upon, the next generation of AI will be defined not just by what it was trained on, but by what it continues to learn.

CHAPTER SEVEN

The Power of Text Generation

Mechanics of Generative Models

At the heart of the modern AI revolution lies a deceptively simple yet profoundly powerful question: "*What word comes next?*"
Generative models, especially large language models (LLMs), are built to answer this question — and by doing so at scale and with nuance, they give rise to creative, coherent, and context-aware text generation that rivals, and sometimes surpasses, human output.

Understanding the mechanics of how this generation works is critical — not only for appreciating their capabilities, but also for building, customizing, and safely deploying them across domains.

1. Probabilistic Foundations: The Core Principle

Generative language models operate on probabilistic principles. At their core, they estimate the likelihood of a word (or token) given a preceding sequence. Instead of retrieving facts or pre-written answers, they calculate the conditional probability distribution over the vocabulary and *sample* from it.

Formally, given a sequence of tokens x1,x2,...,xn−1x_1, x_2, ..., x_{n-1}x1,x2,...,xn−1, the model tries to predict the next token xnx_nxn such that:

P(xn ∣ x1,x2,...,xn−1)P(x_n | x_1, x_2, ..., x_{n-1})P(xn ∣ x1,x2,...,xn−1
)

This process is repeated iteratively — generating one token at a time, appending it to the context, and using that updated context to predict the next token — until a termination condition is met (such as an end-of-sequence token or length limit).

2. Tokenization: Language as Numbers

Before generation begins, the input text must be transformed into a machine-readable format. This involves *tokenization* — breaking down the text into subword units (tokens) using techniques like Byte-Pair Encoding (BPE) or WordPiece.

Each token is assigned a unique numerical ID from the model's vocabulary, enabling it to be processed by the neural network. These token embeddings capture not just spelling, but frequency, structure, and contextual meaning — all compressed into high-dimensional vectors.

3. Neural Architecture: The Transformer Engine

Modern generative models rely on the **Transformer architecture**, introduced in the seminal 2017 paper *"Attention Is All You Need"*. Transformers differ from earlier sequence models like RNNs or LSTMs by processing input as a whole using self-attention mechanisms.

In a Transformer-based generative model like GPT:

- The input tokens are embedded and passed through multiple layers of Transformer blocks.
- Each layer uses **multi-head self-attention**, allowing the model to weigh different parts of the input context differently — giving it the ability to capture long-range dependencies, such as references many sentences apart.
- **Feedforward networks**, **residual connections**, and **layer normalization** refine and stabilize the transformations at each layer.

During generation, the model uses a **causal mask** to prevent access to future tokens, ensuring that generation is left-to-right and autoregressive.

4. Decoding Strategies: From Probabilities to Words

The output of a generative model at each step is a probability distribution over all possible tokens. Converting this distribution into coherent and meaningful text is where **decoding strategies** come in.

Several methods are commonly used:

- **Greedy Decoding**: Always pick the highest-probability token at each step. Fast, but often repetitive and lacks creativity.
- **Beam Search**: Maintains multiple candidate sequences (beams) and explores combinations. More accurate, but can still become deterministic and dull.
- **Top-k Sampling**: Limits sampling to the top k most likely tokens. Introduces randomness while constraining poor choices.
- **Top-p (Nucleus) Sampling**: Samples from the smallest set of tokens whose cumulative probability exceeds p. More adaptive and fluent.
- **Temperature Scaling**: Adjusts the sharpness of the distribution. Lower temperature means more deterministic; higher means more diverse.

By fine-tuning these decoding techniques, developers can control the creativity, coherence, and risk profile of generated text.

5. Prompting: The Input Matters

Generative models are not static question-answering machines. They are **prompt-driven** systems — and the prompt plays a decisive role in shaping the output. Prompting is how humans "program" the model in natural language.

Effective prompting relies on:

- **Clarity**: Phrasing instructions precisely.
- **Context**: Providing relevant background or examples.
- **Continuity**: Designing prompts that reflect the desired tone, format, or logic.

Even slight changes in prompt structure can yield significantly different results — making prompt engineering a critical skill for building generative applications.

6. Inference Time Behavior: Stateless but Context-Aware

Generative models are **stateless by default**. Each generation session doesn't remember prior interactions unless context is explicitly provided. However, within a single prompt or conversation, the model can retain and use context efficiently up to its context window limit — which now exceeds **100,000 tokens** in advanced models.

This means:

- You can feed long documents, dialogues, or source code as context.
- The model reasons about the content holistically.
- But memory is ephemeral unless stored and re-fed — unless wrapped with **external memory systems** or **retrieval-augmented generation (RAG)** techniques.

7. Finetuning vs. In-Context Learning

There are two primary ways to adapt generative models for specific use cases:

- **Finetuning**: Training the model further on domain-specific data. This updates model weights and gives it long-term knowledge or behavior aligned to a domain or task.
- **In-context learning**: Teaching the model via examples embedded in the prompt. This requires no retraining and exploits the model's ability to generalize patterns from just a few demonstrations (a hallmark of LLMs).

In practice, **prompt engineering**, **instruction tuning**, and **reinforcement learning with human feedback (RLHF)** are often used together to shape and constrain generative behavior.

8. Agentic Text Generation: Toward Autonomous Intelligence

As generative models become more sophisticated, they are increasingly being embedded in **agentic frameworks** — where the model doesn't just generate a reply but performs multi-step reasoning, maintains internal goals, uses tools (like search or code execution), and adapts based on outcomes.

In this setting:

- Text generation is a *means*, not the end.
- The model reasons through chains of prompts, reflections, memory calls, and API invocations.
- Generation becomes *interactive*, *contextual*, and *action-oriented.*

These agents can autonomously write code, query data, draft reports, carry out customer interactions, or even explore scientific hypotheses — moving from passive generation to goal-directed cognition.

9. Risks and Guardrails: Generation Gone Wrong

The same flexibility that makes generative models powerful also makes them risky. Without proper safeguards, they can:

- Hallucinate facts or fabricate references.
- Generate toxic, biased, or inappropriate content.
- Mislead users with confident but incorrect outputs.
- Be manipulated through adversarial or misleading prompts.

To mitigate these risks, responsible deployment requires:

- **Content filters** and **moderation layers**.
- **Red-teaming** and **stress testing** for edge cases.
- **Alignment training** using human preferences.
- **Auditing and monitoring** in real-time use.

10. The Bottom Line: Generation as Intelligence

Text generation is not just a mechanical process of stringing words together. In the LLM era, it is a form of **emergent reasoning** — a manifestation of learned knowledge, world models, statistical inference, and linguistic fluency.

Every generated paragraph is the output of:

- Vast unsupervised training across global knowledge and discourse.
- Billions of parameters encoding patterns, associations, and logic.
- Complex token-by-token probabilistic prediction shaped by prompt context.

This is why the ability to generate high-quality, grounded, and adaptive text is considered one of the strongest signals of general-purpose intelligence in machines today. And it is why text generation sits at the heart of everything from enterprise automation to autonomous agents to scientific discovery.

Prompt Engineering and In-Context Learning

At the heart of modern text generation lies a deceptively simple principle: how you ask is just as important as what you ask.

Large Language Models (LLMs), like GPT and its variants, are not rigid programs. They don't rely on hard-coded rules or traditional APIs. Instead, they operate as probabilistic engines, shaped by billions of text examples and capable of generating fluent, meaningful responses. But to steer this power toward useful outcomes, one must learn the emerging art and science of **prompt engineering** — the crafting of inputs that guide the model's outputs — and its powerful complement, **in-context learning**.

Together, these techniques define how humans "program" LLMs — not with code, but with language.

Prompt Engineering: The New Language of Instruction

Prompt engineering is the practice of designing and refining the input text provided to an LLM to elicit the most accurate, coherent, or creative response possible. In this paradigm, natural language becomes a kind of meta-programming language — a flexible, expressive interface for instructing the model.

There are no fixed APIs, endpoints, or parameter calls. Instead, the prompt carries all the instructions:

- What task to perform (summarize, translate, generate, classify).

- How to format the output (bullet points, formal tone, JSON).
- What constraints to follow (word count, style, level of detail).
- What role the model should assume (a teacher, a lawyer, a customer agent).

For example, a single sentence — *"Summarize the following legal paragraph in plain English."* — transforms a general-purpose model into a legal simplifier. The prompt is the interface, the instruction set, and the control layer, all in one.

This simplicity hides a powerful truth: prompt engineering is an act of intent design. It forces users to articulate what they want with precision, clarity, and foresight. In many ways, it's a rediscovery of linguistic precision — not for poetry, but for utility.

From Craft to Discipline: The Maturation of Prompt Engineering

In its early stages, prompt engineering was mostly trial-and-error: asking questions, tweaking phrasing, observing results. But over time, patterns and best practices emerged:

- **Few-shot prompting**: Including a few examples of inputs and outputs within the prompt to guide the model's behavior.
- **Chain-of-thought prompting**: Asking the model to show its reasoning step-by-step, rather than jumping to conclusions.
- **Role-based prompting**: Framing the model as a persona or expert (e.g., "You are a cybersecurity analyst...").
- **Constraint prompting**: Explicitly stating conditions like format, tone, style, or prohibited content.
- **Iterative prompting**: Refining and re-prompting based on initial outputs, enabling dynamic collaboration with the model.

These techniques have transformed prompt engineering into a repeatable, teachable, and increasingly standardized practice — one that enterprise users, developers, analysts, and domain experts can learn and apply without deep machine learning expertise.

In fact, entire startups and platforms have emerged around prompt optimization, validation, versioning, and safety — a new layer in the software development stack.

In-Context Learning: Models That Learn Without Training

In traditional machine learning, learning means weight updates — models are trained, fine-tuned, or retrained based on data and feedback. This is time-consuming, expensive, and often impractical in real-time environments.

In contrast, **in-context learning** allows large language models to *learn* new tasks, patterns, or behaviors on the fly, within the scope of a single prompt, without changing their internal parameters.

This capability is astonishing in its implications.

For example, suppose you provide the model with three examples of email classifications (spam, promotional, transactional) and then ask it to classify a new one. The model uses the examples as *implicit instruction* — not by updating weights, but by recognizing patterns from the context and extending them.

This means LLMs can:

- Adapt to new domains or languages without retraining.
- Follow task instructions without hard-coding.
- Generalize from very few examples — even just one (one-shot) or none (zero-shot).

In practical terms, in-context learning gives LLMs "short-term memory." You can teach them a new skill within seconds, as long as the prompt includes enough guidance or structure. This is particularly powerful for dynamic use cases where models must handle diverse data, changing user needs, or emerging topics.

Prompt Engineering + In-Context Learning = Emergent Agency

When prompt engineering is paired with in-context learning, something remarkable happens: the model begins to behave not just like a responder, but like a reasoning agent.

Given the right prompt, an LLM can:

- Follow a workflow or process across multiple steps.
- Assume roles and switch strategies mid-task.
- Generate code, run simulations, or structure data.
- Chain tasks together — summarize → analyze → generate.
- Reflect on its own output and revise (via recursive prompting or tool use).

This emergent agency — the ability to act, reason, and adapt within a session — is a foundational building block for **agentic AI** systems. These are not static bots or deterministic engines, but *dynamic collaborators* that evolve with the conversation and context.

Enterprise Relevance: The Democratization of AI via Language

In the enterprise world, the power of prompt engineering and in-context learning is transformational:

- Business analysts can automate document review without retraining models.
- Customer service teams can fine-tune tone and escalation protocols via prompts.
- Healthcare professionals can instruct models on how to prioritize symptoms or generate structured summaries.
- Marketers can tailor content generation to tone, audience, or brand guidelines — all within a prompt.

This means teams no longer need an army of data scientists or custom-trained models for every task. Instead, they can rely on general-purpose LLMs, steered precisely via prompt design.

And because the interface is language — not code — the tools are accessible to domain experts, linguists, consultants, and even frontline workers. This is what makes prompt engineering and in-context learning revolutionary: they collapse the gap between capability and usability.

The Future of Prompting: From Static Inputs to Interactive Agents

As language models evolve into interactive, multimodal agents, the notion of a prompt is also evolving:

- Prompts can be **dynamic**, adapting based on prior outputs or real-time data.
- Prompts can be **multimodal**, including not just text, but images, code snippets, or audio.
- Prompts can be **contextualized**, enriched by memory, history, or user preferences.
- Prompts can be **autonomous**, generated by other agents or systems as part of a broader workflow.

Eventually, the line between a prompt and a program may blur entirely — especially as LLMs integrate with tools, APIs, and real-world sensors. But at their core, they will still rely on the foundational idea: that natural language can steer intelligent behavior.

Final Thoughts: Programming with Words

Prompt engineering and in-context learning mark a paradigm shift. They redefine what it means to *use* an AI system. No longer confined to model retraining cycles or rigid UIs, users now shape intelligence with language itself.

It is an invitation — to business leaders, creatives, educators, developers, and everyone else — to think deeply about how we express intent, frame tasks, and collaborate with artificial minds.

In a world where every prompt is a possibility, the future of AI begins not with algorithms, but with words.

Storytelling and Content Generation

At the heart of human expression lies the art of storytelling. For millennia, stories have shaped civilizations, preserved knowledge, sparked revolutions, and transmitted culture across generations. In today's digital world, this innate human tradition is being reimagined and accelerated through AI — specifically, through the generative capabilities of large language models.

LLMs have brought us to a remarkable threshold: machines that can co-author stories, create new narratives, generate original content, and adapt their tone, structure, and style to suit virtually any audience or objective. This evolution goes beyond automation. It represents the rise of **machine-augmented creativity** — where imagination is no longer confined by human bandwidth.

The Genesis of AI-Powered Storytelling

Traditional content creation has always been constrained by time, talent, and translation. Writers face creative blocks, editors work under deadlines, and scaling storytelling across formats, cultures, and languages has long been a challenge. LLMs dismantle many of these constraints by generating coherent, contextually relevant, and stylistically diverse narratives within seconds.

These models don't "think" or "feel" in the human sense. But they are statistically fluent in the art of storytelling. Trained on billions of words — from novels, scripts, poems, and blogs to news articles, speeches, and social media — LLMs internalize patterns of narrative arc, emotional pacing, character development, and voice modulation. They learn the cadences of comedy, the structure of suspense, and the economy of language in journalism.

In essence, they become *probabilistic mirrors* of human creativity — reflecting our vast textual traditions, while remixing them into new, generative possibilities.

Types of Storytelling LLMs Can Enable

LLMs today can create a wide array of story-driven outputs, including:

- **Fictional storytelling** in genres such as science fiction, romance, fantasy, horror, or drama.
- **Narrative world-building** for video games, metaverses, and interactive simulations.
- **Marketing stories** that align with brand voice, emotional resonance, and product journeys.
- **Educational storytelling**, where complex concepts are simplified through metaphor, narrative framing, and persona-based learning.
- **Scenario generation** for simulations in fields like healthcare, defense, and finance.

- **Dialogue-driven storytelling** for screenwriting, theater, podcasts, or virtual companions.

What makes LLM-generated stories truly powerful is their adaptability. They can instantly shift tone, rewrite from a new perspective, modify reading levels, or align with regional sensibilities — at scale and speed that human teams cannot match.

Human-AI Collaboration in Creativity

Rather than replacing human authors, the real power of LLMs lies in *augmenting* them. Writers can use LLMs as:

- **Idea generators**, to explore plot twists, develop characters, or brainstorm headlines.
- **Writing companions**, to suggest sentence completions, alternative phrasings, or stylistic enhancements.
- **Co-creators**, that write drafts, expand outlines, or create variations for A/B testing.
- **Rewriting engines**, that localize or personalize content across demographics or markets.

This synergy creates a new creative paradigm — *interactive ideation* — where the writer and the model engage in a dynamic, iterative loop. The human sets the intent, context, or theme; the model responds with possibilities. The human edits, refines, and re-asks; the model recalibrates. The result is faster output, more diverse content, and often, surprising bursts of originality.

For enterprises, this workflow is a game-changer. Marketing teams can produce dozens of campaign variants in minutes. Publishing houses can scale personalized fiction. Game studios can populate worlds with rich, dynamic lore. E-learning platforms can tailor stories to each learner's profile.

Risks and Responsibilities in AI-Driven Narratives

But with this power comes critical responsibility. Because LLMs draw from vast, uncontrolled datasets, they can inadvertently reproduce stereotypes, cultural biases, or inappropriate content. If prompted carelessly, they may generate misleading stories, reinforce harmful tropes, or produce emotionally flat narratives masked in persuasive language.

Therefore, human oversight is not optional. Editorial review, prompt engineering, and responsible deployment must remain core components of any AI-driven content generation workflow. This is especially important when the stakes are high — such as content for children, mental health storytelling, or politically sensitive narratives.

Ethical storytelling in the AI age requires both transparency and intention. Readers and consumers should know when they're interacting with machine-generated narratives. And creators must be thoughtful about the emotional and cognitive impact of those narratives.

The Future of Storytelling with LLMs

Looking forward, storytelling is poised to become even more immersive and personalized:

- **Interactive narratives** where LLMs dynamically adapt stories in real time based on reader feedback or emotional response.
- **Agentic characters** powered by LLMs that remember past interactions and evolve their dialogue and worldview.
- **Multimodal storytelling** where text is just one thread among video, audio, and visual elements — all co-generated and synchronized.
- **Hyper-personalized content** where stories are tailored to individual personalities, histories, or moods.

This is not science fiction. Already, AI-generated bedtime stories, personalized journals, and virtual therapy bots are emerging in real-world products. Enterprises are embedding generative storytelling in advertising, training, and even strategic scenario planning.

In developing countries, where access to quality education and content is limited, LLM-driven storytelling can democratize learning — crafting compelling narratives in local languages and dialects, aligned with cultural context, and delivered via mobile.

Conclusion: The Renaissance of Storytelling

Creative storytelling and content generation are no longer confined to human imagination alone. With LLMs, we are entering a new renaissance — one where every voice can find amplification, every idea can find expression, and every user can become a creator.

But it is not a replacement. It is a reimagining.

By blending the emotional intelligence of humans with the linguistic intelligence of machines, we are not just creating content at scale. We are crafting a new medium — one where imagination meets computation, and creativity becomes collaborative.

The pen is no longer just mightier than the sword. It is now embedded in silicon, distributed across the cloud, and augmented by algorithms — waiting to co-write the next chapter of human creativity.

Chatbots, Agents, and Conversational Interfaces

Among the most transformative applications of text generation powered by Large Language Models (LLMs) is the emergence of intelligent conversational systems — chatbots, virtual assistants, and more recently, autonomous agents. These systems, once limited to pre-scripted replies and rigid command structures, are now becoming dynamic, context-aware, and capable of engaging in open-ended, intelligent dialogue across tasks, languages, and domains.

From Rule-Based Scripts to Generative Intelligence

Early chatbots operated like decision trees: they followed fixed, rule-based flows that could only respond to narrowly defined user inputs. Phrases had to match predefined keywords; ambiguity was not tolerated. While these systems were suitable for handling routine queries (e.g., checking account balances or booking appointments), they failed catastrophically in the face of unexpected inputs, complex questions, or human emotion.

The advent of neural language models, and eventually transformers, changed this paradigm. These models don't merely retrieve or match answers — they *generate* them. They interpret the user's intent, extract context from prior interactions, and synthesize responses on the fly. This transition from static to generative opened the door to rich, natural, and human-like conversations that feel less transactional and more collaborative.

Chatbots Reimagined with LLMs

Modern LLM-powered chatbots are not just virtual helpdesk assistants — they are multi-skilled communication layers that span industries, functions, and languages. These systems can:

- Hold multi-turn conversations with memory and continuity.
- Understand nuances in tone, sentiment, and implied meaning.
- Adapt to different user personas (technical, novice, emotional).
- Personalize responses based on user history or role.
- Perform reasoning, summarization, explanation, and decision support.

For example, a banking chatbot can now not only answer "What is my balance?" but also understand, "Can I afford this trip to Bali if I withdraw from my savings?" — interpreting context, extracting relevant account data, projecting future expenses, and offering recommendations.

In healthcare, LLM-powered bots can screen symptoms, explain medical terms in layman's language, and provide empathy — not just information. In retail, they can act as shopping concierges, blending product knowledge with customer behavior and stylistic preferences.

These aren't just improvements in interface design — they reflect a deeper shift in capability. Chatbots are becoming first-line problem solvers, recommendation engines, and knowledge navigators.

Rise of Agentic Conversational Interfaces

The evolution from chatbots to *agents* marks another frontier. An agent is not merely reactive, but proactive. It can:

- Set goals, plan tasks, and execute steps autonomously.
- Use external tools (e.g., APIs, databases, calendars) to act on behalf of the user.
- Maintain long-term memory and develop personalized strategies.
- Reason across sessions, modalities, and objectives.

In this agentic paradigm, conversation becomes a control surface for complex behavior. A travel agent powered by an LLM doesn't just reply with flight options — it searches, compares, books, manages changes, and follows up — all within a natural conversation flow. An HR agent can conduct onboarding, answer policy queries, guide form-filling, and detect intent shifts like frustration or confusion, adjusting tone and escalation paths dynamically.

These agentic systems are not just helpful — they begin to feel collaborative, even co-intelligent. They reason, adapt, and participate in workflows like a digital colleague, rather than a rigid command-line.

Interfaces That Disappear

The naturalness of LLM-generated language enables interfaces that become nearly invisible. Instead of forcing users to learn UI workflows, menu trees, or query syntax, these systems meet users where they are — in language. Whether through text or speech, users can simply *say what they need*, and the system adapts.

This is especially powerful in:

- **Low-literacy environments**, where visual interfaces may intimidate.
- **Voice-first use cases**, such as on-the-go interactions or accessibility support.
- **Multi-lingual populations**, where code-switching and dialectal variance are common.
- **Hands-free scenarios**, such as industrial maintenance or healthcare rounds.

Language, in these cases, is not just an interface — it's a liberation from complexity.

Global and Inclusive Applications

The potential of generative conversational systems is particularly profound in developing economies, where smartphone penetration is high but digital literacy is low. LLM-powered agents can:

- Explain government schemes in local languages and dialects.
- Help farmers understand weather forecasts, pricing trends, or subsidy eligibility.

- Guide job seekers through resume creation or skill development pathways.
- Assist women, seniors, and marginalized communities in accessing digital services without navigating apps, forms, or bureaucracy.

These systems, when designed with cultural and linguistic sensitivity, can bridge the last-mile digital divide. They turn smartphones into personal advisors. Text generation thus becomes not just a technical triumph, but a social equalizer.

Limitations and Ethical Concerns

Despite their promise, LLM-powered conversational systems are not infallible. They can:

- Hallucinate incorrect information with high confidence.
- Perpetuate biases present in training data.
- Struggle with factuality, especially in domains requiring precision.
- Be exploited for misinformation, phishing, or social manipulation.

Moreover, when used as customer-facing interfaces, the risk of over-reliance must be managed carefully. Enterprises must ensure robust fallbacks to human agents, clear disclosures, and strict safety filters. Transparency, feedback loops, and red-teaming are vital to build trust and maintain responsible deployment.

The Future of Conversational Interfaces

Looking forward, LLM-powered conversational systems will evolve across three major vectors:

1. **Memory and Personalization**: Persistent memory will allow these agents to evolve with the user, remember preferences, adapt tone, and refine their assistance over time — like a true digital companion.
2. **Multimodality**: Integration of voice, video, image, and code capabilities will make these systems even more expressive, useful, and intuitive. Imagine explaining a problem with a photo or getting a visual walkthrough narrated by an agent.

3. **Agentic Autonomy**: These systems will go beyond chat. They'll schedule meetings, send emails, fill forms, trigger workflows, and learn from outcomes. They'll blend reasoning, action, and language in a unified, seamless experience.

In sum, chatbots and conversational agents powered by LLMs are not simply a user interface improvement — they represent a fundamental rethinking of how humans and machines interact. From call centers to classrooms, from local governance to global enterprises, these systems are redefining what it means to have an intelligent conversation — one where the machine doesn't just understand your question but helps you move toward a meaningful outcome.

The future of human-computer interaction is not GUI — it's language. And thanks to text generation, that future is already speaking.

Language Translation and Localization

In a world that is increasingly interconnected yet linguistically diverse, the ability of machines to translate and adapt language across cultures is one of the most profound applications of large language models (LLMs). Text generation technologies have revolutionized how we approach translation—not merely as a mechanical conversion of words from one language to another, but as a deeply nuanced process of **localization**, **contextual adaptation**, and **cultural fluency**.

From Rule-Based Translation to Generative Intelligence

Historically, machine translation relied on rule-based systems and phrase-based statistical models. These systems could parse grammar structures and map common phrases between languages, but they struggled with idioms, ambiguity, context, and style. The output often felt robotic, literal, and culturally tone-deaf.

Large language models mark a radical shift. Trained on multilingual corpora spanning diverse dialects, domains, and contexts, modern LLMs like GPT-4, mBERT, and NLLB (No Language Left Behind) don't just substitute vocabulary—they **generate linguistically and culturally coherent responses** in the target language. They go beyond sentence-level translation and begin to understand **intent**, **audience**, **register**, and **tone**.

This transition from **machine translation** to **generative localization** is a turning point, especially for global enterprises.

Why Translation Alone Is Not Enough

True language adaptation requires more than swapping words. For global products, services, and communications, **localization** is the art of making content feel native. This involves:

- **Cultural adaptation**: Adjusting references, metaphors, and humor to suit local norms.
- **Contextual understanding**: Preserving the original meaning while adapting tone and flow.
- **Regulatory compliance**: Aligning content with regional laws, especially in legal, healthcare, and financial domains.
- **Emotional resonance**: Ensuring that messages evoke the right sentiment and trust in different cultural contexts.

A simple marketing slogan might need a completely different rewrite in another language—not just for clarity but to avoid cultural missteps or missed impact. Traditional translation tools fall short here. Generative models step in with **semantic flexibility** and **creative control**.

How LLMs Excel at Translation and Localization

Modern LLMs use **multilingual pretraining** and **cross-lingual transfer learning**, meaning they don't treat each language in isolation. Instead, they learn shared linguistic patterns and structures across languages, enabling them to:

- Translate between languages even with limited data.
- Maintain contextual coherence across long documents.
- Infer cultural nuance, gender, and formality from minimal prompts.
- Perform zero-shot or few-shot translations—translating between two languages they were never explicitly trained to connect.

For example, an LLM can translate a business memo from English to Swahili with domain-appropriate terminology, even if training examples for that exact task are sparse. This enables **scalable translation** for underserved and low-resource languages—a key development in inclusivity and digital equity.

Use Cases Across Industries

1. Customer Support and CX
Global enterprises can instantly localize chatbot interactions, helpdesk responses, and FAQs. This ensures that customers across regions receive empathetic, clear, and culturally appropriate support—often in real time.

2. E-commerce and Marketing
Product listings, promotional campaigns, and brand storytelling can be adapted to local languages and sentiments. A tagline that works in the U.S. might be awkward in Japan, but with LLMs, campaigns can be dynamically rephrased to resonate locally—at scale.

3. Healthcare and Telemedicine
In multilingual societies, delivering medical instructions or patient education materials in native languages isn't just a convenience—it's a safety requirement. LLMs can help generate medically accurate, locally understandable, and culturally sensitive materials.

4. Government and Public Services
For policy documents, public health advisories, or legal notices to reach diverse populations, translation must preserve legal nuance and intent. Generative models can help democratize access to essential information.

5. Media, Entertainment, and Education
Subtitles, transcripts, and learning materials can be localized with emotional accuracy and idiomatic clarity. This makes global content accessible and relatable to learners and audiences everywhere.

Challenges in Generative Translation

While generative LLMs offer immense power, they are not infallible. Key challenges include:

- **Hallucination**: The model might generate fluent but factually incorrect or misleading translations.
- **Bias replication**: Training data might reflect cultural or gender stereotypes, which can be amplified in translation.

- **Loss of domain-specific precision**: Technical language—legal, scientific, medical—requires careful preservation of meaning.
- **Over-literalness or over-creative errors**: Some translations may either stick too close to source syntax or drift too far in rephrasing.

These risks underline the importance of **human oversight**, **feedback loops**, and **hybrid systems** that combine LLMs with domain-specific rules or validation layers.

The Future: Towards Real-Time, Context-Aware Translation

Generative models are evolving toward:

- **Context-aware translation**: Adapting meaning based on conversation history, user profile, and task-specific goals.
- **Multimodal translation**: Interpreting and translating speech, images, gestures, and text in an integrated fashion—critical for global accessibility.
- **Personalized translation**: Adjusting tone and formality based on user preferences or prior interactions.
- **On-device, offline translation**: Compressing powerful models for low-latency, low-bandwidth environments—vital for inclusion in developing regions.

Conclusion: A Borderless Future Built on Language

Text generation has moved translation from an auxiliary function to a strategic enabler. With LLMs, businesses can speak to users, partners, and stakeholders in their own language—*not just in words, but in meaning*. This isn't about converting language. It's about *preserving intent, delivering clarity*, and *fostering trust* across borders.

In a world where language is the final frontier of digital transformation, generative AI is making the world not just smaller, but more human. And in doing so, it is helping build a more inclusive, accessible, and linguistically respectful global future.

Summarization, Paraphrasing, and Style Transfer

One of the most impactful capabilities of large language models is their ability to transform, compress, or reframe text while retaining — or intelligently altering — its original meaning. This transformative power, at the heart of many real-world applications, can be distilled into three key generative functions: **summarization**, **paraphrasing**, and **style transfer**. Together, they enable more than just content production — they unlock a form of intelligent communication refinement.

Summarization: Distilling Meaning from Noise

In an era where enterprises, governments, and individuals are overwhelmed with information, the ability to extract the essence of lengthy or complex content is invaluable. Summarization is the process of compressing a body of text into a concise version that retains its key information.

Language models can perform two types of summarization:

- **Extractive summarization** identifies and pulls out the most relevant sentences from the original text, essentially filtering the content without changing its wording.
- **Abstractive summarization**, on the other hand, generates entirely new sentences to capture the core ideas in a more human-like way, mimicking how a person might retell a story in their own words.

Abstractive summarization is where LLMs truly shine. These models learn to internalize the meaning, structure, and importance of the source material and then regenerate it as a coherent, compact output. For enterprises, this means:

- **Meeting transcripts** can be condensed into action points.
- **Legal documents** can be summarized for decision-makers without loss of legal nuance.
- **News articles** can be repackaged for regional audiences in fewer words.
- **Customer feedback** can be distilled into high-level themes for product teams.

Unlike earlier rule-based or statistical methods, LLM-powered summarization can adapt dynamically to the user's intent — whether they want a **brief overview**, a **technical summary**, a **creative abstract**, or a **multi-document synthesis** across sources. The same input can produce different summaries tailored to different stakeholders.

The capacity for real-time, domain-sensitive summarization at scale is rapidly becoming a competitive differentiator across industries.

Paraphrasing: Rewriting Without Losing Meaning

Paraphrasing is the ability to rephrase a sentence or paragraph using different words and structure while preserving its underlying meaning. This goes beyond lexical substitution (i.e., swapping words) and requires a deep semantic understanding of the text. It is a sophisticated linguistic skill — and a key competency for LLMs.

Enterprises use paraphrasing to:

- Generate **variations of marketing copy** for A/B testing.
- Reframe **support responses** to match tone and clarity requirements.
- Improve **search engine optimization** by rewriting content semantically.
- Assist **non-native speakers** in improving grammar and fluency.
- Help students, researchers, and analysts **restate ideas** to build better comprehension.

Unlike summarization, which compresses, paraphrasing retains the full scale of the message but refashions its form. LLMs can execute paraphrasing in ways that are subtle or radical:

- **Light paraphrasing**: Only minor rewordings or syntactic shifts.
- **Deep paraphrasing**: Significant reordering, idiomatic transformation, or rhetorical reframing.

This capability is vital for content moderation, regulatory compliance (e.g., rewording sensitive claims), content deduplication, and knowledge base diversification. Importantly, paraphrasing also contributes to **plagiarism detection and mitigation**: by generating alternate versions of a known text, LLMs can assist in identifying or preventing unethical reuse.

When controlled via prompting or fine-tuning, LLMs can even paraphrase with specific constraints — such as limiting vocabulary to a target reading level, aligning to a brand voice, or reflecting regional dialects.

Style Transfer: The Art of Linguistic Transformation

Style transfer is where language models transition from utilitarian assistants to creative collaborators. It involves taking a piece of text and altering its **style** while preserving its **meaning**. This may involve shifting:

- Tone (formal ↔ casual)
- Persona (professional ↔ playful)
- Audience (child ↔ adult)
- Medium (spoken ↔ written)
- Emotion (neutral ↔ enthusiastic or empathetic)
- Cultural framing (e.g., localizing to a region's norms or idioms)

Where paraphrasing focuses on structure and wording, style transfer alters **how** something is said without altering **what** is said.

Consider these enterprise scenarios:

- A global HR team adapts internal policy documentation into more approachable language for regional offices.
- An AI writing assistant rewrites a CEO's message for different stakeholder groups — investors, employees, and media — each with distinct expectations.
- A chatbot rewrites the same answer in a humorous, serious, or empathetic tone based on user sentiment or urgency.
- A tutoring app transforms scientific explanations into simpler language for K-12 learners or a more advanced tone for graduate students.

Language models trained on vast and stylistically diverse corpora can identify and replicate such stylistic signatures with remarkable fidelity. With prompt engineering or auxiliary classifiers, we can instruct these models to adopt custom styles — from the succinctness of Hemingway to the flourish of Shakespeare or the clarity of corporate communication guidelines.

Critically, style transfer also serves **inclusivity**: adapting content for accessibility (e.g., for people with cognitive disabilities), simplifying for low-literacy users, or localizing for non-native speakers.

The Agentic Angle: Controlled Generation at Scale

Summarization, paraphrasing, and style transfer form the core building blocks for **autonomous communication agents**. These agents can:

- Listen to a conversation, extract and summarize action points.
- Rewrite the output in the stakeholder's preferred style and tone.
- Adapt responses based on cultural context, communication preferences, or brand standards.

This is where the agentic paradigm shifts from passive response generation to **goal-oriented communication**: the system not only processes text but understands the context, purpose, and recipient of that communication.

This transforms how we build:

- **AI copilots** for sales, HR, and customer support.
- **Intelligent editors** for journalism and marketing.
- **Compliance-aware writers** for regulated industries like finance or healthcare.

The model is no longer just a language engine; it becomes a communication strategist — optimizing tone, clarity, and purpose dynamically.

Closing Thoughts

The ability to summarize, paraphrase, and shift linguistic style is not just a linguistic parlor trick — it's a foundation for intelligent, adaptive, and inclusive human-AI interaction. In enterprise, it translates to productivity, personalization, localization, and regulatory safety. In everyday use, it supports understanding, empathy, and expression.

In the hands of an agentic AI, these capabilities are not static functions but dynamic, goal-aware tools — enabling communication that is not only accurate but also effective, resonant, and human-centered.

Risks of Hallucination and Misinformation

As the capabilities of text generation grow, so too do the complexities and consequences of its misuse or misfire. Among the most pressing challenges in this domain are **hallucination** and **misinformation** — phenomena that can distort truth, mislead users, and erode trust in AI systems. These risks are not peripheral or rare; they are core limitations that arise directly from how large language models (LLMs) are trained and how they operate.

What Is Hallucination in LLMs?

In the context of LLMs, *hallucination* refers to a model generating outputs that are syntactically fluent, stylistically appropriate, and seemingly authoritative — but factually incorrect, logically incoherent, or entirely fabricated.

For example:

- A model might state that "Marie Curie won three Nobel Prizes," when in reality she won two.
- It might invent quotes from public figures, cite nonexistent research papers, or attribute policies to governments that never enacted them.
- It could fabricate URLs, legal clauses, or even describe companies and products that do not exist.

What makes hallucination especially dangerous is that the output often appears convincing. Unlike traditional software bugs, hallucinations are not obviously erroneous to the casual reader — they carry the subtle hazard of *plausible falsehoods.*

Why Do LLMs Hallucinate?

To understand hallucination, we must first understand how LLMs work. These models are trained on massive corpora of text — spanning books, articles, websites, transcripts, code, and more — using a method called *next-token prediction.* In simple terms, the model learns patterns in sequences of words and uses probability to predict what comes next.

However, this training method has fundamental implications:

- **No grounding in external reality:** LLMs do not "know" what is true or false. They generate text based on statistical patterns, not verified facts.
- **No dynamic awareness:** Once trained, the model does not update itself with real-time facts unless explicitly fine-tuned or augmented with external tools.
- **Generalization beyond data:** When asked novel or specific questions, the model may interpolate an answer that sounds right but is not based on any true reference.

In essence, hallucination is not a glitch; it is an expected byproduct of a model that prioritizes linguistic coherence over epistemic accuracy.

Hallucination vs. Misinformation

It's important to distinguish between hallucination and misinformation:

- **Hallucination** is unintentional. The model isn't trying to mislead — it simply lacks the ability to differentiate fact from fiction. It produces fluent nonsense because it's optimized for pattern-matching, not truth.
- **Misinformation** can be intentional or unintentional, and in the hands of malicious actors, it can be engineered using LLMs. This includes disinformation campaigns, deepfakes in text, propaganda bots, or targeted fake news generators.

While hallucinations emerge from the model's limitations, misinformation often emerges from misuse — and both can be amplified at scale by the generative prowess of LLMs.

Why This Matters in the Real World

In consumer or creative use-cases, a hallucinated poem or fantasy story might be harmless or even entertaining. But in enterprise, government, healthcare, or legal domains, hallucination and misinformation can have **grave consequences**:

- A medical assistant powered by an LLM might suggest a contraindicated drug interaction.
- A legal draft might cite fabricated case law or misinterpret statutes.
- A financial report summary might contain made-up figures that influence market decisions.
- A chatbot might confidently provide incorrect immigration advice to a vulnerable user.

Even in less critical contexts, hallucination can undermine credibility, confuse users, and trigger unintended outcomes.

The Trust Gap

As LLMs become embedded into search engines, enterprise tools, customer service agents, and decision support systems, the line between *machine output* and *trusted information* begins to blur. This creates what some call the **trust gap** — a space where users are unsure whether they can rely on what the AI tells them.

This gap is exacerbated by the persuasive fluency of LLMs. Unlike traditional search engines that show sources and snippets, generative models often produce confident prose with no citations or verification trail. Users may mistake eloquence for accuracy — a cognitive bias that LLMs unintentionally exploit.

Mitigation Strategies

Addressing hallucination is a multi-pronged effort that spans model design, system architecture, user experience, and policy. Some of the most promising strategies include:

1. **Retrieval-Augmented Generation (RAG):** Instead of relying purely on static model memory, RAG systems retrieve relevant, up-to-date documents during inference, grounding the generated text in verifiable information.
2. **Tool-augmented LLMs:** By allowing LLMs to call APIs, query databases, or run code, systems can delegate factual reasoning to reliable tools instead of relying on the model's internal approximations.

3. **Citation and Attribution:** Including source references alongside generated text helps users assess credibility. This is especially critical in enterprise or scientific use-cases.
4. **Fact-checking Pipelines:** Post-processing layers can analyze generated outputs, flagging or correcting factual inconsistencies using external knowledge bases.
5. **Fine-tuning with Reinforcement Learning from Human Feedback (RLHF):** Aligning models with human expectations of truthfulness and coherence can reduce hallucinations, though not eliminate them entirely.
6. **User Interfaces That Signal Uncertainty:** Subtle UI cues — such as confidence levels, disclaimers, or traceable explanations — can guide users in interpreting model outputs more critically.

The Human-in-the-Loop Imperative

Ultimately, no model — however powerful — can yet replace human judgment, especially in high-stakes settings. The role of humans is not just to consume AI outputs, but to supervise, verify, and calibrate them. Enterprises must design workflows where **AI augments decisions, not automates them blindly**.

Governments, too, must develop policies and standards that address the ethical and informational risks of generative models — especially as they influence public discourse, democratic processes, and societal trust in digital content.

A Caution and a Call

The power of LLMs to generate language is akin to giving machines a voice — one that can inform, persuade, entertain, and mislead. Like all powerful tools, it demands careful stewardship.

We are only beginning to understand the cognitive, social, and informational impacts of machines that can generate language at scale. Hallucination and misinformation are not just technical challenges to be solved — they are *sociotechnical problems* that sit at the intersection of design, intent, context, and consequence.

Addressing them will determine whether LLMs elevate human intelligence — or distort it.

Guardrails, Grounding, and Feedback Loops

Text generation is arguably the most visible superpower of large language models (LLMs). It enables machines to craft articles, generate code, simulate conversations, summarize documents, and more — all through language. But as their outputs become more fluent and human-like, so does the risk of hallucination, bias, manipulation, or misinformation. The challenge is no longer whether a model *can* generate text, but whether it *should* — and *how* to ensure it does so safely, truthfully, and responsibly.

This is where **guardrails**, **grounding**, and **feedback loops** become essential pillars of trust, usability, and performance in generative AI systems.

Guardrails: Keeping Generation Within Safe and Useful Bounds

Guardrails refer to any mechanisms — algorithmic, design-driven, or policy-based — that restrict, shape, or supervise what an LLM can and cannot do. Without these controls, even the most powerful models can veer into unsafe territory, producing:

- Biased or offensive language.
- Factually incorrect or fabricated statements.
- Incoherent, ambiguous, or misleading responses.
- Malicious content like phishing emails or harmful instructions.

In enterprise and high-stakes use cases, these failures are unacceptable. **There are three main types of guardrails:**

1. **Instructional Guardrails (Prompt Engineering and Templates)**
   These include carefully crafted prompts that set constraints on tone, topic, or length — such as:
   - "Respond in formal language suitable for legal correspondence."
   - "Summarize this without using personal opinions or speculations."

- "Avoid making any medical diagnosis or recommendation."

Instructional guardrails help align the model's output with specific context and intent, narrowing the generation space from infinite possibilities to bounded, relevant responses.

1. **Architectural Guardrails (Fine-tuning and Reward Models)**
   These involve modifying the underlying model itself — through supervised fine-tuning or reinforcement learning with human feedback (RLHF) — so that its behavior reflects predefined values and norms.

   For example:

   - Teaching the model to refuse unethical requests ("How do I make a fake ID?").
   - Penalizing hallucinated or unverifiable claims during training.
   - Reinforcing structured reasoning and factual accuracy in long-form answers.

3. **Runtime Guardrails (Post-processing and Filtering)**
   These are safety mechanisms applied *after* the model generates a response:

   - Profanity filters.
   - Hate speech detectors.
   - Fact-checking systems.
   - Role or persona boundaries (e.g., refusing to give financial advice without disclaimers).

These dynamic constraints are particularly useful in live applications like customer support, conversational agents, or collaborative writing tools.

Guardrails don't just protect users; they protect enterprises from liability, reputational harm, and ethical backlash. They are the moral and operational scaffolding that turn a powerful model into a dependable product.

Grounding: Anchoring Text Generation in Verified Knowledge

A core limitation of LLMs is their reliance on probabilistic language modeling rather than real-time knowledge retrieval. In other words, they generate based on patterns they've learned — not on current, verifiable facts. This leads to what is commonly called **hallucination**: output that sounds plausible but is factually incorrect or fabricated.

Grounding addresses this by ensuring that text generation is **anchored in trusted, authoritative data sources.** It brings the model back to reality.

There are several ways to achieve grounding:

1. **Retrieval-Augmented Generation (RAG)**
   Instead of relying solely on the model's internal parameters, RAG systems retrieve relevant documents, web pages, or knowledge base entries in real-time and use them as additional context for generation.

   Example:

   Before answering a legal question, the model retrieves and reads clauses from the relevant regulation. The output is then generated with references to those sections.

2. **Contextual Injection of Enterprise Data**
   For internal applications, grounding is done by embedding private company data (emails, reports, tickets, policies) into the prompt or memory of the model. This transforms a general-purpose model into a domain-aware assistant — without retraining.

   Example:

   A customer service agent asks, "What's the latest refund policy?" The LLM responds by citing the exact paragraph from the company's current policy document.

3. **Citation and Evidence-Based Generation**
   A grounded model not only produces text but supports its claims with links, sources, or document snippets. It becomes explainable and auditable.

Example:

A model writes, "Based on Section 4.3 of your employee handbook, unused vacation days roll over to the next year."

Grounding enables enterprise-grade reliability. It turns language models from plausible guessers into trustworthy communicators. When users know the AI's outputs are backed by data they can verify, trust and adoption increase significantly.

Feedback Loops: Making Language Models Learn and Improve Over Time

No language model is perfect at launch. Their outputs are shaped by their training data, and their behavior reflects the limitations and assumptions embedded within. However, what makes modern LLMs especially powerful is their ability to **learn and adapt** post-deployment through structured **feedback loops**.

Feedback loops turn static models into evolving systems.

Types of feedback loops include:

1. **Human-in-the-Loop (HITL)**
    - Users or moderators review and rate outputs.
    - Missteps are logged and used to fine-tune future responses.
    - Reinforcement Learning with Human Feedback (RLHF) incorporates these signals into ongoing model improvement.
2. **Implicit User Feedback**
    - Clicks, dwell time, edits, rephrasings — all serve as signals.
    - For instance, if a user consistently rewrites the AI's summary, the system may learn to simplify or highlight different aspects.
3. **Automated Evaluation Systems**
    - Models are benchmarked continuously on accuracy, coherence, tone, and factuality.
    - Failures trigger alerts or retraining pipelines.

4. **Closed-Loop Enterprise Systems**

    - In a business context, feedback loops are often domain-specific.
    - For example, when an AI agent drafts emails for support teams, every human-corrected draft is fed back into the system, allowing for personalization and refinement at scale.

Feedback loops ensure that LLMs stay relevant, reduce error rates, adapt to domain language, and improve alignment with user expectations. In agentic systems — where the model not only responds but *acts* — feedback loops are essential to prevent drift, detect anomalies, and course-correct in near real-time.

The Triad in Practice: Guardrails + Grounding + Feedback

When combined, these three mechanisms — guardrails, grounding, and feedback loops — create a virtuous cycle of **safety, relevance, and learning**:

- **Guardrails** keep generation within safe, ethical, and context-appropriate boundaries.
- **Grounding** ensures outputs are tied to reality, improving trust and reducing hallucinations.
- **Feedback loops** enable continuous adaptation and performance tuning in real-world settings.

This triad transforms LLMs from creative engines into reliable enterprise collaborators. It enables **agentic AI** systems to act autonomously yet remain accountable. It empowers developers, policy-makers, and end-users to steer AI behavior without needing to retrain from scratch.

Looking Ahead

As the adoption of LLMs accelerates across sectors — from healthcare to finance, legal to education — the importance of these control systems will only grow. The sophistication of text generation is no longer the bottleneck; **the challenge now lies in governance**. Building with guardrails, grounding, and feedback loops is how we move from experimental demos to trustworthy deployment — responsibly, inclusively, and at scale.

In the age of AI, language is not just a medium; it is an interface to intelligence. But without control, that intelligence becomes unpredictable. These frameworks ensure that the language of machines can serve humanity with clarity, truth, and purpose.

CHAPTER EIGHT

MULTIMODAL INTELLIGENCE — BEYOND TEXT

Introduction to Multimodality

While language is central to human thought, it is not our only mode of communication. We see the world through images. We hear emotions in voices. We interpret body language, read charts, listen to music, navigate videos, and write code. Human intelligence is *inherently multimodal.* Our understanding of the world arises not from a single stream of input, but from the fusion of multiple sensory and symbolic channels.

For decades, artificial intelligence systems operated in silos. One model for language. Another for vision. A separate one for speech. These models were narrow and single-purpose, optimized for specific formats and limited use cases. A chatbot couldn't interpret an image. A vision model couldn't understand a question. A voice assistant couldn't comprehend a chart or a diagram.

Multimodal intelligence changes that. It marks a decisive step toward a more *general*, *flexible*, and *human-like* form of artificial intelligence — one that perceives, reasons, and responds across multiple forms of input and expression.

Why Multimodality Matters

To grasp the significance of multimodality, imagine a simple real-world example:

You receive a message that contains:

- A voice note from a customer expressing frustration,
- A screenshot of an app with an error message,
- A short text describing the issue,
- A link to a video demo of the bug.

A traditional AI system would require different subsystems to process each part — and no unified understanding would emerge. A multimodal AI system, in contrast, can ingest all inputs as a coherent whole, interpret the relationships between them, and generate a meaningful response — just like a human would.

This ability is transformative. It allows AI to:

- Understand richer, real-world contexts,
- Provide more accurate and relevant outputs,
- Interact with humans in ways that feel intuitive and intelligent,
- Bridge the gap between perception and cognition.

Multimodal systems are not just a technical innovation; they represent a closer alignment with how humans process the world.

From Modal Silos to Integrated Intelligence

Each mode — text, image, audio, video, code — carries its own structure, signal, and semantics. For example:

- Text captures syntax, logic, and abstraction.
- Images encode spatial relationships and visual patterns.
- Audio conveys rhythm, tone, and emotion.
- Video adds motion and temporal context.
- Code encodes executable logic and intent.

Historically, AI models trained on these formats have been isolated, optimized only for their modality. But recent breakthroughs in **transformer-based architectures** and **representation learning** have made it possible to unify these modalities into a single system — where diverse inputs are converted into shared embeddings that models can reason over jointly.

This is the essence of multimodal learning: enabling AI systems to learn *joint representations* from *disjoint inputs* — and to understand the *relationships* between them.

A multimodal AI doesn't just see a picture or read a caption. It understands how they relate — whether the caption is accurate, sarcastic, or misleading. It doesn't just transcribe audio; it can understand whether the speaker is angry, confused, or excited. It doesn't just process a chart; it can explain the insight hidden in the trend.

Catalyst for Agentic AI

Multimodal intelligence is not only an enhancement of perception — it is a prerequisite for *agentic AI*.

Why? Because an intelligent agent must:

- **Perceive** its environment across modalities,
- **Understand** and contextualize complex, multi-source inputs,
- **Plan** appropriate actions based on high-dimensional information,
- **Communicate** naturally and appropriately across modes.

A customer support agent powered by a multimodal LLM can handle voice complaints, read screenshots, analyze PDFs, extract data from dashboards, and respond with synthesized speech — all in real time. A digital tutor can watch a student's facial expressions, listen to their spoken questions, read their answers, and provide corrective feedback through voice, text, or animated diagrams.

Multimodality moves us closer to intelligent systems that do not just process commands, but participate in human workflows, assist in creative endeavors, and collaborate on complex decisions.

LLMs Go Multimodal

The leap from language-only models to multimodal LLMs is already underway. Models like GPT-4, Gemini, Claude, and others can now interpret and generate across formats. A prompt can include text and images; the output might be code, prose, or even structured data. Some models can analyze graphs, generate audio, describe visual scenes, or carry out tasks based on mixed inputs.

Multimodal models are also better at *grounding* — anchoring language in the real world. When an AI can "see" a street sign, "hear" an instruction, or "watch" a behavior, its understanding of language becomes less synthetic and more situational. This improves reasoning, reduces hallucination, and enables safer, more context-aware systems.

For enterprises, this opens new frontiers:

- In **healthcare**, a model can combine radiology scans with clinical notes and patient dialogue.
- In **finance**, it can explain a chart using historical context and user queries.
- In **education**, it can read a student's handwritten notes, listen to a spoken explanation, and provide multimodal feedback.
- In **retail**, it can analyze product photos, customer reviews, and audio queries to assist buyers in real time.

Looking Ahead

Multimodal intelligence is not a luxury or niche feature — it is the foundation for the next generation of AI systems that interact with the world as we do.

It shifts AI from being merely reactive to being perceptive and proactive. It allows machines to move beyond interpreting isolated symbols to grasping the fabric of human expression. And it enables intelligent agents not just to understand our words, but to *see what we see, hear what we hear, and respond in ways that resonate across channels.*

As we move deeper into an era of immersive, always-on computing, where AI is embedded in phones, glasses, homes, vehicles, and workflows, multimodality will be the standard — not the exception.

The future of language models is not just *linguistic*. It is *sensory, cognitive, and interactive*. And it begins with understanding that language, in the broader sense, is not just what we speak — but everything we use to make sense of the world.

Vision + Language: Image Captioning and Visual Question Answering (VQA)

While language has historically served as the core substrate of intelligence in machines, the world we live in is inherently multimodal. Humans don't experience life solely through words — we interpret facial expressions, diagrams, gestures, photographs, charts, videos, and environments in parallel with language. True artificial intelligence, therefore, must extend beyond textual fluency to **multimodal understanding**: the ability to learn, reason, and generate across multiple sensory inputs — especially vision and language.

This convergence is no longer aspirational. With advances in large multimodal models (LMMs), the AI landscape is rapidly moving into an era where systems can not only *read* but also *see* — and crucially, link what they see to what they say. Two of the most transformative and mature capabilities in this space are **image captioning** and **visual question answering (VQA)**.

Image Captioning: Giving Language to Vision

Image captioning is the task of generating natural language descriptions for visual inputs. It might seem straightforward at first — describe what's in an image — but under the hood, this task demands a deep, layered form of intelligence.

To generate a useful caption, an AI system must:

1. **Perceive the image accurately** — recognizing objects, scenes, spatial relationships, actions, and attributes.
2. **Interpret context and intent** — discerning which elements are salient and meaningful to the viewer.
3. **Generate coherent language** — producing fluent, grammatically correct, and semantically appropriate sentences that align with human expectations.

For instance, given a photo of a child holding a melting ice cream cone on a sunny street, a model might caption it as:
"A young girl enjoys her ice cream on a warm summer day."
This caption doesn't just identify objects (girl, ice cream) — it adds inferred

context (enjoyment, summer, warmth). This is where the model transitions from seeing to *understanding*.

Why It Matters

Image captioning has widespread impact across domains:

- **Accessibility**: Automatically describing images for visually impaired users.
- **Content moderation**: Detecting inappropriate or harmful content in visual platforms.
- **E-commerce**: Auto-generating product descriptions from photos.
- **Surveillance and forensics**: Summarizing footage or still images.
- **Digital asset management**: Tagging and indexing visual archives with natural language metadata.

At its core, image captioning exemplifies the **alignment of perception with cognition** — a hallmark of intelligent systems.

Visual Question Answering (VQA): Multimodal Reasoning in Action

If image captioning is descriptive, **visual question answering (VQA)** is interactive. VQA involves providing a natural language answer to a question posed about an image. For example:

- *"How many people are in the photo?"*
- *"What color is the car behind the man?"*
- *"Is this person likely at a formal event?"*

This capability requires significantly deeper processing than captioning. The system must:

1. **Parse the question linguistically** — understanding the semantics, intent, and scope.
2. **Attend to the relevant visual regions** — using visual grounding to link phrases in the question to areas in the image.
3. **Reason across modalities** — bridging what it sees with what it understands from language and prior knowledge.

4. **Generate or select an answer** — in natural language or structured form, often under constraints like yes/no, multiple-choice, or free-form.

A high-performing VQA system must resolve ambiguity, understand abstract relationships, and sometimes even make common-sense inferences. For example, if asked:

- *"What is the man likely doing?"* (with an image of a man with a briefcase at a train platform),
  the system must combine visual cues (attire, environment) with world knowledge to respond:
- *"He is waiting for a train."*

Why VQA Is a Breakthrough

VQA marks a transition from perception to **cognitive interaction**. It's no longer about identifying or describing — it's about engaging. This is fundamental to agentic AI, where models must operate not just as passive describers but as active participants in human workflows.

VQA use cases span:

- **Education**: Interactive tutoring systems that combine diagrams and questions.
- **Healthcare**: Radiology assistants answering queries on X-rays or scans.
- **Retail and search**: Allowing customers to ask questions about product images.
- **Surveillance and defense**: Analysts querying specific behaviors or anomalies in visual feeds.
- **Legal and compliance**: Reviewing visual evidence with natural language prompts.

In enterprise contexts, VQA empowers users to extract structured insights from unstructured visual data — turning static images into dynamic knowledge assets.

How It All Works: Under the Hood

Multimodal models that power captioning and VQA typically integrate **vision encoders** (like convolutional neural networks or vision transformers) with **language models** (transformers trained on text). These systems use shared embeddings or attention mechanisms to fuse visual and linguistic inputs into a common representation space.

A modern architecture might look like this:

- **Vision encoder** processes the image and outputs dense feature vectors.
- **Language encoder** or decoder takes the question or prompt and learns to align it with visual features.
- **Fusion layer** (via attention or cross-modal transformers) integrates the signals.
- **Output generator** produces a caption, answer, or text response.

Importantly, these systems can be pretrained on vast multimodal datasets (e.g., image-text pairs from the web) and fine-tuned for domain-specific tasks — allowing generalization with minimal labeled data. This pretrain-then-specialize approach, already dominant in pure NLP, is proving equally powerful in multimodal AI.

The Road Ahead: Toward More Grounded, Agentic Systems

As the field evolves, we're witnessing a shift from single-shot captioning and Q&A to **interactive multimodal agents**:

- Systems that **see**, **listen**, **speak**, and **reason** in context.
- Models that can navigate visual environments, track objects over time, and hold conversations grounded in sensory input.
- Assistants that help doctors interpret scans *and* draft notes, or help students understand *and* explore visual content.

This is not just multimodal — it's **embodied cognition**, where intelligence is situated in space, time, and interaction. Image captioning and VQA are merely stepping stones toward a future where language and vision coalesce to power intelligent, intuitive, and universally accessible machines.

In this unfolding future, the interface to intelligence will not be keyboards or dashboards — it will be natural: *a glance, a question, a comment, a gesture*. And AI will respond — not just with words, but with understanding.

Audio, Video, and Sensor Fusion

Text has been the traditional anchor for language models, but human intelligence is profoundly multimodal. We perceive and interpret the world not just through words but through **sounds, visuals, gestures, and physical sensations**. Our conversations are shaped by vocal intonation, facial expressions, body language, and even the tactile feel of our environment. Intelligence, both human and artificial, becomes significantly more potent when it can synthesize multiple sensory modalities into a coherent understanding of the world.

This is where **audio, video, and sensor fusion** come into play — the integration of heterogeneous data types into a unified AI system. In the domain of large language models, this expansion beyond text unlocks the ability to **perceive, reason, and act** more like humans do. It is foundational to building truly **agentic AI** that can operate autonomously across environments, adaptively process real-time signals, and engage meaningfully with humans in a broad spectrum of contexts.

Audio: Hearing Is Understanding

Audio data introduces a new dimension to language understanding: **prosody, emotion, rhythm, stress, pitch**, and **intonation** — all of which influence meaning but are invisible in written text. For example, the same sentence can be interpreted as sincere or sarcastic purely based on tone.

Multimodal LLMs that ingest audio are capable of:

- **Speech recognition and transcription** (converting spoken language into text).
- **Speaker identification** (recognizing who is speaking based on voice).
- **Emotion detection** (identifying sentiment or mental state).
- **Sound event detection** (e.g., detecting alarms, footsteps, or environmental noise).

Modern LLMs can process raw waveform audio, spectrograms, or tokenized phonemes using models such as **whisper-like encoders**, often combined with transformers that map audio into a shared embedding space with text. This enables **cross-modal grounding**, where models can align what is said (text) with how it is said (audio).

For enterprise applications, this unlocks numerous use cases:

- **Voice assistants** that understand user intent beyond words.
- **Call center analytics** that track tone, frustration, or compliance.
- **Real-time transcription with speaker-aware summarization.**
- **Low-bandwidth voice-based interfaces** for populations with limited literacy.

For agentic systems in low-resource environments, audio processing enables **on-device voice command understanding**, particularly useful for those with limited text-based interaction capability.

Video: Seeing Context and Action

Video introduces temporal and spatial reasoning into LLMs. A single frame may contain rich visual data, but a sequence of frames (i.e., a video) contains **action, change, causality, and intention** — core elements of intelligence.

To process video, multimodal systems must:

- Parse both **individual frames (images)** and **motion across time**.
- Align **speech, subtitles, and sound** with visual context.
- Understand **scene dynamics**, such as who is doing what, where, and when.
- Recognize **microexpressions, gestures, posture, gaze**, and more.

Video fusion with LLMs enables systems to not only describe what they see, but **generate reasoning** about the unfolding narrative. For example:

- In education: automatically summarize a lecture by watching and listening to it.
- In healthcare: interpret patient interactions in telemedicine.
- In security: detect anomalies in surveillance without manual tagging.
- In entertainment: generate highlights, detect inappropriate content, or personalize recommendations.

Technically, this often involves **vision transformers (ViT)** or **spatiotemporal convolutional networks**, which are fused with language models via shared embeddings or cross-attention layers. The challenge lies in synchronizing timelines — aligning visual cues with spoken or written language in real time.

For low-end environments, efficient compression, **frame sampling**, and **audio-only approximations** can support video-light deployments that retain high informational value while reducing computational load.

Sensor Fusion: Touching the Physical World

Beyond sight and sound lies a vast realm of data from **sensors**: GPS, accelerometers, gyroscopes, magnetometers, LiDAR, ultrasonic sensors, temperature, pressure, haptics, and biosignals like heart rate or EEG. These sensors bring AI into **embodied intelligence** — the ability to understand and interact with the physical world.

Sensor fusion in the context of LLMs means:

- Embedding **contextual state awareness** (e.g., location, orientation, motion).
- Responding to **external stimuli** (e.g., vibration indicating danger).
- Detecting **user behavior** (e.g., posture while using a phone).
- Making sense of **non-linguistic but structured signals** in real time.

Imagine an agentic AI deployed in:

- **Autonomous vehicles**, where LiDAR, cameras, and GPS must be fused with real-time reasoning.
- **Wearables**, where health signals like heart rate variability inform stress detection.
- **Industrial IoT**, where equipment vibration, noise, and temperature indicate maintenance needs.
- **Smart homes**, where multiple inputs (motion sensors, voice commands, ambient noise) converge to predict user needs.

Sensor fusion involves aligning **heterogeneous data streams** that may be asynchronous, noisy, and high-dimensional. Integrating them with LLMs allows these models to reason about **cause and effect, context-aware**

decision-making, and even **multi-agent collaboration** in physical environments.

When fused with language, this sensor-derived knowledge becomes **actionable**:

- "The machine is overheating" can now be tied to vibration patterns and thermal readings.
- "The user appears drowsy" can be inferred from eye movement and seating posture data.

For edge scenarios, particularly in emerging markets, sensor fusion enables **resilient intelligence** in offline environments — where local models must respond autonomously to audio-visual-sensor inputs without connectivity to the cloud.

From Perception to Action: Multimodal Reasoning

Multimodal fusion is not just about perceiving multiple modalities — it's about **reasoning across them**. A robust agentic AI must answer not just:

"What is being said?"

but

"Who is saying it, how are they saying it, where are they, what are they doing, and why?"

This cross-modal reasoning is the next frontier in AI:

- In medicine: combining audio (symptoms), video (movement), and vitals (sensors) for early diagnosis.
- In education: using tone (audio), engagement (video), and device usage (sensor) to adapt instruction.
- In security: integrating voice, facial cues, and geolocation to detect fraud or threats.

Each modality offers partial insight. Fused together, they provide **situational awareness** — the essential substrate for intelligent, autonomous behavior.

Conclusion: Toward Embodied, Situated Intelligence

Audio, video, and sensor fusion move LLMs beyond their textual origins into a **holistic understanding of human experience**. This is not a shift in input format — it's a shift in cognitive depth. It allows AI to become more than a chatbot or text generator. It becomes a **perceptual agent** — one that sees, hears, senses, and reasons.

As this capability matures, we edge closer to a future where AI systems don't just respond with linguistic fluency, but **act with situational intelligence**. Whether assisting a farmer in a remote village, guiding a factory operator through diagnostics, or helping a child learn to read through gestures and sound, **multimodal intelligence is the enabler** of real-world, embodied AI.

And it all begins by teaching our machines not just to read and write — but to listen, to see, to sense, and to understand.

Multimodal Transformers and Cross-Modal Learning

The intelligence of the real world is not confined to a single medium. Humans learn by seeing, listening, touching, reading, and even smelling — often all at once. When a child learns the word "apple," they don't just hear it spoken or see it written. They observe its color, feel its texture, taste its flavor, and smell its sweetness. Language, in our world, is deeply entwined with other modalities. To build machines that understand the world as richly and holistically as we do, we must go **beyond text**.

This is where **multimodal learning** and **multimodal transformers** come into play — a transformative shift in AI that extends language models from pure-text understanding to a multi-sensory, contextual intelligence that can interpret images, audio, video, and beyond. These models are no longer just *language* models; they are *world* models.

The Rise of Multimodal Transformers

Multimodal transformers are extensions of the now-ubiquitous transformer architecture — originally designed for natural language — to handle multiple input modalities. They are built to jointly process and reason across different types of data: text, images, speech, videos, code, and more.

The central challenge here is heterogeneity: each modality has a distinct structure and information density. Text is symbolic and sequential. Images are spatial and dense. Audio is temporal and continuous. Videos blend spatial and temporal dimensions. How do we build one unified model that can understand and operate across all of them?

The answer lies in the transformer's core design principle: **attention.** Attention allows the model to weigh the importance of different inputs dynamically, regardless of sequence type. By adapting the attention mechanism to multimodal inputs — often using modality-specific encoders that convert diverse inputs into a shared representation space — we enable powerful forms of cross-modal interaction and alignment.

Multimodal transformers, therefore, don't just fuse information — they create an emergent intelligence that learns to associate words with visuals, tones with emotions, or gestures with intent. This fusion unlocks a range of capabilities far beyond what unimodal systems can achieve.

Understanding Multimodal Processing

At the core of a multimodal transformer is the ability to **ingest**, **align**, **fuse**, and **reason** across multiple data types. This typically involves three high-level stages:

1. **Encoding**: Each modality — say, an image and a sentence — is first processed through a dedicated encoder. For example, images might be processed through a vision transformer (ViT) or CNN, while text is processed through a standard language encoder. These produce dense vector representations, often called embeddings, that capture the essential features of each input.
2. **Alignment**: These embeddings are then mapped into a **shared latent space**, allowing the model to understand that the word "dog" and a photo of a dog refer to the same concept. This alignment is crucial for tasks like image captioning, visual question answering, or video summarization.
3. **Fusion and Reasoning**: Using a cross-modal attention mechanism, the model then integrates the aligned representations. This is where actual reasoning happens — the model can attend to specific parts of an image based on a question in natural language, or generate descriptive text based on visual or audio cues.

The beauty of multimodal transformers lies in their flexibility. Once modalities are embedded in the same conceptual space, the model can operate across them seamlessly — describing, interpreting, comparing, or even translating from one modality to another.

Cross-Modal Learning: Learning Across Senses

Cross-modal learning is the principle that knowledge gained in one modality can inform or enhance learning in another. In biological systems, this is natural — we often associate a sound with a visual, or a texture with a word. In AI systems, enabling this requires both architectural design and data-driven learning.

At its core, cross-modal learning is about *transfer and generalization.* It involves three main paradigms:

1. **Cross-Modal Retrieval**: The system learns to retrieve one modality given another. For instance, finding the right image when given a caption or locating the appropriate audio clip when given a transcript.
2. **Cross-Modal Generation**: The model generates content in one modality from another — such as generating a video narration from a script, or synthesizing an image from a description.
3. **Cross-Modal Reasoning**: Perhaps the most advanced use case, this involves answering questions that require information from multiple modalities. For example: "*What emotion is the person showing in the image, and how does it contrast with the tone of their speech?*"

Cross-modal learning requires not just large amounts of multimodal data but also thoughtful supervision — from contrastive losses (e.g., CLIP) to paired caption-image datasets (e.g., COCO, LAION), or temporally synchronized video-audio-text datasets (e.g., HowTo100M, AudioSet). These resources enable the models to learn rich and robust associations between modalities.

Implications of Multimodal and Cross-Modal Systems

The implications of these systems are profound, especially in real-world, enterprise, and mission-critical domains:

- **Accessibility**: Systems that understand speech, vision, and gesture together can assist users with disabilities far more effectively — such as reading text from images aloud for the visually impaired or translating sign language into speech.

- **Security and Surveillance**: Cross-modal reasoning allows intelligent systems to flag anomalies in behavior or conversation, combining visual feeds with audio context.
- **Healthcare**: Multimodal models can analyze radiology images, understand textual medical histories, and interpret doctor-patient conversations to assist in diagnostics.
- **Retail and E-commerce**: Multimodal systems can enable richer product discovery (e.g., "Show me shoes like this image but in red"), virtual try-ons, or immersive shopping via augmented reality.
- **Media and Content Creation**: Creative professionals can use language prompts to generate images, videos, or entire scenes, accelerating ideation and storytelling.
- **Education**: Cross-modal tutors can combine voice, gesture, diagrams, and language to deliver highly adaptive, personalized learning experiences across diverse learner profiles.

But the power of multimodal AI also raises new challenges. Biases can amplify across modalities. Misalignment between modalities can lead to hallucinations or incoherence. And data privacy concerns become more complex when text, speech, and images are simultaneously processed. These are not just technical challenges — they are ethical imperatives.

A New Frontier for Intelligent Agents

Multimodal transformers are not just better interfaces — they are foundational to building truly **agentic AI**. An agent that can understand your words, see what you're pointing at, hear the tone of your voice, and act accordingly is exponentially more capable — and more natural — than one that only processes static text.

In enterprise contexts, this is transformative:

- A customer service agent that analyzes a customer's voice and facial cues alongside their spoken complaints.
- A field technician assistant that sees the equipment via a phone camera, understands a spoken query, and gives step-by-step guidance.
- A compliance agent that watches a video conference, reads accompanying documents, and flags risk in real-time.

These are not futuristic fantasies. With the advent of models like GPT-4 with vision, Gemini, and Claude's image and document understanding, we are already seeing these capabilities emerge — albeit in controlled settings. The next wave will make them real-time, robust, and pervasive.

In summary, **multimodal transformers and cross-modal learning** represent a major leap in the evolution of machine intelligence — from linguistic fluency to sensory comprehension, from passive models to collaborative agents. They are the scaffolding upon which future AI will be built — inclusive, embodied, and contextually rich.

Fusion Techniques: Early, Late, and Hybrid

In the evolving landscape of artificial intelligence, **multimodal intelligence** stands out as a transformative leap beyond text-centric models. Multimodal models empower AI systems to interpret, integrate, and generate insights across multiple data types — text, images, audio, video, sensor data, and more. This ability to "see," "hear," and "read" simultaneously mimics human perception more closely than ever before, unlocking richer, more nuanced interactions and capabilities.

At the heart of building these multimodal systems lies a crucial design decision: **how to fuse information from different modalities.** Fusion — the process of combining data from distinct sources into a coherent representation — defines the system's effectiveness in understanding complex real-world phenomena and delivering seamless user experiences.

There are three primary fusion techniques in multimodal AI: **early fusion, late fusion, and hybrid fusion.** Each approach has its strengths and challenges, and choosing among them depends on factors like data characteristics, computational resources, task requirements, and deployment scenarios.

Early Fusion: Integrating Modalities at the Input Level

Early fusion involves combining raw or low-level features from different modalities into a unified representation *before* any high-level processing occurs. In other words, data from text, images, audio, and other sources are transformed into a compatible format and merged at the outset, then fed together into a single model pipeline.

This approach mirrors how human sensory data is integrated early in the brain's processing stages. For example, when reading a news article accompanied by images, your brain rapidly combines the textual content and visual cues to form a coherent understanding.

Advantages of Early Fusion:

- **Rich Interactions:** By merging raw features, early fusion allows the model to learn intricate correlations and cross-modal dependencies at a fine-grained level. This can improve the AI's ability to disambiguate subtle contextual cues.
- **Unified Representation:** It forces the system to create a single, shared embedding space where multimodal information is tightly coupled, enabling more seamless reasoning across modalities.
- **End-to-End Training:** Early fusion supports end-to-end learning, allowing gradients to flow across all modalities simultaneously, which often leads to better optimization and model performance.

Challenges with Early Fusion:

- **Heterogeneous Data Alignment:** Different modalities vary widely in format, scale, and timing. Aligning them precisely at the feature level can be difficult — for example, synchronizing video frames with spoken words or sensor data with textual metadata.
- **High Dimensionality:** Combining raw features from multiple modalities often results in very large input vectors, which increases computational complexity and memory usage.
- **Data Quality Disparities:** If one modality's data is noisy or missing, it can degrade the entire fused input representation, making the system less robust.

Early fusion is often preferred in scenarios where tight integration of sensory signals is critical, such as in autonomous driving (combining camera images, LiDAR scans, and radar data) or in medical diagnostics (integrating imaging scans with patient notes and lab results).

Late Fusion: Combining Decisions or Outputs

In contrast, **late fusion** takes a modular approach, processing each modality independently through specialized sub-models before combining their outputs or decisions. Instead of merging raw data, late fusion aggregates the predictions, features, or embeddings generated by individual modality-specific models.

This approach is akin to how humans might first analyze text and images separately before synthesizing conclusions or making decisions.

Advantages of Late Fusion:

- **Modularity and Flexibility:** Each modality can be modeled with its best-suited architecture and trained independently. For instance, convolutional neural networks (CNNs) can handle images, recurrent or transformer models can handle text, and separate audio models can analyze speech.
- **Robustness to Missing Modalities:** If one data stream is missing or corrupted, the other models can still function, making late fusion systems more resilient.
- **Simpler Integration:** Combining outputs (e.g., via weighted voting, concatenation of embeddings, or ensemble methods) is often easier than merging raw features, facilitating scalable system design.

Challenges with Late Fusion:

- **Limited Cross-Modal Interaction:** Because modalities are processed independently until the end, the system may miss deeper correlations or complementary patterns that only emerge through early joint processing.
- **Suboptimal End-to-End Learning:** Late fusion often requires separate training of modality-specific models, which can lead to less coordinated representations and limit the potential gains from joint optimization.

Late fusion is particularly useful when modalities are loosely coupled or when computational constraints require parallel pipelines — for example, combining video analysis and natural language queries in a surveillance system or merging sensor data streams in IoT devices with textual command inputs.

Hybrid Fusion: Combining the Best of Both Worlds

Hybrid fusion methods aim to leverage the strengths of both early and late fusion by integrating modalities at multiple points within the architecture. This strategy acknowledges that some features or modalities benefit from early integration, while others are best processed independently and combined later.

Hybrid fusion architectures often include multiple stages:

- **Initial early fusion** of closely related or synchronous modalities (e.g., combining audio and video frames).
- **Separate modality-specific processing** for higher-level feature extraction.
- **Subsequent late fusion** layers that merge embeddings or decision scores for final prediction or generation.

Advantages of Hybrid Fusion:

- **Balanced Complexity:** By selectively fusing some modalities early and others later, hybrid approaches control input dimensionality while still enabling rich cross-modal interactions.
- **Improved Robustness:** The system can rely on independent processing where needed, enhancing tolerance to missing or noisy data.
- **Hierarchical Understanding:** Hybrid fusion supports multi-level reasoning where low-level sensory features interact early, and abstract semantic features integrate later, reflecting the hierarchical nature of many real-world tasks.

Challenges with Hybrid Fusion:

- **Architectural Complexity:** Designing and tuning hybrid fusion models is more complex, requiring careful coordination between different fusion points and training regimes.
- **Resource Intensive:** Hybrid models may demand more computational resources and engineering effort compared to simpler early or late fusion systems.

Hybrid fusion is rapidly gaining traction in domains requiring nuanced understanding and dynamic flexibility. Examples include advanced virtual assistants that combine speech, facial expressions, and contextual text, or autonomous systems that integrate sensor data with high-level maps and mission objectives.

Choosing the Right Fusion Strategy

Selecting among early, late, and hybrid fusion techniques depends on several considerations:

- **Nature of the Data:** Are the modalities synchronous (e.g., audio and video) or asynchronous (e.g., images and text documents)?
- **Task Requirements:** Does the application demand fine-grained joint reasoning or is high-level decision fusion sufficient?
- **System Constraints:** What are the computational and latency budgets? Are models deployed on edge devices or cloud servers?
- **Robustness Needs:** How critical is tolerance to missing or noisy modalities?

For enterprises integrating multimodal AI, these decisions affect everything from system architecture and training pipelines to deployment and user experience.

Fusion Techniques in Practice: Real-World Examples

- In **healthcare**, early fusion of medical imaging and electronic health record data enables precise diagnostics, while late fusion of patient history and real-time sensor data supports dynamic monitoring.
- In **customer service**, hybrid fusion blends real-time speech analysis (early fusion of audio features) with text chat logs and sentiment scores (late fusion) to provide proactive, empathetic responses.
- In **autonomous vehicles**, early fusion of LiDAR and camera data aids immediate obstacle detection, while late fusion of navigation maps and sensor alerts informs higher-level path planning.

The Future of Fusion: Towards Dynamic and Adaptive Integration

Emerging research explores **adaptive fusion**, where models dynamically select or weight modalities based on context, confidence, or task phase. This aligns with the vision of **agentic AI** that actively reasons about which inputs to prioritize and when, enabling even more efficient and intelligent multimodal systems.

As multimodal models evolve, fusion strategies will become more sophisticated — balancing computational efficiency, robustness, and deep semantic understanding to power AI systems that can truly perceive and reason about the richness of our complex world.

Applications in Accessibility, Creativity, and Robotics

As large language models evolve, their capabilities extend far beyond text. The future of artificial intelligence lies in **multimodal intelligence** — systems that can understand, integrate, and generate multiple types of data simultaneously: language, images, audio, video, and even sensor information. This fusion of modalities is transforming how machines perceive and interact with the world, unlocking new possibilities across accessibility, creativity, and robotics.

Accessibility: Empowering Inclusion Through Multimodal AI

One of the most profound impacts of multimodal intelligence is its potential to **break down barriers for people with disabilities** and improve universal access to information and communication.

- **Visual Accessibility:** Multimodal AI can convert images and videos into rich, descriptive language. This enables visually impaired users to "see" the world through detailed audio descriptions generated on the fly. For example, a smartphone camera combined with a multimodal AI can narrate scenes, identify objects, recognize faces, or even describe the emotions of people in a room, fostering greater independence.
- **Hearing Accessibility:** Similarly, multimodal systems improve accessibility for the deaf or hard of hearing by providing real-time

transcription and sign language recognition. By combining audio input with visual cues such as lip movements or gestures, AI can generate accurate captions or even translate sign language into spoken words, making conversations and multimedia content accessible.

- **Cognitive and Learning Support:** Multimodal AI can assist users with learning disabilities by adapting content presentation to suit different cognitive styles. For instance, educational material can be transformed into interactive, multimodal experiences combining text, audio narration, visual aids, and interactive elements. This personalized approach helps learners grasp complex concepts more intuitively.
- **Cross-Lingual Accessibility:** By integrating audio, visual, and textual inputs, multimodal AI enables seamless real-time translation that includes cultural and contextual cues. This facilitates communication across language barriers, making services and information globally accessible, especially in multilingual and underserved communities.

In all these scenarios, multimodal AI systems operate as intelligent intermediaries — translating complex, heterogeneous data into human-understandable formats tailored to individual needs, thereby fostering true inclusion.

Creativity: Amplifying Human Imagination and Expression

Multimodal intelligence is revolutionizing **creative industries** by augmenting the creative process, enabling novel forms of artistic expression, and democratizing creativity.

- **Visual and Textual Synthesis:** Artists, designers, and writers can now collaborate with AI systems that simultaneously process text and images. For example, a writer can describe a scene, and the AI generates corresponding artwork, or a visual artist can upload a sketch and receive poetic or narrative descriptions to inspire further development. This bidirectional interplay expands the creative toolkit and accelerates ideation.
- **Music and Sound Generation:** Beyond visual and textual data, multimodal models incorporate audio to compose original music or soundscapes inspired by textual prompts or images. Musicians can experiment with AI-generated accompaniments, or filmmakers can

generate custom sound effects synchronized with video content — all powered by cross-modal understanding.

- **Interactive Storytelling:** Multimodal AI enables dynamic narratives that respond to user input in real time, combining text, images, and sound to create immersive stories or games. These experiences adapt to audience reactions, offering personalized journeys that blend human imagination with machine creativity.
- **Content Creation at Scale:** Enterprises benefit from multimodal AI by automating the production of marketing materials, educational content, or social media posts that combine text, images, and video. This enhances efficiency while maintaining creativity, allowing human creators to focus on strategic and conceptual innovation.
- **Cultural Preservation and Innovation:** Multimodal AI aids in documenting and revitalizing endangered languages and cultures by linking spoken word, traditional art, and storytelling. This fusion ensures heritage is preserved not only through text but also through rich multimedia expressions accessible to future generations.

By harnessing multiple data modalities, AI no longer passively follows scripts but actively co-creates with humans — inspiring new forms of art and expanding the boundaries of creative expression.

Robotics: Multimodal Intelligence for Physical Interaction and Autonomy

In robotics, multimodal intelligence is a game-changer, enabling machines to **perceive, reason, and act in complex, dynamic environments** with human-like flexibility and situational awareness.

- **Sensory Integration:** Robots equipped with cameras, microphones, tactile sensors, and sometimes radar or LIDAR generate a continuous stream of heterogeneous data. Multimodal AI fuses these inputs to create a unified understanding of surroundings — recognizing objects, interpreting spoken commands, detecting obstacles, and even reading human emotions or gestures. This integrated perception is essential for safe and intuitive human-robot interaction.
- **Natural Language Understanding and Dialogue:** Combining speech recognition with contextual visual cues allows robots to understand

ambiguous commands or answer questions grounded in their immediate environment. For example, a household robot can interpret "Pick up the red book next to the lamp" by visually identifying objects and localizing language references, enabling precise, context-aware responses.

- **Manipulation and Dexterity:** Multimodal AI informs robotic control systems to adjust grip, force, and movement based on tactile feedback combined with visual input. This enables delicate tasks such as assembling electronics, handling fragile objects, or performing medical procedures with greater finesse than previously possible.
- **Learning from Interaction:** Through multimodal feedback—visual observation, spoken instructions, and tactile signals—robots can learn new tasks via demonstration or natural conversation, reducing the need for complex programming. This makes robotics more adaptable to diverse applications, from manufacturing lines to eldercare.
- **Autonomous Navigation:** Robots combine multimodal data to navigate unpredictable environments — fusing maps, live camera feeds, auditory signals (e.g., alarms, voices), and spatial sensors. This allows autonomous vehicles or drones to operate safely in urban settings, warehouses, or disaster zones, adapting to real-time changes.
- **Human-Robot Collaboration:** Multimodal intelligence enables robots to work alongside humans by recognizing gestures, gaze, and vocal tone to anticipate needs and coordinate actions seamlessly. In industrial or healthcare settings, this leads to safer and more efficient workflows, where robots act as partners rather than tools.

The integration of multimodal AI into robotics marks a shift from rigid automation toward **context-aware, interactive, and learning systems** that can safely and effectively operate in real-world environments. This is the foundation of truly intelligent machines capable of complex tasks alongside humans.

In Summary

Multimodal intelligence is the bridge between isolated AI capabilities and holistic, human-like understanding. By integrating language, vision, audio, and sensory data, these systems unlock new frontiers in accessibility, empowering those with disabilities and bridging communication gaps; in creativity, fueling new art forms and democratizing content creation; and in robotics, enabling machines to perceive and act with situational awareness and adaptability.

As enterprises adopt these technologies, they will redefine what it means to interact with machines — not as users commanding tools but as collaborators co-creating value across diverse domains. The future of AI is not just about words, but about the seamless fusion of all the senses, giving rise to truly intelligent, multimodal agents.

Multimodal Agents in the Enterprise

As artificial intelligence advances beyond the realm of text-based interactions, the emergence of **multimodal intelligence** marks a pivotal evolution in how machines perceive, understand, and act within complex environments. Multimodal agents are AI systems that integrate and process multiple types of data — text, images, audio, video, and even structured sensor signals — simultaneously. This fusion empowers them to interpret the world more like humans do: holistically and contextually.

In the enterprise context, multimodal agents unlock transformative capabilities across industries by enabling richer insights, more intuitive interactions, and deeper automation. They bridge the gap between siloed data streams and human-centric workflows, driving efficiency, innovation, and strategic advantage.

The Essence of Multimodal Agents

Traditional AI and language models primarily focused on one modality — usually text — limiting their ability to fully understand or interact with real-world scenarios. Enterprises, however, generate and rely on a diverse mix of data types daily: images from manufacturing lines, audio recordings of customer calls, video surveillance, PDFs of contracts, sensor data from IoT devices, and unstructured text notes.

A **multimodal agent** integrates these disparate inputs into a unified understanding, enabling it to:

- **Interpret complex situations** by combining visual, auditory, and textual cues.
- **Cross-reference information** across formats — for example, correlating a customer's complaint email with a recorded call and product image.

- **Generate richer outputs** that may include text summaries, annotated images, or synthesized video explanations.
- **Interact naturally** with humans through multiple sensory channels such as voice, text, and gestures.

This multimodal fusion not only enhances accuracy and comprehension but also expands the range of tasks an AI can autonomously perform.

Multimodal Agents in Enterprise Use Cases

Enterprises benefit from multimodal agents in a variety of critical domains:

1. Customer Experience and Support

Multimodal agents revolutionize customer service by understanding and responding to inputs beyond typed messages or spoken queries. For example, a customer can upload a photo of a defective product, and the agent can visually inspect it while simultaneously analyzing the accompanying chat conversation. It can listen to voice messages, detect emotional tone, and even recognize urgency from speech patterns.

By integrating these data streams, the agent delivers personalized, empathetic, and context-aware support, accelerating issue resolution and increasing customer satisfaction. Multimodal agents also power next-generation virtual assistants that combine speech, gesture recognition, and visual understanding for seamless, natural interactions across channels.

2. Intelligent Document Processing and Compliance

Regulatory environments require enterprises to process vast amounts of unstructured data: scanned contracts, handwritten notes, multimedia evidence, and more. Multimodal agents can analyze text alongside images, signatures, and document layouts, extracting critical information accurately even from poor-quality scans.

For compliance teams, this means faster audit preparation, automatic detection of inconsistencies, and real-time monitoring of regulatory adherence. Multimodal AI can highlight key contract clauses while simultaneously cross-checking related email threads and voice call transcripts, enabling holistic risk management.

3. Manufacturing and Quality Assurance

In manufacturing, multimodal agents monitor production lines by combining sensor data, high-resolution images, video feeds, and operator logs. They can detect defects through computer vision while correlating that with machine sensor anomalies and human operator notes.

This integrated analysis allows predictive maintenance, reducing downtime and improving product quality. Multimodal AI-powered robots and assistants can also guide workers with voice instructions complemented by visual cues, enhancing safety and productivity.

4. Healthcare and Diagnostics

Healthcare is inherently multimodal — doctors rely on patient histories (text), medical imaging (X-rays, MRIs), lab results (structured data), and spoken observations. Multimodal agents assist clinicians by synthesizing these diverse inputs into comprehensive diagnostic support.

For instance, an AI assistant can review radiology images alongside doctors' notes and patient interviews, helping to flag anomalies, suggest treatment plans, and prioritize cases. Such agents improve diagnostic accuracy, reduce clinician workload, and support telemedicine by processing video consultations combined with patient data.

5. Security and Fraud Detection

Enterprises tasked with securing assets and detecting fraud benefit from multimodal agents that analyze video surveillance, access logs, transaction records, and voice communications concurrently. For example, an agent can detect suspicious activity by combining facial recognition from video with unusual patterns in transaction data and verbal cues from intercepted calls.

This fusion enables faster threat detection and more nuanced risk assessments, enhancing enterprise cybersecurity and fraud prevention efforts.

Designing Multimodal Agents for the Enterprise

Building multimodal agents for enterprises involves several critical considerations:

Data Integration and Preprocessing

Enterprises generate enormous and heterogeneous data streams. Effective multimodal AI requires robust pipelines to ingest, synchronize, and preprocess data from diverse sources — whether structured or unstructured, real-time or batch.

This includes harmonizing time-stamped sensor data with textual logs, standardizing image formats, and extracting features relevant for cross-modal analysis. Ensuring data quality, privacy, and compliance during this process is paramount.

Model Architecture and Fusion Techniques

Multimodal agents rely on advanced neural architectures capable of encoding each data modality effectively while learning to combine their representations meaningfully. This often involves transformer-based encoders for text and vision, convolutional networks for images and video, and specialized layers for audio or sensor data.

Fusion can happen at multiple levels:

- **Early fusion:** combining raw input features.
- **Late fusion:** integrating modality-specific model outputs.
- **Hybrid fusion:** iterative integration throughout layers.

The choice depends on the use case, data characteristics, and computational resources.

Context Awareness and Reasoning

Enterprises require agents that understand context — business goals, regulatory constraints, user intent, and situational variables. Multimodal agents need mechanisms to maintain state, reason across modalities, and adapt dynamically.

This often involves layering multimodal perception with symbolic reasoning, knowledge graphs, or reinforcement learning to support complex decision-making.

User Interaction and Explainability

Multimodal agents in enterprise settings interact with diverse users: frontline workers, analysts, executives. Designing intuitive interfaces that support multimodal input and output (e.g., voice commands combined with visual dashboards) enhances usability.

Moreover, explainability is crucial — stakeholders must trust the AI's decisions. Multimodal agents should provide transparent rationales, highlight evidence from multiple modalities, and allow users to interrogate outputs.

Privacy, Security, and Ethics

Handling multimodal data raises significant privacy and security challenges. Enterprises must safeguard sensitive visual, audio, and textual data, comply with regulations such as GDPR and HIPAA, and address ethical concerns related to bias and fairness across modalities.

Responsible AI governance frameworks should be embedded from design through deployment.

The Strategic Impact of Multimodal Agents

The integration of multimodal intelligence into enterprise workflows does not merely optimize individual processes — it catalyzes strategic transformation.

- **Enhanced Decision-Making:** By synthesizing richer data inputs, multimodal agents provide deeper insights, reducing uncertainty and enabling proactive strategies.
- **Increased Automation:** Multimodal AI unlocks new automation frontiers, tackling tasks previously thought too complex or nuanced for machines.
- **Competitive Differentiation:** Organizations that harness multimodal intelligence gain agility and innovation capacity in customer engagement, risk management, and product development.
- **Improved Collaboration:** Multimodal agents facilitate seamless human-machine teaming by interpreting natural human signals and responding accordingly.

Looking Ahead: The Future of Multimodal Enterprise AI

As foundational models evolve and multimodal capabilities mature, the boundary between AI and human intelligence will blur further. Enterprises will increasingly deploy **agentic, self-learning multimodal systems** capable of continual adaptation and cross-domain reasoning.

Future multimodal agents will:

- Integrate real-time sensor and IoT data for hyper-contextual awareness.
- Leverage advances in spatial and temporal understanding from video and audio.
- Support personalized and culturally aware interactions across global teams.
- Embed ethical frameworks that dynamically assess and mitigate bias and misinformation.

The journey to multimodal intelligence in the enterprise is not only about technology — it's about reimagining workflows, culture, and business models in an AI-powered world.

Challenges: Alignment, Latency, and Interpretability

As large language models evolve, their scope is expanding far beyond text alone. The next frontier of AI is **multimodal intelligence** — the ability to understand, integrate, and generate information across multiple data types, including images, audio, video, sensor data, and structured inputs. Multimodal models hold transformative potential for enterprise solutions, enabling richer, more intuitive interfaces and unlocking insights from complex, diverse data sources.

However, this expansion also brings profound challenges. Three of the most critical are **alignment**, **latency**, and **interpretability**. These challenges must be addressed thoughtfully for multimodal AI to fulfill its promise safely, effectively, and responsibly.

1. Alignment: Ensuring Cohesive, Relevant Understanding Across Modalities

Alignment in multimodal AI refers to the capacity of the model to consistently and correctly relate information from different input sources and modalities, ensuring the output is coherent, relevant, and trustworthy.

Unlike unimodal models that handle a single input type (e.g., text only), multimodal models must reconcile vastly different data forms. For instance, an image and a textual description might convey related but not identical information. Ensuring the model "understands" this relationship and aligns its outputs accordingly is complex.

Challenges in Alignment:

- **Semantic Consistency:** Different modalities often have different levels of abstraction and noise. For example, a blurry photo and a vague caption may conflict or provide incomplete information. The model must learn to prioritize and integrate these inputs accurately.
- **Cross-Modal Representation:** Achieving a shared representation space where features from text, vision, and audio can interact meaningfully is difficult. Models must translate raw sensory data and symbolic language into compatible vectors while preserving essential meaning.
- **Contextual Awareness:** Alignment requires understanding context not only within each modality but across modalities. For example, the tone of spoken words combined with facial expressions or gestures can drastically alter the meaning.
- **Domain Adaptation:** Different industries have unique modalities and jargon — medical imaging combined with doctor's notes, or manufacturing sensor data combined with maintenance logs. Ensuring alignment in these specialized domains requires careful dataset curation and fine-tuning.

Why Alignment Matters:

Misalignment can lead to incorrect inferences, inconsistent outputs, or hallucinations — where the model invents details that do not exist or contradict inputs. In critical applications such as healthcare diagnostics, legal document analysis, or security monitoring, these errors can have serious consequences.

Robust alignment mechanisms involve multimodal pretraining on well-curated datasets, architectural innovations like cross-attention layers that explicitly model relationships between modalities, and post-processing validation techniques. Ongoing research explores self-supervised learning and contrastive methods that teach models to recognize which elements from different modalities correspond.

2. Latency: Balancing Speed and Complexity in Real-Time Multimodal AI

Latency refers to the time delay between receiving input and producing output. In many enterprise applications — customer support chatbots, live video analytics, voice assistants, or safety-critical monitoring systems — low latency is essential for a responsive user experience and operational effectiveness.

Multimodal models inherently face increased latency challenges compared to unimodal ones due to:

- **Data Processing Complexity:** Handling multiple data streams (e.g., video frames, audio signals, textual context) requires more computational resources and sophisticated preprocessing pipelines.
- **Model Size and Complexity:** Multimodal architectures often combine multiple deep neural networks specialized for each modality, increasing inference time.
- **Integration Overheads:** Fusion mechanisms that combine different modality representations add additional computational steps.

Challenges in Managing Latency:

- **Hardware Constraints:** Especially in on-device or edge computing scenarios (such as mobile phones, IoT devices, or embedded systems), hardware limitations restrict how large or complex the model can be.
- **Network Dependencies:** Cloud-based AI services face latency from network communication, especially in regions with unstable or slow internet connections.
- **Real-Time Synchronization:** When modalities arrive asynchronously (e.g., live video with separate audio streams), synchronizing them without adding delays is non-trivial.
- **Energy Efficiency:** Reducing latency often involves increasing computational throughput, which can conflict with power constraints on mobile or battery-powered devices.

Approaches to Reducing Latency:

- **Model Optimization:** Techniques such as model pruning, quantization, and knowledge distillation reduce model size and complexity without significant performance loss.
- **Efficient Architectures:** Designing lightweight transformer variants or hybrid models tailored to specific modalities and tasks.
- **Edge-Cloud Collaboration:** Offloading heavy computations to the cloud when possible while maintaining low-latency responses through on-device caching and pre-processing.

- **Asynchronous Processing:** Architectures that can handle modalities independently and fuse information opportunistically as it arrives.

Addressing latency is crucial not only for usability but also for safety and compliance in scenarios like real-time fraud detection or voice call spam identification, where delays can undermine effectiveness.

3. Interpretability: Making Multimodal AI Transparent and Trustworthy

Interpretability — the ability to understand and explain why an AI system produces a particular output — is a central concern in AI adoption, especially for complex, high-stakes enterprise applications.

Multimodal intelligence magnifies interpretability challenges because it combines opaque neural network decisions across heterogeneous data types. Stakeholders — from engineers and business leaders to regulators and end-users — must be able to trust these systems, understand their strengths and limitations, and diagnose errors when they occur.

Interpretability Challenges in Multimodal AI:

- **Opaque Fusion Layers:** Deep learning models integrate modalities through dense vector representations and attention mechanisms that are difficult to directly interpret.
- **Complex Attribution:** Determining which modality or input feature influenced a decision most is harder when multiple streams converge.
- **Dynamic Contexts:** Multimodal models often operate in changing environments, making it harder to trace cause-effect chains for specific outputs.
- **Lack of Ground Truth:** For many multimodal tasks, annotated datasets with detailed explanations are scarce, limiting supervised interpretability research.

Why Interpretability Matters:

- **Accountability:** Enterprises must be able to explain AI-driven decisions to customers, regulators, and internal auditors.
- **Debugging and Improvement:** Understanding failure modes is essential for model refinement and reducing bias or error.

- **User Trust:** Transparent models foster confidence and willingness to adopt AI systems.
- **Ethical Compliance:** Interpretability helps detect and mitigate unintended biases and harmful outputs.

Methods to Enhance Interpretability:

- **Attention Visualization:** Mapping attention weights across modalities to identify which inputs influenced predictions.
- **Saliency and Feature Attribution:** Using techniques like SHAP or LIME adapted for multimodal data to highlight key features.
- **Model Simplification:** Employing surrogate models that approximate complex models with interpretable logic.
- **Human-in-the-Loop Systems:** Combining AI outputs with expert feedback to validate and explain decisions.
- **Explainable Multimodal Architectures:** Designing models with modular components and explicit reasoning paths that facilitate explanation.

As AI systems increasingly touch sensitive domains such as healthcare, finance, and legal, interpretability moves from a “nice to have” to a regulatory and ethical imperative.

Conclusion

Multimodal intelligence promises to revolutionize how machines perceive and interact with the world — bridging the gap between raw data and meaningful understanding. However, realizing this vision requires overcoming significant hurdles in aligning disparate modalities into coherent understanding, ensuring responsive, low-latency interactions, and making complex AI decisions transparent and interpretable.

In enterprise contexts, addressing these challenges is not just a technical necessity but a foundation for responsible AI adoption, user trust, and sustained impact. By investing in research and development around alignment strategies, latency optimization, and interpretability techniques, organizations can harness the full power of multimodal AI — building systems that are not only smart but also reliable, timely, and accountable.

The journey toward truly intelligent, multimodal AI is challenging but essential. It is where the future of human-machine collaboration will be defined — creating new possibilities that transcend text and enable richer, more human-centered AI experiences.

CHAPTER NINE

REAL-WORLD IMPACT OF LLMS

Enhancing Knowledge Work: Search, Research, and Retrieval

One of the most transformative applications of large language models (LLMs) lies in their ability to revolutionize knowledge work — the complex, often unstructured tasks that involve finding, interpreting, synthesizing, and applying information. In today's data-driven world, knowledge workers face a deluge of information across multiple formats, sources, and languages. The challenge is no longer just access to data, but the ability to **extract actionable insight efficiently and accurately**.

LLMs have emerged as powerful tools to augment search, research, and retrieval processes, reshaping how organizations and individuals interact with knowledge.

The Traditional Bottlenecks in Knowledge Work

Before diving into the impact of LLMs, it is important to understand the traditional challenges knowledge workers face:

- **Information overload:** Vast volumes of documents, emails, reports, and databases create noise, making it difficult to locate relevant information quickly.
- **Unstructured data:** Much of the world's knowledge exists in unstructured formats — natural language text, audio transcripts, images,

or video captions — which traditional keyword search struggles to index effectively.

- **Context loss:** Keyword-based or Boolean search techniques often miss the context or intent behind queries, leading to irrelevant or incomplete results.
- **Fragmentation:** Knowledge is often siloed across different platforms, repositories, and formats, requiring manual cross-referencing.
- **Language and terminology barriers:** Domain-specific jargon, synonyms, acronyms, and multilingual content complicate retrieval.
- **Time constraints:** Business decisions often require rapid insights, which lengthy manual research cannot provide.

These pain points slow down decision-making, reduce productivity, and increase the risk of errors — all of which can have tangible economic and strategic consequences.

How LLMs Transform Search and Retrieval

Large language models address these bottlenecks by leveraging deep understanding of language, context, and semantics. Unlike traditional search engines that rely primarily on keyword matching, LLMs can:

- **Understand intent and nuance:** LLMs interpret the meaning behind user queries, including implied questions or complex information needs. For example, a query like "What are the risks of the new data privacy law on customer retention?" is understood as a request for a contextual risk assessment, not just documents containing those keywords.
- **Enable natural language querying:** Users can ask questions or issue commands in everyday language without needing to structure searches precisely. This lowers the barrier for non-technical users and speeds up interactions.
- **Summarize and synthesize:** Instead of simply listing documents, LLMs can generate concise summaries, compare viewpoints, or highlight critical points drawn from multiple sources, turning raw data into insight.
- **Extract entities and relationships:** By recognizing names, dates, events, and their connections, LLMs enable more granular retrieval and exploration of knowledge graphs.

- **Handle multilingual and domain-specific content:** Fine-tuned LLMs can bridge language gaps and adapt to industry-specific terminologies, expanding accessibility.
- **Improve search ranking through relevance:** By modeling semantic similarity, LLMs rank documents and passages not just by keyword frequency but by conceptual relevance.

The result is an enriched search experience that helps knowledge workers quickly locate precise, contextually relevant information.

Use Cases Across Industries

Enterprise knowledge management is a primary beneficiary of LLM-powered search and retrieval. Imagine a legal team searching across thousands of case files, precedents, contracts, and regulatory texts. LLMs can enable:

- Finding exact clauses relevant to a particular dispute or regulation.
- Generating concise briefings synthesizing multiple legal opinions.
- Flagging potential compliance risks hidden in dense documents.

Similarly, in **healthcare**, clinicians can retrieve patient histories, treatment protocols, and research articles quickly, aided by LLMs that understand medical terminology and context. This can support diagnosis, personalized treatment planning, and medical research.

In **finance**, analysts can interrogate market reports, earnings calls transcripts, and news articles to identify trends, risks, and opportunities — all while cutting through jargon and dense language.

In **scientific research**, LLMs help sift through the ever-growing corpus of academic papers, patents, and experimental data, enabling researchers to discover relevant work, detect emerging trends, or propose hypotheses faster.

Revolutionizing Research Workflows

LLMs do not simply improve search; they fundamentally alter how research is conducted:

- **Interactive exploration:** Instead of static queries, knowledge workers can engage in iterative, conversational research. Asking follow-up questions, requesting clarifications, or narrowing the scope becomes seamless.
- **Cross-referencing disparate data:** LLMs can connect dots across different repositories and data types — text, tables, audio transcripts, and more — offering integrated perspectives.
- **Automated literature reviews:** Generating comprehensive overviews of topics, identifying gaps in research, and suggesting future directions can be done semi-automatically.
- **Reducing cognitive load:** By offloading repetitive or routine information retrieval tasks, LLMs free up researchers to focus on creative and analytical aspects of their work.

Enhancing Retrieval with Memory and Personalization

The latest LLM applications increasingly incorporate **memory modules** that retain context across sessions or users, enabling personalized retrieval experiences:

- **Contextual continuity:** The model remembers previous queries or preferences, making retrieval smarter and more relevant over time.
- **User adaptation:** Search and research tools can adapt to user expertise, domain, or language preferences.
- **Collaborative knowledge:** Teams can share insights and annotations that inform retrieval, fostering collective intelligence.

Challenges and Considerations

Despite these advances, deploying LLMs for knowledge work involves critical challenges:

- **Data privacy and security:** Sensitive corporate or personal information requires secure handling and on-premise or hybrid deployments.
- **Accuracy and hallucination:** LLMs may generate plausible but incorrect information; verification and human oversight remain essential.

- **Bias and fairness:** Models can inadvertently reflect biases present in training data, affecting search fairness or inclusivity.
- **Scalability and latency:** Serving complex queries across massive datasets with low latency requires optimized infrastructure and model architectures.
- **Integration with legacy systems:** Enterprises need smooth integration with existing document management, CRM, ERP, and communication platforms.

Toward the Future of Knowledge Work

As LLMs continue to evolve, their impact on knowledge work will deepen. Upcoming advances such as **multimodal understanding**, **real-time summarization**, **interactive agentic assistants**, and **federated knowledge systems** promise to further break down barriers in search, research, and retrieval.

By turning raw data into actionable insight, large language models empower knowledge workers to navigate complexity with speed and precision — transforming information overload into informed decision-making, creativity, and innovation.

Code Generation and Software Engineering

In the evolving landscape of artificial intelligence, large language models (LLMs) are rapidly reshaping the domain of software engineering. What was once a painstakingly manual, detail-oriented, and sometimes error-prone craft is now being augmented and accelerated by AI systems capable of generating, debugging, documenting, and even architecting code. This transformation is not only technical but cultural, heralding a new era where human creativity and machine precision combine to redefine how software is built, maintained, and scaled.

The Traditional Software Engineering Challenge

Software engineering has always been a complex interplay of logic, creativity, and discipline. Developers must translate abstract ideas and business requirements into precise instructions a machine can execute. This process involves:

- Understanding requirements clearly.
- Designing system architecture and components.
- Writing syntactically correct and semantically meaningful code.
- Testing for correctness, security, and performance.
- Documenting for maintainability and collaboration.
- Debugging and refactoring over iterative development cycles.

These tasks require significant expertise and time. Even skilled engineers face bottlenecks—debugging subtle bugs, onboarding new developers, or translating legacy code into modern frameworks. The cumulative effect is a costly, time-consuming process vulnerable to human error.

Enter Large Language Models: Coding as a Language Task

At their core, LLMs are trained on vast corpora of text, which increasingly includes massive datasets of source code from public repositories, documentation, Q&A forums, and educational resources. This allows them to learn the syntax, semantics, and idiomatic usage patterns of dozens of programming languages—Python, JavaScript, Java, C++, and more.

Unlike traditional rule-based code completion tools, LLMs can:

- Understand contextual prompts describing desired functionality in natural language.
- Generate multi-line, logically coherent code snippets.
- Translate between programming languages.
- Suggest unit tests.
- Provide inline explanations and documentation.
- Identify and even fix bugs by reasoning over error messages or code behavior.
- Assist in architectural design through iterative dialogue with developers.

This marks a paradigm shift: coding is treated as a **language generation** problem rather than just a sequence prediction or autocomplete task.

Practical Applications in Software Development

1. Code Autocompletion and Snippet Generation
Modern IDEs (Integrated Development Environments) equipped with LLM-powered extensions enable developers to write code faster by predicting entire blocks from short prompts. For example, typing a comment like "function to parse JSON and validate schema" can trigger a complete implementation, dramatically reducing boilerplate coding.

2. Automated Code Review and Debugging
LLMs can analyze existing code for potential bugs, style inconsistencies, or security vulnerabilities. By integrating with testing frameworks, they suggest fixes or improvements, thereby reducing technical debt and improving software robustness.

3. Documentation and Knowledge Transfer
Good documentation is vital but often neglected. LLMs automatically generate docstrings, usage examples, and explanations in plain language. This improves code maintainability and accelerates onboarding for new team members.

4. Language Translation and Legacy Modernization
Migrating legacy systems to newer technologies is costly and risky. LLMs can translate legacy codebases (e.g., from COBOL to Python) while preserving logic, enabling smoother modernization efforts.

5. Intelligent Pair Programming and Mentoring
Developers can interact with AI copilots conversationally, asking for guidance, alternatives, or best practices in real time. This democratizes programming knowledge, making advanced techniques accessible to less experienced engineers.

Impact on Developer Productivity and Business Outcomes

The infusion of LLMs into software engineering workflows yields multiple benefits:

- **Accelerated Development Cycles:** Faster prototyping and iteration.
- **Improved Code Quality:** Early detection of errors and adherence to standards.
- **Cost Reduction:** Less time spent on routine coding and debugging.

- **Enhanced Innovation:** Developers focus more on creative problem-solving than repetitive tasks.
- **Greater Accessibility:** Non-experts can participate more easily in software creation, enabling citizen developers and bridging skill gaps.

For enterprises, these translate into faster time-to-market for products, higher software reliability, and greater agility in responding to changing market needs.

Challenges and Considerations

Despite their promise, LLMs for code generation are not infallible. Challenges include:

- **Accuracy and Safety:** Generated code may contain subtle bugs, security flaws, or inefficient constructs requiring expert review.
- **Context Understanding:** Complex, multi-module systems require a global understanding beyond isolated snippets.
- **Intellectual Property:** Use of open-source code for training raises licensing and compliance questions.
- **Explainability:** Developers must understand why a piece of code was generated to trust and maintain it.
- **Ethical Concerns:** Over-reliance on AI may erode critical coding skills; bias in training data can propagate insecure or suboptimal patterns.

Addressing these requires integrating LLMs as **collaborative assistants** rather than autonomous coders, embedding human oversight, and advancing research in model interpretability and validation.

The Future: Toward Agentic AI in Software Engineering

Looking ahead, the convergence of LLMs with other AI techniques promises more agentic, autonomous systems capable of higher-order reasoning about software design, deployment, and maintenance. Imagine AI agents that can:

- Continuously monitor codebases for anomalies or performance degradation.

- Automatically refactor and optimize code in production.
- Coordinate across teams by summarizing project status, blockers, and resource needs.
- Learn and adapt from user feedback to align with evolving coding standards and business goals.

Such systems will not replace developers but will elevate their capabilities — making software engineering more creative, strategic, and impactful.

Conclusion

Large language models have fundamentally changed how machines understand and generate code, catalyzing a new era in software engineering. By bridging the gap between natural language and programming languages, LLMs empower developers to build faster, smarter, and more reliably. While challenges remain, their role as collaborative partners in coding is already transforming enterprises worldwide.

As we continue this journey, understanding and harnessing this technology will be critical for businesses aiming to innovate and compete in the digital age. The language of intelligence is no longer confined to humans; it now extends to the machines we build — and the software they create.

Education, Personalized Learning, and Tutoring

Education is among the most profound areas transformed by artificial intelligence, and large language models (LLMs) are spearheading this revolution. Traditionally, education has followed a one-size-fits-all paradigm, constrained by classroom sizes, limited teacher availability, and standardized curricula. But learning is inherently personal—shaped by individual abilities, interests, cultural backgrounds, and goals. LLMs unlock the potential for truly personalized learning at scale, reshaping how knowledge is delivered, absorbed, and applied.

LLMs as Intelligent Tutors

One of the most impactful applications of LLMs in education is their ability to act as personalized, on-demand tutors. Unlike conventional tutoring, which is often expensive and inaccessible, AI-powered tutoring can be democratized across geographies and socio-economic divides.

LLMs can:

- **Explain complex concepts in multiple ways** until the student understands.
- **Answer questions instantly**, no matter the time of day.
- **Detect misunderstandings or gaps** in knowledge by analyzing student responses.
- **Offer hints and scaffold learning** rather than giving away answers, encouraging critical thinking.
- **Adapt to the learner's pace and style**, whether visual, auditory, or kinesthetic.

For example, a student struggling with algebra can receive step-by-step problem-solving guidance, while another exploring creative writing can get instant feedback on tone, style, or grammar. This dynamic interaction fosters engagement and retention far beyond static textbooks.

Personalized Learning Pathways

LLMs facilitate the design of personalized learning journeys tailored to each student's unique profile:

- **Diagnostic Assessment:** By analyzing a learner's prior knowledge, misconceptions, and interests, LLMs can recommend customized content and exercises.
- **Real-Time Adaptation:** As students progress, AI adjusts difficulty levels, recommends supplementary materials, or revisits earlier topics to reinforce mastery.
- **Multi-Lingual and Multicultural Support:** Large language models trained on diverse corpora can offer education in multiple languages and contexts, making learning inclusive and culturally relevant.
- **Cross-Disciplinary Integration:** LLMs can connect concepts across subjects, showing how math applies to science or literature to history, enriching understanding through interdisciplinary learning.

This personalization is especially transformative for learners in under-resourced or remote settings where expert teachers or diverse educational materials may be scarce.

Content Creation and Curation

In addition to tutoring, LLMs streamline content creation—an often time-consuming task for educators:

- **Generating Exercises and Quizzes:** AI can automatically produce problem sets, multiple-choice questions, or essay prompts aligned with curriculum standards.
- **Summarizing Complex Texts:** LLMs can create concise, student-friendly summaries of dense academic papers or textbooks, making advanced knowledge more accessible.
- **Crafting Lesson Plans:** By understanding educational objectives, LLMs assist teachers in designing coherent lesson plans that integrate activities, assessments, and discussions.
- **Adapting Materials for Different Levels:** From elementary school to university, LLMs can modify the complexity of reading materials to suit varied learner proficiencies.

This reduces teacher workload, allowing educators to focus on mentorship and individualized student support rather than repetitive preparation.

Facilitating Lifelong Learning

Education doesn't stop after formal schooling. LLMs empower learners of all ages to acquire new skills and knowledge:

- **Professional Development:** Workers can receive upskilling through interactive tutorials, simulated scenarios, and instant feedback.
- **Language Learning:** Conversational AI powered by LLMs helps learners practice speaking, listening, and writing in new languages with contextual correction.
- **Accessible Learning for Special Needs:** Tailored interactions assist students with disabilities, including dyslexia, hearing impairment, or

cognitive challenges, making education more equitable.

These capabilities make continuous learning feasible in a fast-evolving world where skills rapidly become outdated.

Enhancing Collaboration and Critical Thinking

LLMs also promote active, collaborative learning:

- **Facilitating Group Projects:** AI can moderate and guide group discussions, suggest resources, and summarize ideas.
- **Encouraging Inquiry:** By providing nuanced answers and posing further questions, LLMs stimulate curiosity and critical reflection.
- **Supporting Debate and Perspective-Taking:** AI can simulate diverse viewpoints, helping learners understand multiple sides of complex issues.

Through these interactions, AI doesn't replace educators but becomes a powerful augmentation, nurturing higher-order thinking and creativity.

Challenges and Ethical Considerations

Despite the promise, the integration of LLMs in education raises important questions:

- **Bias and Fairness:** AI models trained on internet-scale data risk perpetuating biases or stereotypes. Careful evaluation and mitigation are essential to avoid disadvantaging learners.
- **Privacy and Data Security:** Sensitive student information must be protected, requiring transparent data governance frameworks.
- **Dependence vs. Autonomy:** Excessive reliance on AI tutoring could undermine development of independent learning skills or critical skepticism.
- **Equity in Access:** While LLMs can democratize education, disparities in technology access could exacerbate existing inequalities without deliberate policy action.

Addressing these issues requires collaboration between educators, technologists, policymakers, and communities to build responsible, inclusive AI-powered education.

The Transformational Potential

Ultimately, LLMs enable a paradigm shift in education — from standardized, rigid instruction toward flexible, learner-centric experiences. By making expert guidance, personalized feedback, and rich resources available 24/7, AI-powered education holds the promise of unlocking human potential on a global scale.

For learners in developing countries or remote regions with limited educational infrastructure, LLMs can provide a critical lifeline to knowledge and opportunity. For educators, AI can be an indispensable ally, freeing time and energy to foster inspiration, creativity, and mentorship.

As we continue to innovate and iterate, large language models will redefine what it means to teach and learn, creating a more equitable, engaging, and effective educational ecosystem for all.

Customer Experience and Conversational AI

In today's hyper-connected, fast-paced world, **customer experience (CX)** has emerged as a defining factor for business success. Across industries—from telecommunications and finance to healthcare and retail—customers demand instant, personalized, and meaningful interactions. Their expectations are shaped by seamless digital experiences where responses are prompt, accurate, and human-like. At the heart of this transformation lies the rise of **conversational AI**, empowered by large language models (LLMs), which are reshaping how organizations engage, support, and delight their customers.

The Paradigm Shift in Customer Experience

Traditional customer service systems, constrained by rigid scripts and limited understanding, often result in frustration: long wait times, repetitive explanations, and one-size-fits-all responses. Conversational AI changes this by enabling **natural, free-flowing interactions** that understand intent, context, and sentiment, delivering responses that feel personalized and empathetic.

LLMs power these systems by leveraging their ability to comprehend complex language patterns and nuances. This allows enterprises to move beyond keyword matching or rule-based chatbots into a realm where AI can:

- **Understand diverse customer intents**, even when queries are ambiguous or phrased unconventionally.
- **Maintain context across multi-turn conversations**, avoiding repetitive questions and adapting responses as the dialogue evolves.
- **Interpret emotional cues** in language, enabling empathetic and appropriate responses.
- **Provide multilingual support**, crucial for global companies and those serving diverse populations, including low-resource languages.
- **Generate dynamic, personalized content**, tailored to individual customer profiles and preferences.

Conversational AI in Action: Use Cases Transforming CX

1. **Virtual Assistants and Chatbots**

Modern chatbots, powered by LLMs, are no longer scripted machines but **intelligent virtual assistants** capable of handling a wide range of customer inquiries—from billing questions and product recommendations to troubleshooting technical issues and booking appointments.

Unlike early chatbots, these assistants can handle **complex, open-ended conversations**. For example, a telecom subscriber frustrated with frequent dropped calls can explain the problem naturally. The AI assistant will recognize keywords, interpret intent, check service logs, and guide the user through troubleshooting steps or escalate the issue if needed—without the customer ever feeling stuck in an endless loop.

1. **Voice-Enabled Conversational Agents**

Conversational AI is not limited to text. The integration of **automatic speech recognition (ASR)** and **text-to-speech (TTS)** with LLMs enables voice assistants that interact naturally in real time. For many users—especially in developing countries or among older demographics—voice is the preferred or only accessible channel.

These agents can transcribe conversations, detect intent, and respond instantly, all while sounding human and empathetic. This opens new avenues in industries like healthcare, where patients can schedule appointments or get medication reminders over the phone, and banking, where voice verification and conversational banking simplify user experience.

3. **Sentiment Analysis and Real-Time Feedback**

LLMs can analyze customer input not just for content but for **emotional sentiment** and urgency. This capability helps prioritize support tickets, escalate critical issues, or tailor response tone. For example, if a customer's message reveals frustration or anger, the system can flag it for immediate human intervention or switch to a more conciliatory response style.

4. **Personalized Recommendations and Proactive Support**

By combining conversational AI with user profile data and interaction history, LLM-powered systems can **anticipate customer needs** and offer proactive suggestions. For instance, an e-commerce platform might recommend products based on previous purchases and browsing patterns during a conversation. A telecom provider might alert customers about plans that better suit their usage patterns or upcoming service disruptions.

Benefits to Enterprises

- **Scalability:** Conversational AI powered by LLMs can simultaneously serve thousands of customers 24/7, without fatigue or delays, helping enterprises scale support during peak times without proportional increases in human staff.
- **Cost Efficiency:** Automating routine inquiries reduces operational costs and frees human agents to focus on complex, high-value interactions.
- **Consistency:** LLMs ensure consistent quality of service, adhering to compliance and regulatory guidelines, which is especially critical in

sectors like finance and healthcare.
- **Data Insights:** Every interaction provides valuable data that can be analyzed for trends, product improvement, and better customer understanding.

Addressing Challenges and Ethical Considerations

While conversational AI offers transformative benefits, it also raises important challenges:

- **Bias and Fairness:** Language models can inadvertently perpetuate biases present in training data, leading to unfair or offensive responses. Enterprises must adopt robust bias mitigation strategies and continuous monitoring.
- **Privacy and Security:** Conversations often involve sensitive personal data. Systems must ensure secure data handling, compliance with privacy regulations (like GDPR), and transparent data usage policies.
- **Transparency:** Customers should be aware when they are interacting with AI rather than a human, ensuring informed consent and trust.
- **Accessibility:** Conversational AI must cater to users with disabilities, low literacy, or non-standard dialects. Multimodal interfaces and simplified language generation play key roles here.
- **Cultural Sensitivity:** For global enterprises, conversational agents need localization beyond translation—adapting tone, formality, idioms, and cultural references appropriately.

Conversational AI in Developing Countries and Low-End Devices

A critical frontier for conversational AI is delivering these capabilities **on low-end devices and in regions with limited connectivity**, especially in developing countries. This requires:

- **Efficient, lightweight models** that can run on-device or with minimal network dependency.

- **Support for local languages and dialects**, many of which have limited digital resources.
- **Robustness to noisy inputs and accents** to ensure voice assistants work reliably.
- **Innovative notification systems**, such as inaudible voice cues or USSD-based fallback, to bridge infrastructure gaps.

These innovations democratize AI benefits, allowing millions to access quality customer service, financial inclusion, healthcare information, and educational support.

The Road Ahead: Agentic AI and Conversational Ecosystems

Looking forward, conversational AI powered by LLMs is evolving beyond simple assistants into **agentic AI**—autonomous systems that can plan, execute, and learn across multiple tasks and channels. This means:

- AI assistants that proactively manage entire customer journeys, from onboarding to retention.
- Multi-agent systems collaborating behind the scenes, combining expertise in sales, support, compliance, and marketing.
- Integration with IoT and smart devices, allowing natural language control over home appliances, vehicles, and workplace tools.
- Continuous learning from interactions, improving over time without constant human retraining.

Enterprises that harness these capabilities will unlock **new paradigms of customer engagement**—more intuitive, efficient, and human-centered than ever before.

In sum, the integration of LLM-powered conversational AI in customer experience is not just a technological upgrade — it is a strategic imperative that enables enterprises to meet evolving expectations, expand access, and build trust in a digital-first world. Its impact is already profound and only set to deepen as models grow more intelligent, adaptable, and ethical.

Accessibility and Inclusive Interfaces

One of the most profound and socially transformative impacts of large language models (LLMs) lies in their ability to advance **accessibility** and **inclusion**. In a world where billions of people face barriers—be they linguistic, cognitive, sensory, or technological—LLMs offer new pathways to level the playing field, making information and technology truly available to everyone, regardless of ability or background.

The Accessibility Challenge

Accessibility means enabling people with disabilities or different abilities to interact with digital tools, services, and information in ways that respect their needs and dignity. This encompasses a wide range of challenges:

- **Visual impairments:** Blindness or low vision make reading text or navigating graphical interfaces difficult.
- **Hearing impairments:** Deaf or hard-of-hearing individuals often rely on captioning or sign language interpretation.
- **Cognitive disabilities:** Neurodivergent users, such as those with dyslexia, ADHD, or autism, may require simplified language or alternative interaction modes.
- **Motor impairments:** Limited dexterity or mobility can restrict interaction with standard keyboards, mice, or touchscreens.
- **Language barriers:** Non-native speakers or those with limited literacy need tools that can translate, simplify, or contextualize language.

Despite legal frameworks and standards such as the Web Content Accessibility Guidelines (WCAG), many digital platforms remain challenging or inaccessible to significant populations. This gap is not only a social justice issue but also a lost opportunity for businesses, governments, and societies to engage fully with their constituencies.

How LLMs Transform Accessibility

LLMs fundamentally change the game by enabling more natural, flexible, and context-aware interaction with technology. Their ability to understand, generate, and manipulate human language opens doors for multiple accessibility innovations:

1. **Natural Language Interfaces for Everyone**

Traditional interfaces rely heavily on visual elements, menus, and complex workflows. LLMs enable **conversational interfaces** where users can simply *ask* for what they need in their own words. This reduces dependency on technical literacy or navigation skills. Voice assistants powered by LLMs can understand varied accents, dialects, and even non-standard speech patterns, making technology more inclusive.

For example, a user with limited mobility can control smart home devices, schedule appointments, or seek help via natural voice commands instead of manual input. Similarly, those with cognitive impairments benefit from interaction modes that are less overwhelming and more intuitive.

2. Real-Time Captioning and Transcription

LLMs integrated with speech recognition technologies can generate real-time captions for video calls, lectures, and broadcasts. Unlike earlier captioning solutions that struggled with accuracy or domain-specific terms, LLMs contextualize spoken content to improve transcription quality dramatically. This allows deaf and hard-of-hearing users to participate more fully in conversations, educational environments, and workplaces.

Moreover, LLMs can translate these captions into multiple languages, broadening accessibility across linguistic divides.

3. Text Simplification and Explanation

Many complex documents—legal contracts, medical instructions, policy statements—are inaccessible to people with limited literacy or cognitive disabilities. LLMs can **simplify language**, summarize key points, or generate explanations tailored to the user's comprehension level.

For instance, a patient receiving a complex diagnosis can ask an AI assistant to explain medical jargon in plain language. This fosters autonomy, better decision-making, and reduces misunderstandings that can impact health outcomes.

4. Multimodal Accessibility

Modern LLMs are increasingly multimodal — capable of processing and generating text, images, audio, and video. This opens up new avenues for **alternative content presentation**:

- For visually impaired users, AI can describe images or videos verbally.
- For hearing-impaired users, AI can generate sign language avatars from spoken or written content.
- For users with learning disabilities, AI can create interactive, multimedia explanations combining text, visuals, and audio cues.

Such multimodal capabilities ensure that information is not just available but accessible in the most effective form for diverse users.

5. Personalized and Adaptive Interfaces

Every user's accessibility needs and preferences are unique. LLMs enable **adaptive interfaces** that learn from user interactions and tailor communication style, complexity, and delivery mode accordingly. This personalization ensures inclusivity without forcing one-size-fits-all solutions.

For example, an AI assistant might detect when a user struggles with dense text and proactively offer summaries or switch to voice explanations. Or it may adjust responses for a non-native speaker by using simpler vocabulary and clearer sentence structures.

6. Bridging Language and Literacy Gaps

The global diversity of languages and dialects poses a major accessibility challenge. Millions lack access to technology in their native tongues, limiting digital inclusion. LLMs trained on vast multilingual corpora can translate, transliterate, and localize content across hundreds of languages.

This capability enables:

- Access to education and government services in native languages.
- Cross-cultural communication in business and social contexts.
- Preservation and revitalization of underrepresented languages through digital tools.

Beyond literal translation, LLMs understand context and cultural nuance, enabling more natural and respectful language use.

Enterprise and Social Impact

From an enterprise perspective, inclusive AI-driven accessibility interfaces create tangible value:

- **Expanded customer reach:** Serving users with disabilities or in different language groups increases market size.
- **Improved user satisfaction:** Accessible products reduce frustration and improve loyalty.
- **Regulatory compliance:** Meeting accessibility standards avoids legal risks and penalties.

- **Social responsibility:** Building inclusive technology enhances brand reputation and contributes to equity.

For governments and nonprofits, LLM-enabled accessibility fosters greater civic participation, educational equity, and social inclusion. In emerging markets and developing countries, where digital literacy and infrastructure vary widely, accessible AI interfaces can leapfrog traditional barriers and democratize access to knowledge and services.

Challenges and Ethical Considerations

While LLMs offer immense promise, accessibility efforts must be approached responsibly:

- **Bias and fairness:** Models must be trained and evaluated to avoid linguistic or cultural biases that could marginalize users.
- **Privacy and security:** Sensitive accessibility data requires robust protections.
- **User autonomy:** AI interfaces should empower users without enforcing paternalistic constraints or replacing human judgment.
- **Transparency:** Users should understand when AI is involved and have control over its behavior.

Ongoing collaboration with disability advocates, linguistic experts, and diverse user communities is critical to building truly accessible and inclusive AI.

Conclusion

Accessibility and inclusion are not afterthoughts — they are core design principles for the future of AI. Large language models are powerful enablers of this vision, turning natural language into a universal interface that adapts to the diverse realities of human ability and culture.

By harnessing LLMs for accessible, personalized, and multimodal communication, we can create technology that respects and amplifies human dignity. This transformation is not just technical — it is a step toward a more equitable digital society where everyone, regardless of ability, language, or background, can participate, create, and thrive.

AI in Science, Healthcare, and Legal Domains

Large Language Models have transcended the realm of theoretical innovation to become pivotal tools across some of society's most critical and complex domains — science, healthcare, and law. These fields are traditionally knowledge-dense, heavily reliant on precision, and require nuanced understanding and interpretation of vast textual and data sources. LLMs, by virtue of their ability to understand, generate, and reason with human language, are reshaping how professionals in these areas work, innovate, and serve communities globally.

AI in Scientific Research: Accelerating Discovery

Scientific research is an iterative process of hypothesis, experimentation, analysis, and publication — all underpinned by language. Researchers publish papers, share data, write grant proposals, and communicate complex findings in precise terms. Navigating the ever-expanding scientific literature is a growing challenge, and here LLMs are proving transformative.

Literature Review and Summarization:
LLMs can parse thousands of scientific articles, extracting key insights, summarizing results, and highlighting trends or contradictions. This ability drastically reduces the time researchers spend on literature reviews, allowing them to focus more on experimentation and innovation.

Hypothesis Generation and Experimental Design:
By analyzing existing data and publications, LLMs can suggest novel hypotheses or experimental pathways, effectively acting as intelligent research assistants. They can cross-reference findings from disparate fields, identifying connections that may elude human researchers.

Data Interpretation and Code Generation:
Many scientific tasks require data analysis using specialized code or statistical software. LLMs can generate or debug scripts in languages like Python or R, making computational analysis more accessible, especially for scientists without deep programming expertise.

Collaborative Research and Accessibility:
Language models help bridge linguistic and technical barriers, translating scientific work across languages and formats, democratizing access to knowledge globally, including in under-resourced institutions and

developing countries.

Challenges and Considerations:
Scientific accuracy and reproducibility are paramount. While LLMs can synthesize information, their outputs must be carefully validated to avoid propagation of errors or unsupported claims. The risk of hallucination—where models generate plausible but false information—necessitates rigorous human oversight.

AI in Healthcare: Enhancing Diagnosis, Treatment, and Patient Care

Healthcare generates an immense amount of unstructured text: clinical notes, diagnostic reports, research literature, insurance claims, and patient communications. LLMs are uniquely positioned to unlock the value hidden in this data to improve outcomes and operational efficiency.

Clinical Documentation and Summarization:
Physicians spend significant time documenting patient encounters. LLMs can automate this process by transcribing and summarizing doctor-patient conversations in real-time, freeing clinicians to focus more on care and less on paperwork. They can also extract key clinical findings from historical records to support decision-making.

Diagnostic Assistance and Decision Support:
By synthesizing patient data and the latest medical literature, LLMs can assist doctors in diagnosing complex conditions or suggesting personalized treatment plans. They can flag potential drug interactions, highlight overlooked symptoms, and generate alerts for critical conditions.

Patient Communication and Education:
LLMs power chatbots and virtual assistants that provide patients with understandable explanations of their health conditions, medication instructions, and appointment scheduling. This increases engagement, adherence, and health literacy, especially in underserved populations.

Medical Research and Drug Discovery:
Similar to their role in broader science, LLMs accelerate biomedical research by summarizing vast datasets, identifying potential drug candidates, and proposing new clinical trial designs. They can analyze genomic sequences and biological data to suggest novel therapeutic targets.

Ethical and Privacy Imperatives:
The healthcare domain demands the highest standards of privacy, accuracy,

and fairness. LLMs deployed in clinical settings must comply with regulations such as HIPAA and GDPR, ensure unbiased recommendations across demographics, and provide transparent explanations to earn trust from practitioners and patients alike.

AI in the Legal Domain: Revolutionizing Practice and Access to Justice

The legal profession revolves around dense, complex language in statutes, contracts, case law, and briefs. Legal practitioners invest countless hours interpreting language and precedent. LLMs are rapidly becoming indispensable tools in this field by automating routine tasks and augmenting legal reasoning.

Contract Analysis and Drafting:
LLMs can review contracts, flag risky clauses, suggest revisions, and even generate first drafts of standard agreements. This reduces manual review times and helps ensure compliance with evolving regulations.

Legal Research and Precedent Identification:
LLMs scan through massive databases of case law and statutes to identify relevant precedents and legal principles. They can answer specific legal questions or generate comprehensive legal memos, making research faster and more thorough.

Litigation Support and Document Review:
During discovery and litigation, attorneys must sift through enormous document repositories. LLMs streamline this process by classifying documents, extracting key information, and identifying potentially privileged or relevant content.

Access to Justice:
By powering chatbots and automated legal aid tools, LLMs increase accessibility for individuals who cannot afford traditional legal counsel. These tools can help draft simple wills, prepare court forms, or provide guidance on common legal issues.

Regulatory Compliance and Risk Management:
Enterprises use LLMs to monitor changes in laws and regulations, automatically updating compliance documentation and alerting risk managers to potential liabilities.

Caveats and Responsibilities:
The legal domain demands precision and interpretability. Misinterpretation

can have serious consequences. Hence, LLM outputs must be treated as assistive rather than authoritative, and legal professionals must maintain oversight. The ethical use of AI in law also requires transparency to avoid biases that could disadvantage certain groups.

Cross-Domain Synergies and the Future

In these domains, the impact of LLMs is not isolated. Scientific research fuels healthcare innovation, healthcare outcomes inform legal regulations, and legal frameworks shape scientific funding and healthcare delivery. LLMs provide a common language and intelligence layer that can bridge these traditionally siloed fields.

Multimodal and Agentic Extensions:
Future models will integrate text with images, genomic data, medical imaging, legal diagrams, and real-time voice input, creating richer, more contextual insights. Agentic AI will enable models to plan, execute tasks, consult external databases, and interact with human experts seamlessly.

Towards Responsible AI in Critical Domains:
As these models become embedded into life-changing workflows, responsible design — emphasizing fairness, privacy, explainability, and continuous validation — becomes a non-negotiable priority. Institutions must partner with AI developers to co-create frameworks that balance innovation with societal trust.

Summary

Large Language Models are catalyzing profound transformations across science, healthcare, and law. By understanding and generating human language at scale, they are accelerating discovery, enhancing patient care, and democratizing access to legal services. Their ability to digest vast unstructured data, generate insights, and interact naturally with professionals positions LLMs as foundational technologies of the modern knowledge economy.

Yet, their power demands respect and responsibility. With careful stewardship, these models can usher in a new era where AI not only augments human intelligence but also elevates the quality, fairness, and accessibility of some of society's most vital domains.

Decision Support and Business Intelligence

In today's data-driven world, the ability to make informed, timely decisions is critical to business success. Organizations across industries—from finance and healthcare to telecommunications and retail—rely heavily on insights extracted from vast volumes of data to guide strategy, operations, and customer engagement. Yet, despite advances in analytics, many decision-makers still struggle to access the right information at the right time, to synthesize complex datasets, or to interpret nuanced trends buried in unstructured data.

Large Language Models (LLMs) are fundamentally reshaping the landscape of **decision support and business intelligence (BI)** by bridging the gap between raw data and actionable knowledge through natural language understanding and generation. Their ability to comprehend, summarize, and reason with diverse textual and numeric inputs offers unprecedented opportunities to augment human decision-making across organizational hierarchies.

From Data to Decisions: The Challenge

Traditional BI systems often depend on structured data warehouses, pre-built dashboards, and SQL queries—tools that require significant technical expertise and upfront design. While these systems excel at tracking key performance indicators (KPIs) or generating static reports, they frequently fall short when users need to explore complex "what-if" scenarios, integrate unstructured data like emails or customer feedback, or understand the rationale behind emerging trends.

Moreover, in many enterprises, valuable insights remain locked in disparate silos: product development notes, customer service transcripts, competitor news articles, regulatory filings, social media chatter, and internal knowledge bases. The challenge is not just to collect data but to **contextualize** it — to connect dots across sources, detect signals amid noise, and present findings in a way decision-makers can trust and act upon quickly.

How LLMs Enhance Decision Support

LLMs serve as a transformative interface that unlocks the full spectrum of business intelligence by translating complex data narratives into **clear, conversational insights**. Unlike traditional BI tools, they can:

- **Interpret unstructured data:** Extract meaningful information from emails, documents, customer reviews, social media, and technical reports, synthesizing qualitative and quantitative inputs.
- **Summarize complex reports:** Condense lengthy documents into executive summaries or bullet points tailored to the user's context and preferences, saving time and improving comprehension.
- **Answer natural language queries:** Instead of navigating dashboards or writing code, users can ask questions in plain language — "What were the key drivers of revenue growth last quarter?" or "Which customer segment showed the highest churn risk?" — and receive precise, data-backed responses.
- **Generate scenario analyses:** Assist in exploring hypothetical business scenarios by simulating outcomes based on input parameters, market trends, or historical data, facilitating proactive strategy development.
- **Provide explainability:** Go beyond black-box outputs by clarifying the reasoning behind predictions or recommendations, increasing transparency and trust.

Through these capabilities, LLMs act as **intelligent knowledge assistants**, enabling business leaders, analysts, and frontline workers alike to access insights without specialized training or dependence on data engineers.

Applications Across Industries

Finance and Banking

In financial services, decision support powered by LLMs is revolutionizing risk assessment, investment strategies, and regulatory compliance. By analyzing market reports, earnings calls transcripts, news sentiment, and historical data, LLMs help portfolio managers understand market dynamics and assess risks dynamically. They can generate natural language explanations of complex models—such as credit scoring or fraud detection—making insights accessible to non-technical stakeholders and regulators alike.

Healthcare

Healthcare executives and clinicians face an overwhelming volume of clinical studies, patient records, treatment guidelines, and medical literature. LLMs facilitate evidence-based decision-making by synthesizing this information to support diagnostic, therapeutic, and operational decisions. For instance, a hospital administrator might query patient flow bottlenecks or resource allocation with natural language, receiving actionable recommendations that improve care quality and reduce costs.

Retail and E-commerce

In retail, LLM-driven BI tools analyze consumer feedback, social media trends, inventory data, and sales performance to identify shifting customer preferences and optimize supply chains. Decision-makers can generate dynamic reports on product performance or regional sales disparities through simple conversational queries, enabling faster responses to market changes.

Telecommunications

Telecom operators leverage LLMs to analyze vast CDRs (call detail records), customer service logs, network performance data, and competitor moves to inform pricing strategies, churn prediction, and fraud detection. By integrating structured and unstructured data streams, LLMs provide nuanced insights that drive subscriber retention and network investment decisions.

The Power of Conversational BI

A revolutionary aspect of LLMs in decision support is the rise of **conversational business intelligence**—interfaces that allow decision-makers to interact with data through dialogue rather than complex tools. This democratizes data access, empowering stakeholders at all levels to ask questions, request updates, or generate reports on demand without waiting for analyst support.

This conversational approach also fosters iterative exploration. Users can drill down into answers by asking follow-up questions or requesting alternative perspectives, creating a dynamic feedback loop that traditional static dashboards cannot match.

Integrating LLMs with Existing BI Ecosystems

Enterprises don't need to replace their entire BI infrastructure to benefit from LLMs. Instead, LLMs complement and enhance existing systems by:

- **Augmenting data ingestion:** Parsing unstructured text and integrating insights into data lakes.
- **Enhancing reporting:** Auto-generating narratives for dashboards and alerts.
- **Automating routine queries:** Reducing analyst workload by handling common data requests.
- **Supporting decision workflows:** Embedding intelligent assistants in collaboration platforms for real-time, contextual advice.

Such integration accelerates enterprise AI adoption by blending innovation with familiar workflows and governance controls.

Challenges and Considerations

While LLMs offer tremendous promise, enterprises must approach their deployment thoughtfully to mitigate risks:

- **Data quality and bias:** LLMs reflect the data they are trained on. Ensuring the underlying data is accurate, representative, and free from harmful biases is critical to avoid misleading or unfair insights.
- **Explainability:** Business decisions often require transparency. Enterprises must choose or build models that provide clear reasoning paths rather than inscrutable outputs.
- **Security and compliance:** Sensitive business data must be protected throughout ingestion, processing, and storage, especially in regulated industries.
- **Human-in-the-loop:** LLMs should augment rather than replace human judgment. Embedding expert review and feedback loops enhances decision quality and trust.
- **Continuous learning:** Business environments are dynamic. Models need ongoing updates to remain relevant and accurate as new data and contexts emerge.

Looking Forward: Towards Autonomous Decision Systems

The integration of LLMs with other AI capabilities—such as reinforcement learning, causal inference, and multi-agent systems—is pushing enterprises towards **autonomous decision support** platforms. These systems can proactively monitor data streams, detect anomalies, recommend actions, and even execute routine decisions within predefined guardrails.

Imagine a telecom operator whose AI continuously analyzes subscriber behavior and network performance to autonomously adjust pricing, launch targeted campaigns, or flag fraud — all while providing human supervisors with natural language summaries and alerts.

Such hybrid human-AI decision ecosystems will enable organizations to respond faster, innovate continuously, and maintain competitive advantage in an increasingly complex global landscape.

Conclusion

Large Language Models are redefining business intelligence and decision support by transforming how organizations access, interpret, and act on data. Their unique ability to handle unstructured language data, generate contextual insights, and interact conversationally bridges the gap between humans and machines, making data-driven decisions more accessible and actionable.

As enterprises adopt these technologies, the focus must remain on **ethical, transparent, and collaborative AI**—ensuring LLMs amplify human intelligence, foster trust, and serve as catalysts for sustainable, inclusive growth.

In the chapters that follow, we will explore more domains where LLMs are making a profound impact, including programming assistance, education, customer support, and beyond — further illustrating the transformative power of language intelligence in the real world.

LLMs in Finance, E-Commerce, and Marketing

Large Language Models (LLMs) have moved from academic curiosities and experimental prototypes into powerful engines driving transformation across multiple industries. Their ability to understand, generate, and reason with human language enables them to disrupt traditional workflows, unlock new efficiencies, and create richer customer experiences. In this chapter, we explore the profound impact LLMs are having in three major sectors—finance, e-commerce, and marketing—highlighting practical applications, challenges, and future possibilities.

LLMs in Finance: Revolutionizing Decision-Making and Risk Management

The financial sector is among the earliest and most intensive adopters of AI, given the industry's reliance on massive textual data and the need for rapid, high-stakes decisions. LLMs enhance finance by transforming how information is processed, analyzed, and acted upon.

1. Financial Research and Analysis

Investment analysts and portfolio managers traditionally spend hours reading earnings reports, market news, regulatory filings, and economic forecasts. LLMs automate this laborious process by rapidly summarizing dense documents, extracting key insights, and even generating natural-language briefs tailored to decision-makers' specific interests. This accelerates research cycles and helps uncover trends that may be buried in unstructured data.

2. Risk Assessment and Compliance

Regulatory compliance is a labyrinth of evolving rules, dense policy documents, and risk disclosures. LLMs can parse these complex documents to identify potential compliance risks or regulatory changes that might affect portfolios or operations. They support anti-money laundering (AML) efforts by analyzing transaction logs, communications, and customer data to flag suspicious activity with higher precision. This mitigates regulatory penalties and financial losses.

3. Customer Interaction and Personalization

Banks and financial institutions use LLM-powered chatbots and virtual assistants to provide 24/7 customer service. These systems can handle complex queries—ranging from balance inquiries to loan advice—by understanding nuanced customer intent and context. They also enable hyper-personalized financial advice by integrating customers' transaction histories, goals, and risk preferences, helping democratize access to financial planning.

4. Fraud Detection and Prevention

LLMs help detect fraud patterns by analyzing transactional language and metadata for anomalies that are difficult to identify with rule-based systems alone. For example, natural language in support calls, emails, or chat transcripts can reveal social engineering attempts or suspicious behavioral cues. By combining text analysis with other AI modalities, financial institutions enhance their ability to protect customers and assets.

5. Algorithmic Trading and Market Sentiment Analysis

Financial markets react to news, social media, and geopolitical events expressed in language. LLMs process vast streams of textual data to gauge market sentiment, identify emerging risks, or spot trading opportunities. This natural language understanding complements quantitative models by integrating qualitative factors that often precede market moves.

LLMs in E-Commerce: Elevating Customer Experience and Operational Efficiency

E-commerce thrives on understanding customer needs, predicting preferences, and delivering seamless interactions—domains where LLMs excel. The fusion of vast product catalogs, customer reviews, and transactional data creates a fertile ground for language models to create value.

1. Personalized Recommendations and Search

Traditional recommendation engines often rely on explicit purchase history or simple collaborative filtering. LLMs enrich these systems by interpreting natural language queries, understanding customer reviews, and capturing contextual preferences that go beyond surface-level patterns. For example, a customer searching for "lightweight running shoes with good arch support" can receive precise recommendations informed by product descriptions and user feedback analyzed by an LLM.

2. Conversational Shopping Assistants

Chatbots powered by LLMs offer interactive, human-like shopping experiences. They can answer detailed questions about product specifications, availability, and delivery timelines. Moreover, these assistants can handle complex multi-turn dialogues, helping customers narrow down choices, compare products, and even upsell complementary items — all in natural language.

3. Content Creation and Management

E-commerce platforms require continuous content generation: product descriptions, marketing copy, FAQs, and review summarizations. LLMs automate much of this workload by generating high-quality, SEO-optimized text at scale. This not only reduces operational costs but also improves content consistency and freshness, which are critical for search rankings and customer trust.

4. Customer Feedback Analysis and Sentiment Mining

Millions of product reviews, support tickets, and social media mentions are a goldmine of insights but overwhelming to analyze manually. LLMs classify and summarize customer sentiment, identify emerging product issues, and even extract feature requests or competitive intelligence. This real-time feedback loop helps brands adapt their offerings and resolve issues proactively.

5. Localization and Multilingual Support

Global e-commerce businesses face the challenge of serving diverse markets with different languages and cultural contexts. Multilingual LLMs facilitate accurate translation and localization of product information, customer communications, and marketing content, enabling brands to expand internationally without compromising quality or user experience.

LLMs in Marketing: Driving Creativity, Precision, and Engagement

Marketing is fundamentally about language — crafting messages that resonate, influence, and convert. LLMs amplify marketers' capabilities by combining data-driven insights with creative generation and automation.

1. Automated Content Generation

Marketers need a steady stream of content — blogs, emails, social media posts, ads, whitepapers — often under tight deadlines. LLMs can generate draft copy, headlines, and creative ideas that marketers can refine and personalize, significantly speeding up campaign development. They enable rapid A/B testing of different tones, messages, and formats.

2. Audience Segmentation and Targeting

By analyzing customer data, social media interactions, and purchase histories expressed in natural language, LLMs uncover nuanced audience segments based on preferences, behaviors, and sentiment. This granular understanding allows marketers to tailor messages with precision, improving engagement and conversion rates while minimizing waste.

3. Social Media Monitoring and Brand Reputation Management

Brands operate in a constant stream of public opinion. LLMs monitor social media platforms, forums, and review sites to detect shifts in sentiment, emerging trends, or potential PR crises early. By automatically summarizing public discourse, these models empower marketing teams to respond swiftly and strategically.

4. Personalized Customer Engagement

Beyond broad campaigns, LLMs enable personalized, context-aware customer interactions across email, chat, and voice channels. For example, email campaigns powered by LLMs can dynamically adjust content based on recipients' past interactions, preferences, and real-time engagement signals, improving relevance and ROI.

5. Market Research and Competitive Intelligence

LLMs assist in scanning and synthesizing vast volumes of market reports, competitor websites, and customer reviews. They extract actionable insights on market trends, emerging needs, and competitive positioning. This accelerates strategic planning and helps marketers identify white spaces for innovation.

6. Ethical and Responsible Messaging

As marketing messages become increasingly personalized and generated at scale, ethical considerations come to the forefront. LLMs offer tools to audit content for bias, compliance with advertising standards, and cultural sensitivity, helping organizations maintain trust and avoid reputational risks.

Challenges and Considerations Across Sectors

While the impact of LLMs in finance, e-commerce, and marketing is transformative, it is accompanied by challenges that enterprises must address:

- **Data Privacy and Security:** Handling sensitive customer and financial data demands rigorous governance to prevent leaks and misuse.
- **Bias and Fairness:** Models trained on historical data may propagate biases, necessitating careful evaluation and mitigation strategies.
- **Explainability:** For high-stakes decisions in finance especially, understanding the rationale behind model outputs is crucial for regulatory compliance and trust.

- **Integration with Legacy Systems:** Embedding LLM capabilities into existing IT infrastructures requires thoughtful design to maximize benefits and minimize disruptions.
- **Cost and Resource Efficiency:** Large models require substantial computational resources, which must be balanced with operational budgets and sustainability goals.

The Road Ahead: Expanding Horizons

The convergence of LLMs with other AI modalities—vision, speech, structured data—and the development of agentic AI capable of autonomous reasoning promise even deeper integration of language intelligence in these sectors. Financial advisors powered by LLMs may soon offer real-time portfolio management recommendations based on market news and client goals. E-commerce platforms could feature fully conversational shopping experiences with AI agents that understand customer lifestyles and preferences holistically. Marketing may evolve towards hyper-personalized omnichannel campaigns orchestrated by AI systems that continuously learn and adapt.

The real-world impact of LLMs in finance, e-commerce, and marketing is just the beginning. These models are reshaping industries by transforming how organizations understand data, engage with customers, and make decisions — paving the way for a future where human creativity and machine intelligence amplify each other in unprecedented ways.

Human + AI Collaboration in the Workplace

The integration of Large Language Models (LLMs) into the workplace marks a profound shift in how humans and machines interact to produce value, solve problems, and innovate. Far beyond mere automation or tool augmentation, LLMs enable a new paradigm of collaboration where human creativity, judgment, and empathy combine with AI's scalability, speed, and data-driven insights. This chapter explores how this evolving partnership transforms workflows, empowers knowledge workers, and redefines roles across industries.

The New Collaboration Model: Augmentation, Not Replacement

One of the most important clarifications about LLMs in the workplace is that they are not designed to replace humans but to augment human capabilities. While early waves of automation threatened routine jobs, modern AI is increasingly focused on enhancing complex cognitive work — enabling humans to focus on higher-value activities that require contextual understanding, ethics, and emotional intelligence.

LLMs serve as collaborative partners that assist in processing vast amounts of information, generating options, and enabling more informed decision-making. This shift moves the workplace from a human-versus-machine mindset to one of human-plus-machine synergy.

Enhanced Productivity and Efficiency

At the most immediate level, LLMs amplify productivity by automating time-consuming language-based tasks. This includes drafting emails, summarizing documents, generating reports, translating content, and extracting key insights from unstructured data sources such as meeting transcripts or customer feedback.

Because LLMs can adapt to diverse formats and languages, they reduce bottlenecks caused by linguistic or knowledge barriers — a critical factor in globalized enterprises and emerging markets. For example, employees who once spent hours parsing through dense legal contracts can rely on AI to highlight relevant clauses and flag risks, freeing them to concentrate on negotiation strategy rather than manual review.

Moreover, LLMs' ability to generate contextual suggestions and reminders during writing or coding tasks transforms the nature of work itself. They act like a knowledgeable assistant who anticipates needs and offers just-in-time expertise, drastically reducing cognitive load.

Empowering Knowledge Workers and Creatives

In knowledge-intensive roles — such as research, law, finance, healthcare, and marketing — LLMs open new frontiers of creativity and insight. By surfacing relevant data points from vast corpora, LLMs enable experts to formulate hypotheses faster and with broader context. For instance, scientists can accelerate literature reviews, doctors can quickly cross-reference symptoms and treatment protocols, and financial analysts can generate detailed risk assessments based on real-time data streams.

Creative professionals also benefit from AI collaboration. Writers, designers, and content creators use LLMs as brainstorming partners to generate fresh ideas, draft narratives, or explore alternative phrasings. This interaction fuels iterative creativity, where human judgment shapes AI-generated outputs into refined, high-quality work.

Importantly, the collaborative workflow is bidirectional. Humans guide the AI with prompts, edits, and ethical oversight, while AI expands the range of possibilities and reduces friction.

Democratization of Expertise

One of the most profound societal impacts of LLMs is the democratization of knowledge and expertise. AI-powered workplace tools lower the barriers to entry for complex tasks that traditionally required years of specialized training. For example, customer service representatives can handle more complex inquiries with AI-suggested responses; small business owners can generate professional marketing content without hiring expensive agencies; frontline workers can access instant language translation and domain knowledge support.

This democratization enables enterprises to unlock latent talent and foster more inclusive workplaces. It also supports development goals by empowering users in emerging markets with tools previously out of reach.

Collaboration Across Language and Culture

Language is often a major barrier in multinational organizations and global markets. LLMs' multilingual capabilities help bridge this gap by offering near-real-time translation, localization, and cultural adaptation of text and speech. This fosters smoother communication among diverse teams and more effective engagement with customers worldwide.

The AI's ability to understand nuanced language also supports better sentiment analysis and cultural context interpretation, which is vital in crafting sensitive communications or marketing strategies tailored to local audiences.

Facilitating Learning and Continuous Improvement

Workplace collaboration with AI is not static but adaptive and continuous. LLMs improve over time with fine-tuning, feedback loops, and integration of organizational data. This ongoing learning helps AI align more closely with company goals, compliance requirements, and unique workflows.

Furthermore, AI systems facilitate continuous learning for employees themselves by providing on-demand explanations, training modules, and just-in-time coaching. For example, a sales professional preparing for a call can use AI to rehearse responses and receive feedback on tone or phrasing. This real-time assistance supports skill development and boosts confidence.

Ethical Collaboration and Transparency

As AI becomes a collaborator rather than a mere tool, the ethical dimension of workplace AI use grows more important. Transparency about when and how AI contributes to decisions is critical to maintaining trust among employees, customers, and regulators. Organizations must ensure that AI outputs are explainable, fair, and free from harmful biases — particularly in decisions affecting hiring, promotions, or customer treatment.

Moreover, human oversight remains essential. While LLMs can surface options or draft responses, ultimate judgment and responsibility rest with humans. Training programs should prepare workers to understand AI's strengths and limitations, fostering a culture of responsible AI use.

Challenges in Adoption and Integration

Despite its promise, AI collaboration in the workplace faces several challenges:

- **Data privacy and security:** Sensitive corporate information must be protected as LLMs process and generate text.
- **Change management:** Employees may fear job displacement or distrust AI recommendations; transparent communication and training are key.
- **Bias mitigation:** AI systems trained on vast datasets can inherit social biases; proactive auditing and correction mechanisms are necessary.
- **Integration complexity:** Embedding LLMs into existing workflows, software, and enterprise architecture requires careful design and

customization.

Addressing these challenges is essential to realizing the full potential of human + AI collaboration.

Looking Ahead: The Future Workplace

The trajectory is clear: AI will become an indispensable collaborator in the workplace, transforming not only how work is done but also what work means. Roles will evolve as humans focus more on strategy, creativity, and empathy, supported by AI's ability to handle scale, complexity, and detail.

As models become more agentic — able to plan, reason, and interact over extended conversations and workflows — workplaces will shift toward dynamic partnerships between humans and AI systems. This will create new opportunities for innovation, inclusion, and productivity that were previously unimaginable.

Conclusion

Human + AI collaboration in the workplace is already reshaping industries worldwide, blending human ingenuity with artificial intelligence's transformative power. By embracing this partnership thoughtfully — balancing efficiency with ethics, automation with empathy — organizations can unlock unprecedented value and build future-ready workforces capable of navigating a complex, interconnected world.

CHAPTER TEN

Responsible AI — Ethics, Safety, and Governance

Bias and Fairness in Language Models

As artificial intelligence becomes deeply integrated into daily life and critical business functions, the stakes for ethical and fair AI systems have never been higher. Among the most pressing ethical challenges in AI—especially in large language models (LLMs)—are issues of **bias** and **fairness**. Understanding these concepts, their origins, and their implications is vital for responsible AI development and deployment.

What is Bias in Language Models?

Bias in language models refers to the presence of systematic and unfair prejudices embedded within the AI's behavior, outputs, or decision-making processes. These biases often reflect historical, societal, or cultural inequalities found in the data the models are trained on. Since LLMs learn from massive text corpora sourced from the internet, books, articles, social media, and other publicly available content, they inevitably absorb both explicit and subtle biases present in human language.

These biases can manifest in several ways, including:

- **Stereotyping:** Assigning specific attributes or roles to particular groups based on gender, ethnicity, religion, nationality, or other identity factors.
- **Discrimination:** Producing outputs that disadvantage or marginalize certain populations.
- **Exclusion:** Ignoring or underrepresenting minority voices and experiences.
- **Overgeneralization:** Applying learned patterns too rigidly without contextual nuance, thereby reinforcing harmful narratives.

Because language is so deeply tied to culture, identity, and power structures, the presence of bias in language models can have profound social consequences. This is especially critical when AI systems are used in sensitive domains like hiring, healthcare, law enforcement, credit scoring, and content moderation.

Sources of Bias

Bias in language models arises primarily from three interconnected sources:

1. **Training Data:**
   The datasets used to train LLMs are vast and often scraped from publicly available internet sources. These texts contain historical prejudices, cultural assumptions, and unbalanced representations. For instance, literature and online discourse may disproportionately feature certain demographics or viewpoints, while others are marginalized or stereotyped. Models trained on such data mirror these biases, sometimes amplifying them unintentionally.
2. **Model Architecture and Training Processes:**
   Although model architectures like Transformers are designed to capture statistical patterns in language, they lack true understanding or judgment. During training, optimization objectives focus on predicting the next word or sentence, which can reinforce common but biased associations. Without intervention, models learn and propagate these statistical regularities without questioning their fairness or accuracy.
3. **Deployment Context and User Interaction:**
   The way models are fine-tuned, prompted, or integrated into applications can influence biased behavior. User queries, cultural context, and the specific task can expose or mitigate bias. Furthermore,

feedback loops can emerge where biased outputs shape human responses, which in turn influence future training data or usage.

Fairness: What Does It Mean for AI?

Fairness in AI implies that models should treat all individuals and groups equitably, without favoritism or prejudice, ensuring that the benefits and harms of AI systems are distributed justly. However, fairness is a complex, context-dependent concept that varies across cultures, legal systems, and ethical frameworks.

Key considerations in AI fairness include:

- **Equality of Treatment:** Ensuring that the AI system's outputs do not disproportionately disadvantage any group.
- **Equity of Outcome:** Recognizing that equal treatment may not suffice if historical disadvantages require corrective measures.
- **Transparency:** Making model behavior understandable so stakeholders can assess fairness.
- **Accountability:** Establishing mechanisms to address harms and correct bias.

In practice, fairness involves a delicate balance. For example, a language model deployed in hiring might need to avoid gender or ethnic bias, but also ensure that relevant skills and qualifications are fairly assessed.

Real-World Impacts of Bias in Language Models

Unchecked bias in language models can have tangible negative impacts across sectors:

- **Hiring and Recruitment:** AI-driven resume screening tools may inadvertently favor candidates from dominant groups, perpetuating workplace inequality.
- **Healthcare:** Language models assisting in diagnostics or patient communication may misunderstand or misrepresent symptoms in minority populations.

- **Legal Systems:** AI tools for case analysis or sentencing recommendations risk reinforcing existing racial or socioeconomic disparities.
- **Content Moderation:** Automated systems may misclassify or censor marginalized voices while failing to flag harmful content from dominant groups.
- **Financial Services:** Credit scoring algorithms powered by language data may discriminate against underserved communities.

In all these cases, biased AI can exacerbate social inequities, damage trust, and create legal and reputational risks for organizations.

Strategies to Mitigate Bias

Addressing bias in language models requires a multi-layered, ongoing approach combining technical, organizational, and societal efforts:

1. **Diverse and Representative Training Data:**
   Curate training datasets that include balanced representation across demographics, languages, cultures, and viewpoints. Techniques such as data augmentation and targeted sampling can help amplify minority voices.
2. **Bias Detection and Measurement:**
   Develop robust metrics and evaluation frameworks to identify biases systematically. Tools like fairness audits, bias benchmarks, and adversarial testing help expose problematic behavior before deployment.
3. **Algorithmic Fairness Techniques:**
   Apply methods such as debiasing embeddings, adversarial training, and differential privacy to reduce learned prejudices. Incorporate fairness constraints during training and fine-tuning to balance accuracy and equity.
4. **Human-in-the-Loop Systems:**
   Maintain human oversight in critical decisions and continuously monitor model outputs. Human reviewers can catch biases that automated tools miss and provide contextual judgment.
5. **Transparent Model Documentation:**
   Publish clear model cards, datasheets, and impact assessments that disclose training data sources, limitations, and known biases.

Transparency builds trust and enables informed decision-making.

6. **Inclusive Design and Stakeholder Engagement:**
   Engage diverse user groups, ethicists, domain experts, and affected communities during model development and deployment. Their perspectives help identify risks and design fairer systems.
7. **Regulatory and Ethical Frameworks:**
   Align AI development with evolving legal standards and ethical guidelines such as GDPR, the AI Act, or industry-specific codes of conduct. Responsible governance ensures accountability.

The Ethical Imperative

Fairness is not a technical detail but a fundamental human value. As AI systems increasingly influence decisions with real-world consequences, it is imperative to design language models that promote social justice rather than reinforce injustice.

Achieving fairness demands continuous vigilance, humility, and a commitment to listening to marginalized voices. It requires balancing innovation with caution and prioritizing the well-being of all stakeholders.

Conclusion

Bias and fairness are among the most critical ethical challenges facing language models today. Understanding their origins, recognizing their impacts, and proactively addressing them is essential for building trustworthy AI systems. As language models become integral to enterprise operations, customer interactions, and societal infrastructures, responsible stewardship of these technologies will define their true value.

By integrating fairness at every stage—from data curation through deployment—developers, businesses, and policymakers can ensure that language models not only amplify human potential but do so equitably, inclusively, and with respect for our shared humanity.

Privacy, Consent, and Data Stewardship

In the era of Large Language Models (LLMs) and AI systems that increasingly interact with human language, privacy, consent, and data stewardship emerge as foundational pillars of responsible AI. These principles not only protect individual rights but also build trust and legitimacy in AI deployments, especially in sensitive domains such as healthcare, finance, telecommunications, and legal services.

As enterprises harness LLMs for tasks ranging from customer support automation to fraud detection, how data is collected, stored, processed, and shared becomes a critical ethical and legal issue. This section explores the challenges and best practices surrounding privacy, consent, and stewardship to ensure AI technologies serve humanity while respecting fundamental rights.

1. Privacy: Protecting Personal and Sensitive Information

Privacy is a fundamental human right recognized globally, enshrined in frameworks such as the EU's General Data Protection Regulation (GDPR), California Consumer Privacy Act (CCPA), and many national laws. It refers to an individual's control over their personal information and freedom from unauthorized intrusion.

AI systems, especially LLMs, rely heavily on data — often unstructured text, voice calls, messages, and interaction logs — that can contain sensitive personal details. Protecting this data from exposure, misuse, or breach is paramount.

- **Data Minimization:** AI models should be trained and operated on the minimum data necessary to achieve their objectives. Avoid collecting or retaining excessive personally identifiable information (PII) unless absolutely essential.
- **Anonymization and De-identification:** Before data enters AI training pipelines or inference environments, it should be stripped of direct identifiers such as names, phone numbers, and addresses. Techniques like tokenization, pseudonymization, and differential privacy help ensure individuals cannot be re-identified from the data.
- **Secure Data Storage and Access Controls:** Enterprise systems must implement strong encryption at rest and in transit, role-based access controls, and audit logs. This limits exposure and tracks any access or usage of sensitive data.
- **Privacy-Preserving AI Techniques:** Emerging methods such as federated learning, homomorphic encryption, and secure multi-party

computation allow AI models to learn from data without directly exposing the raw data itself. These approaches are especially valuable for on-device intelligence and decentralized systems.
- **Risk of Data Leakage from Models:** LLMs trained on large corpora may inadvertently memorize and regurgitate sensitive information seen during training. Rigorous testing, data filtering, and model fine-tuning are required to mitigate these risks.

2. Consent: Empowering Individuals with Agency

Consent is the ethical and often legal basis for collecting, processing, and sharing personal data. It ensures individuals understand how their data will be used and grants permission voluntarily, with full awareness of implications.

- **Informed Consent:** Consent must be meaningful — users should receive clear, accessible explanations about what data is collected, for what purpose, how it will be processed, and for how long it will be retained. Technical jargon or vague statements undermine genuine understanding.
- **Granularity and Choice:** Whenever possible, consent mechanisms should allow individuals to choose which types of data they agree to share and for which purposes. For instance, a customer might consent to data use for customer service but not for marketing.
- **Dynamic and Revocable Consent:** Consent is not a one-time checkbox. Users should be able to review, modify, or withdraw consent at any time, and systems must respect these changes promptly.
- **Special Considerations for Vulnerable Groups:** Extra care must be taken when AI systems process data from minors, marginalized communities, or people with limited digital literacy. Mechanisms for consent must be adapted to protect these groups from exploitation or harm.
- **Transparency Through User Interfaces:** In AI-driven products, consent should be integrated naturally into the user experience — for example, through privacy dashboards, notifications, and real-time prompts before data is collected or shared.

3. Data Stewardship: Ethical Responsibility in Managing Data

Data stewardship extends beyond legal compliance. It encompasses the ethical obligation to handle data with care, respect, and foresight — especially in AI systems whose impact can ripple widely and unexpectedly.

- **Accountability and Governance Structures:** Organizations must designate data stewards and AI ethics officers responsible for overseeing data handling and AI use. This includes monitoring compliance, assessing risks, and addressing harms when they arise.
- **Data Quality and Integrity:** Stewardship means ensuring data used for AI training and inference is accurate, unbiased, and representative. Poor quality or skewed data leads to flawed models that can perpetuate misinformation, discrimination, or faulty decisions.
- **Ethical Use of Data:** Data should never be used to manipulate, deceive, or discriminate against individuals or groups. This includes preventing AI-driven profiling that reinforces social inequalities or violates human dignity.
- **Cross-Border Data Flows and Jurisdictional Challenges:** Many enterprises operate globally, making data stewardship complex across different legal regimes. Organizations must navigate these with respect for local privacy laws while maintaining high standards universally.
- **Transparency and Explainability:** Data provenance — the history of where data came from and how it was processed — should be documented and made available when needed to build trust and enable auditing.
- **Balancing Innovation and Protection:** While data enables innovation in AI, stewardship requires balancing rapid development with cautious, ethical deployment. This might mean staging releases, rigorous testing, and ongoing impact assessments.

4. Practical Implementation in AI and LLM Contexts

When developing and deploying LLM-based AI, integrating privacy, consent, and stewardship principles requires deliberate design and ongoing vigilance.

- **Privacy by Design:** Embed privacy and data protection mechanisms at every stage — from data collection to model training, inference, and deployment.
- **User-Centric Controls:** Provide end-users with tools to view, edit, or delete their data. This builds trust and aligns with regulatory requirements.
- **Audit Trails and Compliance Reporting:** Maintain detailed logs of data processing activities, consent records, and AI model decisions to support compliance and transparency.
- **Ethical Review Boards:** Establish multidisciplinary committees including legal experts, ethicists, data scientists, and community representatives to evaluate AI projects, ensuring privacy and consent standards are upheld.
- **Continuous Monitoring:** Implement systems to detect and respond to privacy breaches, consent violations, or unethical data use in real time.
- **Education and Awareness:** Train AI practitioners, data engineers, and business leaders on privacy principles, consent best practices, and stewardship responsibilities to embed an ethical culture.

5. Challenges and Future Directions

- **Evolving Regulations:** Privacy laws continue to evolve rapidly worldwide, creating a shifting compliance landscape. AI teams must stay informed and agile.
- **Complex Consent in AI Ecosystems:** Consent management grows complicated in multi-party data ecosystems — for example, when data is shared among partners or used to train third-party AI models.
- **Balancing Personalization and Privacy:** AI-driven personalization requires detailed data, which can conflict with privacy preservation. Finding this balance is a key design challenge.
- **Algorithmic Transparency vs. Data Privacy:** Explaining AI decisions often requires revealing data inputs, which can conflict with privacy protections. Developing privacy-respecting explainability methods is an active research area.
- **Cultural Variations in Privacy Expectations:** Privacy norms differ globally; designing AI systems that respect these nuances while

maintaining core ethical standards is critical for global enterprises.

Conclusion

Privacy, consent, and data stewardship are not ancillary considerations but essential cornerstones for responsible AI. They ensure that as language models and AI systems become more powerful, they do so with respect for human dignity, autonomy, and trust.

For enterprises and practitioners, embedding these principles demands deliberate design, rigorous governance, and a commitment to ongoing ethical reflection. Only then can AI's promise be fulfilled — a transformative tool that augments human intelligence while protecting the rights and freedoms that define our humanity.

Transparency and Explainability

As artificial intelligence, particularly large language models (LLMs), become deeply embedded in critical decision-making, communication, and automation processes, the principles of transparency and explainability rise from technical concerns to ethical imperatives. Transparency and explainability are foundational pillars that support trust, accountability, and responsible deployment of AI systems in enterprises, governments, and society at large.

Understanding Transparency in AI

Transparency refers to the openness and clarity around how AI systems function, the data they are trained on, the decisions they make, and the potential limitations and biases they may carry. It's about illuminating the "black box" of AI so that stakeholders — from developers and businesses to regulators and end-users — can understand what the AI is doing and why.

In practice, transparency involves multiple layers:

- **Data transparency:** Clear documentation about the datasets used for training and fine-tuning, including their sources, coverage, representativeness, and any known biases or gaps.

- **Model transparency:** Information about the architecture of the AI models, their training processes, tuning parameters, and updates. While some technical details may be proprietary, sufficient disclosure is necessary to understand capabilities and risks.
- **Decision transparency:** Explanations or rationales for AI-generated outputs, especially when these outputs impact human lives—such as loan approvals, medical diagnoses, or legal recommendations.

Transparency empowers users and regulators to scrutinize AI systems, detect unfairness or errors, and take corrective actions. It is the cornerstone of **accountability**, ensuring that organizations deploying AI remain answerable for its outcomes.

The Challenge of Explainability

While transparency is about revealing what's inside the AI system, **explainability** addresses the "why" and "how" of AI decisions in a way that humans can grasp. Explainability is critical because:

- AI models, especially large and complex ones like LLMs, generate results based on millions or billions of parameters learned from massive data.
- Their reasoning processes are not inherently interpretable by humans; they do not "think" like people but operate through statistical associations and patterns.
- Without explainability, users are left trusting outputs blindly, risking automation bias where humans over-rely on AI without scrutiny.

Explainability means developing methods and tools to provide meaningful, accessible, and actionable insights into the AI's decision process. It can range from:

- **Feature importance analysis:** Identifying which inputs most influenced the model's output.
- **Counterfactual explanations:** Showing how small changes in input would have changed the result.
- **Rule extraction:** Simplifying model behavior into human-readable rules or logic.

- **Example-based explanations:** Presenting similar past cases or outputs that inform current decisions.

Why Transparency and Explainability Matter

1. **Building User Trust**
   Transparency and explainability are prerequisites for building trust with users. When people understand why an AI made a particular decision or recommendation, they are more likely to accept and effectively collaborate with the system. This trust is crucial in sensitive domains like healthcare, finance, and criminal justice, where errors or biases can have profound consequences.
2. **Enabling Ethical and Fair AI**
   Explainability allows organizations to identify and mitigate biases or unfair outcomes embedded in models. For example, if a model disproportionately denies loans to a particular demographic, explainability helps uncover the contributing factors—be it skewed training data or flawed feature selection—and guides remediation.
3. **Facilitating Regulatory Compliance**
   Many jurisdictions are now introducing laws and regulations mandating AI transparency and explainability. For instance, the European Union's AI Act and GDPR's "right to explanation" require organizations to provide clear information about automated decisions affecting individuals. Transparent and explainable AI supports compliance and reduces legal risks.
4. **Supporting Continuous Improvement and Safety**
   Explainability is key for monitoring AI performance post-deployment. By understanding failure modes and decision patterns, organizations can fine-tune models, update data, and improve robustness. It also aids in identifying unintended harmful behaviors early, preventing safety risks.
5. **Empowering Stakeholders Across the Value Chain**
   Transparency is not just for technical teams. Executives, business users, regulators, customers, and civil society all have a stake. Clear and accessible explanations democratize understanding, enabling informed decisions about AI adoption, use, and oversight.

Balancing Transparency with Complexity and Privacy

Achieving transparency and explainability in large language models presents unique challenges:

- **Scale and Complexity:** LLMs can have hundreds of billions of parameters and are trained on vast, heterogeneous datasets. Explaining decisions at this scale is non-trivial and often requires sophisticated approximation methods.
- **Trade-offs Between Accuracy and Interpretability:** Simpler, interpretable models may sacrifice performance, while more accurate models may be less explainable. The key is finding a balance appropriate to the use case, risk level, and user needs.
- **Protecting Intellectual Property:** Organizations may hesitate to disclose detailed model architectures or data due to competitive concerns. Designing transparency frameworks that respect proprietary information while providing sufficient clarity is essential.
- **Data Privacy and Security:** Transparency about data use must also respect user privacy and comply with data protection regulations. Disclosing training data sources should avoid exposing sensitive or personal information.

Emerging Approaches and Best Practices

To address these challenges, the AI community and enterprises are adopting multiple strategies:

- **Explainability Toolkits and Frameworks:** Open-source tools like SHAP (SHapley Additive exPlanations), LIME (Local Interpretable Model-agnostic Explanations), and integrated visualization dashboards help interpret AI outputs.
- **Model Cards and Data Sheets:** Standardized documentation formats that describe model capabilities, limitations, intended use, and ethical considerations. These "model cards" provide transparency in a digestible format.

- **Human-in-the-Loop Systems:** Combining AI with human judgment ensures that critical decisions are reviewed and explanations contextualized.
- **Transparent AI Governance:** Establishing cross-functional AI ethics boards and governance frameworks that oversee transparency policies, audits, and communication with stakeholders.
- **User-Centered Explanations:** Designing explanations that are tailored to different user groups — from technical experts to end-users — using language and formats they understand.

Looking Ahead: Transparency as a Foundation for Trustworthy AI

As AI continues to advance, transparency and explainability will evolve from optional features to foundational requirements embedded in the entire AI lifecycle — from design and development to deployment and ongoing monitoring.

The future promises:

- **Explainable-by-Design Models:** Architectures and training methods that inherently support interpretability without sacrificing performance.
- **Interactive Explanations:** Dynamic, context-aware explanations that adapt based on user feedback and needs.
- **Regulatory Standards:** International norms and legal frameworks that define minimum transparency and explainability requirements.
- **Collaborative AI Systems:** AI systems that work alongside humans with shared understanding and mutual accountability, made possible only through transparent and explainable mechanisms.

Conclusion

Transparency and explainability are not merely technical challenges but ethical commitments. They ensure that AI systems respect human values, empower informed decision-making, and foster trust in an increasingly automated world. For businesses, embracing transparency is not just about compliance—it's about leadership in responsible AI innovation, unlocking

AI's transformative potential while safeguarding society.

By prioritizing transparency and explainability, we pave the way toward AI systems that are not only intelligent but also accountable, fair, and aligned with the best interests of humanity.

Regulatory Landscapes and Compliance

As large language models (LLMs) and AI systems grow in complexity and capability, their integration into business, society, and everyday life brings unprecedented opportunities — but also significant risks. These risks extend beyond technical limitations and encompass critical ethical, legal, and societal concerns. In this evolving environment, regulatory frameworks and compliance mechanisms are essential to ensure AI development and deployment are safe, fair, transparent, and accountable.

Understanding the regulatory landscape is crucial not only for legal adherence but also for building trust with users, customers, and society at large. Compliance with emerging and established regulations shapes how organizations innovate responsibly, mitigate risks, and harness AI's transformative potential.

The Rise of AI Regulation: A Global Overview

Governments, multilateral bodies, and regulatory agencies around the world are actively shaping AI governance. Unlike traditional technologies, AI systems — especially LLMs — challenge existing regulatory paradigms due to their scale, opacity, and unpredictability. Regulations are developing at different paces and scopes across regions, reflecting diverse cultural values, economic priorities, and political systems.

European Union (EU): The EU is at the forefront of comprehensive AI regulation. Its proposed **Artificial Intelligence Act (AI Act)** aims to classify AI systems based on risk levels— from minimal to unacceptable. The AI Act mandates strict requirements for high-risk AI applications, including transparency, documentation, human oversight, robustness, and data quality. For language models, this means rigorous evaluation to prevent harm in critical domains like healthcare, employment, or law enforcement. The EU also enforces the **General Data Protection Regulation (GDPR)**, which governs data privacy and impacts AI training data, model explainability, and user consent.

United States (US): The US regulatory approach is more sector-specific and decentralized. Agencies like the Federal Trade Commission (FTC) focus on preventing deceptive practices, bias, and privacy violations. The National Institute of Standards and Technology (NIST) has developed AI risk management frameworks emphasizing trustworthy AI. At the federal level, multiple bills are under discussion, aiming to set standards for transparency, accountability, and bias mitigation. States like California have introduced privacy laws that affect AI data handling. The US approach encourages innovation while trying to balance ethical concerns.

China: China's regulatory environment for AI emphasizes national security, social stability, and technological leadership. The government enforces strict rules on data sovereignty, content control, and algorithmic transparency. Recent guidelines require companies to disclose how AI systems work, especially those that influence public opinion or user behavior. The Chinese framework aims to control misinformation and promote "positive" AI use aligned with state priorities.

Other Regions: Countries in Asia, Africa, and Latin America are developing diverse AI policies, often inspired by global frameworks but tailored to local contexts. International bodies like the OECD and UNESCO are working to establish global AI ethics guidelines emphasizing human rights, fairness, and inclusiveness.

Key Regulatory Themes Relevant to LLMs and AI Systems

Several recurring themes define regulatory priorities for AI governance, especially for language models that interact with people at scale and process vast amounts of data:

1. **Transparency and Explainability**
   Regulations increasingly demand that AI systems are transparent about how decisions are made. For LLMs, this means disclosing model capabilities, limitations, and potential biases in accessible language. Explainability also involves enabling human users and regulators to understand the rationale behind AI outputs — a challenging task for complex neural architectures. Compliance requires organizations to document model training data, algorithms, and evaluation procedures, and to provide meaningful explanations for automated decisions that affect individuals.

2. **Fairness and Non-Discrimination**
   AI systems must avoid perpetuating or amplifying societal biases related to race, gender, ethnicity, disability, or socioeconomic status. For language models, this involves addressing biased language patterns learned from training data. Regulators require regular audits, impact assessments, and mitigation strategies to ensure fairness. Compliance demands proactive bias testing and adjustments to models and datasets, along with monitoring for disparate impacts post-deployment.
3. **Privacy and Data Protection**
   LLMs depend on massive datasets, often containing sensitive or personal information. Regulations like GDPR impose strict requirements on data collection, processing, consent, storage, and sharing. Organizations must implement privacy-by-design principles and safeguard against unauthorized data use or leakage. Compliance means adopting techniques such as data anonymization, differential privacy, and secure data governance frameworks.
4. **Accountability and Human Oversight**
   Regulatory frameworks emphasize that humans must retain meaningful control over AI systems, especially in high-stakes applications. This includes the ability to intervene, override, or halt automated processes. Organizations are held accountable for AI outcomes, requiring clear governance structures, roles, and responsibilities. Documentation and audit trails must demonstrate compliance with oversight policies.
5. **Safety and Robustness**
   AI systems must be reliable and resilient against errors, adversarial attacks, or misuse. For LLMs, this involves thorough testing to prevent harmful outputs such as misinformation, hate speech, or unsafe recommendations. Regulations mandate robustness standards and incident response protocols to minimize risk to users and society.
6. **Environmental and Social Impact**
   The computational intensity of training and deploying LLMs has significant environmental implications. Increasingly, regulations and industry best practices call for sustainability considerations in AI lifecycle management. Social impact assessments ensure AI contributes positively without exacerbating inequalities or societal harms.

Compliance Challenges for Enterprises

Implementing AI regulation compliance presents complex challenges for businesses adopting LLMs and related AI technologies:

- **Complexity of AI Systems**
  The technical complexity and opaqueness of LLMs make it difficult to achieve transparency and explainability. Organizations need to invest in specialized tools, interdisciplinary teams, and ongoing monitoring.
- **Dynamic and Evolving Models**
  LLMs continuously improve through fine-tuning and updates, complicating efforts to maintain documented compliance status. Enterprises must establish agile governance processes to track changes and reassess risks.
- **Cross-Jurisdictional Regulations**
  Global companies must navigate multiple, sometimes conflicting regulations across countries. Harmonizing compliance efforts while respecting local laws requires coordinated legal, technical, and policy strategies.
- **Data Governance and Privacy**
  Ensuring ethical data sourcing and usage requires end-to-end data governance frameworks, particularly when models are trained on third-party or public datasets.
- **Bias Mitigation**
  Detecting and mitigating bias is an ongoing process that demands specialized expertise and robust evaluation methodologies. Failure to comply can lead to legal penalties and reputational damage.

Strategies for Regulatory Compliance and Responsible AI Governance

To successfully navigate the regulatory landscape, enterprises must embed responsible AI practices into their core operations:

- **Establish AI Governance Frameworks**
  Create dedicated AI ethics and compliance committees that include legal, technical, and business stakeholders. Define clear policies on data

usage, model evaluation, transparency, and accountability.

- **Adopt Risk-Based Approaches**
  Prioritize compliance efforts based on AI system risk classification, focusing resources on high-impact applications.
- **Implement Continuous Monitoring**
  Use automated tools and human reviews to continuously assess AI behavior, fairness, and safety post-deployment.
- **Invest in Explainability Tools**
  Develop or integrate tools that provide interpretable insights into model decisions, tailored for different stakeholders (users, auditors, regulators).
- **Engage with Regulators and Industry Groups**
  Participate proactively in regulatory consultations, standard-setting initiatives, and ethical AI forums to stay ahead of emerging requirements.
- **Educate and Train Workforce**
  Build organizational AI literacy to empower employees at all levels to understand ethical issues and compliance obligations.

The Future of AI Regulation: Balancing Innovation and Protection

Regulatory frameworks around AI are still evolving. Policymakers face the difficult task of balancing innovation incentives with societal safeguards. Too little regulation risks harm, erosion of trust, and misuse; too much can stifle progress and competitiveness.

As AI systems, particularly LLMs, grow more agentic and autonomous, regulation will likely evolve toward:

- Emphasizing **explainability** and **human-AI collaboration**.
- Mandating **robust validation** and **impact assessments** throughout AI lifecycles.
- Expanding scope to include **multimodal and adaptive AI systems**.
- Supporting **international harmonization** to reduce fragmentation.
- Enforcing **ethical AI certification** and **auditability** as standard practices.

Enterprises that embed responsible AI practices early, align with regulatory expectations, and foster transparency and inclusiveness will be best positioned to lead in the AI-powered future.

Summary

Regulatory landscapes and compliance form the backbone of responsible AI governance. They ensure that the transformative power of large language models and AI is harnessed safely, ethically, and equitably. Understanding and proactively managing regulatory requirements empowers organizations to build trustworthy AI systems that respect human rights, uphold fairness, and foster innovation.

As AI technologies reshape industries and societies, regulatory compliance is not merely a legal obligation — it is a strategic imperative for sustainable AI adoption and impact.

Mitigating Risks: Red Teaming and Model Audits

As large language models (LLMs) and AI systems grow in capability and complexity, the imperative to ensure their safe, ethical, and reliable deployment has never been greater. These models influence decisions in healthcare, finance, law, education, and countless other domains, often directly affecting human lives and societal norms. While the transformative potential of AI is vast, it carries inherent risks—bias amplification, misinformation, unintended harms, privacy violations, and adversarial exploitation—that demand proactive mitigation strategies.

Among the most powerful and practical tools in the AI governance toolkit are **red teaming** and **model audits**. These processes enable organizations to identify vulnerabilities, assess ethical risks, and strengthen safeguards before AI systems are widely deployed or embedded into critical workflows.

The Rationale Behind Red Teaming and Model Audits

AI systems, especially those driven by LLMs, operate in complex, often unpredictable ways. Unlike traditional software, where bugs are usually repeatable errors in code logic, AI "failures" can stem from learned patterns in massive datasets or emergent behaviors that arise only under specific contexts. The black-box nature of neural models means that problems may not be apparent during initial testing, and unintended consequences can surface only after deployment.

To address this uncertainty, organizations must rigorously stress-test AI systems — not only for technical robustness but also for ethical alignment, fairness, and compliance with legal and societal standards. This requires adversarial, multidisciplinary, and iterative approaches that combine technical expertise with domain knowledge, user insights, and ethical reasoning.

What Is Red Teaming in AI?

Originating in cybersecurity and military defense, **red teaming** refers to the practice of simulating attacks or adversarial scenarios to uncover vulnerabilities in systems. In the context of AI, red teaming involves a dedicated group of experts intentionally probing and challenging AI models to expose weaknesses, biases, or potential misuse.

Red teams act as internal or external adversaries who test the system under real-world conditions and adversarial inputs — inputs that might exploit blind spots or gaps in the model's training, logic, or safeguards. They explore questions such as:

- Can the model be manipulated to produce harmful or biased content?
- How does the model behave under ambiguous or adversarial queries?
- Are there pathways for the model to leak sensitive or private information?
- Does the model reinforce stereotypes, misinformation, or harmful ideologies?
- How resilient is the model against prompt injections or adversarial attacks?

Red teaming is both a **technical** and **ethical** exercise. It requires diverse expertise spanning AI engineering, social sciences, ethics, law, and domain-specific knowledge (e.g., healthcare, finance). The goal is not only to "break" the model but to generate actionable insights that can inform remediation strategies, improved model design, and more effective user guidelines.

How Red Teaming Is Conducted

A typical red teaming process involves:

1. **Scenario Definition:** Identifying high-risk use cases, sensitive applications, and contexts where the AI's output could cause harm or violate policies.
2. **Adversarial Testing:** Designing adversarial prompts, edge cases, or input manipulations that stress-test the model's responses. This includes attempts to bypass safety filters or exploit model hallucinations.
3. **Behavior Analysis:** Examining model outputs for evidence of bias, toxicity, privacy leaks, or misleading information. This step often involves qualitative human review as well as automated detection tools.
4. **Reporting and Recommendations:** Documenting vulnerabilities and failure modes along with severity assessments, and recommending mitigation steps such as retraining, algorithmic adjustments, or policy changes.
5. **Iterative Improvement:** Incorporating red team findings into the development lifecycle, then retesting after improvements to verify risk reduction.

Some organizations engage **external red teams** to ensure impartiality and bring fresh perspectives, while others build in-house red teams embedded within their AI development cycles.

Model Audits: Systematic Evaluation Beyond Red Teaming

Complementary to red teaming, **model audits** involve comprehensive, structured assessments of an AI system's ethical, technical, and operational attributes. Where red teaming is adversarial and exploratory, audits are formalized and often mandated by regulatory or internal governance frameworks.

Model audits typically cover multiple dimensions, including:

- **Fairness and Bias:** Measuring disparate impacts across demographic groups, analyzing training data representativeness, and evaluating mitigation effectiveness.

- **Safety and Robustness:** Testing the model's reliability under varied inputs, including edge cases and stress conditions.
- **Privacy and Security:** Assessing risks of data leakage, membership inference attacks, or exposure of personally identifiable information.
- **Transparency and Explainability:** Evaluating how well model behavior can be interpreted or explained to stakeholders, users, and regulators.
- **Compliance and Governance:** Ensuring adherence to relevant laws, ethical guidelines, and organizational policies.

Audits are often carried out using a combination of automated tools (e.g., fairness metrics, adversarial testing frameworks), expert review panels, and stakeholder consultations. Increasingly, independent third-party audits are becoming a best practice and may be required for AI systems used in high-stakes or regulated environments.

Why These Processes Matter for Responsible AI

1. **Early Detection of Harm:** Red teaming and audits uncover problems before they reach end users, preventing reputational damage and real-world harm.
2. **Continuous Risk Management:** AI systems evolve through retraining and fine-tuning. Ongoing audits ensure risks are managed throughout the model's lifecycle.
3. **Building Trust:** Demonstrating rigorous risk assessment and mitigation builds confidence among users, customers, regulators, and the public.
4. **Informing Ethical Design:** Insights from red teams and audits guide developers toward more inclusive, transparent, and accountable AI systems.
5. **Regulatory Readiness:** As governments implement AI regulations, evidence from audits and red teams will be essential for compliance and certification.

Challenges and Future Directions

While red teaming and audits are critical, they face several challenges:

- **Scope and Scale:** LLMs are vast, complex, and continuously evolving, making exhaustive testing difficult.
- **Subjectivity in Ethics:** Assessing bias, fairness, and harm involves value judgments that can vary across cultures and stakeholders.
- **Resource Intensive:** Effective red teams require interdisciplinary talent and time-consuming manual reviews.
- **Adversarial Evolution:** Attackers constantly develop new ways to exploit models, requiring adaptive defense strategies.

To address these, the AI community is exploring:

- **Automated Red Teaming Tools:** Leveraging AI to generate adversarial inputs and detect failure modes at scale.
- **Standardized Auditing Frameworks:** Developing universal metrics, benchmarks, and reporting standards for responsible AI.
- **Collaborative Governance:** Engaging diverse stakeholders—including impacted communities—in audits and red team processes.
- **Explainable AI Advances:** Improving transparency to make audits more effective and actionable.

In Summary

Mitigating risks in large language models and AI systems is a multifaceted challenge demanding technical rigor and ethical foresight. Red teaming offers an adversarial, probing approach to uncover hidden vulnerabilities, while model audits provide comprehensive, structured assessments of a model's safety, fairness, and compliance. Together, these methodologies form a critical backbone for responsible AI governance.

In a world increasingly shaped by AI, these processes are not optional—they are foundational. They empower organizations to deploy language models that are not only powerful and useful but also aligned with human values, respect privacy, and safeguard society.

AI Alignment and Control

As artificial intelligence systems grow in capability, sophistication, and autonomy, a fundamental question looms larger than ever: **How do we**

ensure that AI acts in ways that align with human values, ethics, and intentions? This challenge, known as **AI alignment**, is central to responsible AI development. Equally critical is **AI control** — the mechanisms and frameworks that govern how AI systems behave, especially when operating at scale or in safety-critical environments.

Without effective alignment and control, powerful AI systems risk unintended consequences, from subtle biases and unfair outcomes to catastrophic failures or misuse. These risks are amplified in Large Language Models (LLMs) and agentic AI platforms, where language and reasoning capabilities enable AI not only to interact with humans but to autonomously generate decisions and actions.

What Is AI Alignment?

AI alignment refers to the process of designing AI systems so that their goals, behaviors, and outputs consistently reflect the values, preferences, and ethical principles intended by their creators and society at large.

Unlike traditional software, where explicit programming dictates behavior, modern AI systems—especially LLMs—derive their capabilities from complex patterns in data. They learn statistical correlations, probabilistic predictions, and representations of human knowledge without explicit instruction on ethics or societal norms. This creates two key challenges:

1. **Value Specification Problem:** Defining what "aligned" behavior means in precise, operational terms. Human values are nuanced, context-dependent, and often contradictory.
2. **Robustness Problem:** Ensuring that AI systems continue to behave as intended even in new, unforeseen scenarios, or when adversarial conditions arise.

Why AI Alignment Is Difficult

There are several reasons why AI alignment presents a uniquely difficult problem:

- **Ambiguity of Human Values:** Values such as fairness, justice, and privacy vary across cultures, contexts, and individuals. Encoding such rich, evolving concepts into AI systems is inherently complex.
- **Misaligned Incentives:** AI models optimize for objectives defined during training or deployment, often proxy metrics such as accuracy or engagement. These metrics can diverge from ethical or societal goals, leading to outcomes like manipulation or discrimination.
- **Emergent Behaviors:** As LLMs and multimodal AI systems grow larger and more agentic, they can exhibit unexpected behaviors, hallucinations, or reasoning shortcuts that defy simple oversight.
- **Opaque Decision-Making:** Many state-of-the-art models operate as "black boxes," making it challenging to interpret or predict their decision pathways.

Approaches to AI Alignment

Researchers and practitioners pursue multiple complementary strategies to align AI systems with human values:

1. Human-in-the-Loop Training

Including humans actively in the training and feedback process helps guide models toward desired behaviors. Techniques such as Reinforcement Learning from Human Feedback (RLHF) enable models to learn from curated judgments about output quality, ethical acceptability, or safety.

2. Value-Driven Objective Functions

AI systems are designed with explicit objectives that incorporate ethical constraints or fairness metrics. For example, loss functions may penalize biased outputs or incentivize transparency.

3. Interpretability and Explainability

Developing methods to visualize, explain, or audit AI decisions improves trust and allows stakeholders to identify misalignment or harmful outputs. Explainability also facilitates compliance with regulatory requirements around AI accountability.

4. Robustness and Adversarial Training

Systems are stress-tested against edge cases, adversarial inputs, and scenario simulations to ensure stable, aligned performance. This includes training on diverse, representative datasets to mitigate bias and avoid brittle behavior.

5. Ethical Frameworks and Guidelines

Organizations embed alignment principles into design through ethics committees, impact assessments, and governance policies. These frameworks guide AI development from ideation through deployment.

The Challenge of AI Control

Control mechanisms extend alignment by ensuring AI systems behave safely and predictably once deployed. Control is about building **fail-safes**, **oversight tools**, and **intervention protocols** that can:

- Detect and prevent harmful or unintended outputs in real-time.
- Allow humans to override or shut down AI actions if needed.
- Monitor long-term AI behavior to catch gradual drift or scope creep.

Control Paradigms for AI

Several control paradigms are emerging as best practices in managing AI systems:

1. Sandboxing and Isolation

Running AI systems in controlled, monitored environments limits risk during development and testing. Sandboxing restricts access to critical systems, data, or external networks to prevent misuse.

2. Access and Permission Controls

Granular controls determine which parts of an AI system can be accessed or modified by whom. This reduces risk from insider threats or accidental misuse.

3. Continuous Monitoring and Auditing

Automated logging, anomaly detection, and human audits enable ongoing oversight of AI outputs and behaviors. This helps detect early signs of deviation or emergent risks.

4. Interpretable AI and Human Override

Interfaces allow human operators to understand AI rationale and intervene when necessary, ensuring ultimate authority remains with people.

AI Alignment and Control in Enterprise Settings

For enterprises deploying LLMs and AI agents, alignment and control are not abstract goals but concrete requirements:

- **Regulatory Compliance:** Industries such as finance, healthcare, and telecom face stringent rules on fairness, privacy, and transparency.
- **Reputation Management:** AI failures or biased outputs can cause brand damage and legal liability.
- **User Trust:** Customers expect AI-powered services to be ethical, reliable, and respectful of their rights.
- **Operational Safety:** Autonomous AI in critical infrastructure must avoid unsafe decisions that could harm people or systems.

Implementing alignment and control mechanisms requires multidisciplinary collaboration across AI research, ethics, legal, security, and business domains.

Toward a Future of Safe and Aligned AI

The trajectory of AI development demands that alignment and control mature hand-in-hand with capability. As we unlock new possibilities in multimodal, agentic AI systems that interact, reason, and learn continuously, the complexity of alignment will deepen.

Efforts such as **collaborative research across academia and industry**, **open standards for AI safety**, and **inclusive dialogues with global stakeholders** will be crucial.

Moreover, a proactive mindset—anticipating risks before deployment, embedding ethical thinking in every phase, and fostering transparency—will help us harness AI's power for societal good rather than harm.

Conclusion

AI alignment and control are not mere technical challenges but fundamental ethical imperatives. They demand that we build AI systems that not only perform tasks efficiently but also reflect and respect human values, rights, and safety.

As stewards of this transformative technology, we carry the responsibility to ensure AI acts as a trusted partner — augmenting human intelligence without overriding it; amplifying creativity without amplifying harm.

The promise of AI can only be realized when intelligence meets wisdom, when power meets prudence, and when innovation is guided by conscience.

Building Trustworthy and Inclusive AI

As artificial intelligence, especially large language models (LLMs), becomes deeply embedded in society and enterprise ecosystems, the imperative to build AI systems that are trustworthy, safe, and inclusive grows ever stronger. Responsible AI is no longer a theoretical ideal or a compliance checkbox—it is foundational to sustainable innovation, user acceptance, and positive impact.

Why Trustworthiness Matters

Trust is the cornerstone of any meaningful relationship between humans and machines. In AI, trustworthiness hinges on multiple dimensions: reliability, fairness, transparency, privacy, and accountability. Without these, users risk losing confidence, businesses face reputational damage, and societies may suffer from unintended harms.

LLMs, with their ability to generate human-like language, present unique challenges for trust. Their outputs can be persuasive, authoritative, and sometimes indistinguishable from human-generated content. This power raises the stakes:

- **Can the AI be relied upon to provide accurate and unbiased information?**
- **Does the model respect user privacy and data security?**
- **Are the decisions and content generated by AI explainable and auditable?**
- **Is the AI accessible and fair across different languages, cultures, and demographics?**

Building trust means addressing these questions head-on.

Core Principles of Trustworthy AI

1. **Fairness and Mitigating Bias**
   AI models learn from vast datasets reflecting human language and knowledge — and therefore can inherit the biases present in those sources. This includes gender, racial, cultural, and ideological biases that may inadvertently be amplified by LLMs.

Organizations must adopt rigorous bias detection and mitigation strategies, including:

- Diverse and representative training data that includes multiple languages and cultural contexts.
- Regular audits for disparate impact on different groups.
- Incorporating fairness constraints in model design and deployment.
- Transparent communication about model limitations.

Fair AI promotes inclusivity and ensures no group is disproportionately harmed or marginalized.

1. **Transparency and Explainability**
   One of the greatest challenges with large language models is their "black box" nature. Even AI practitioners struggle to fully interpret why a model generated a specific output.

   To foster transparency:

- Clear documentation of model capabilities, training data sources, and known limitations should be publicly available.
- Explainable AI (XAI) techniques should be integrated wherever possible to help users and stakeholders understand how decisions are made.
- User interfaces should provide context or confidence scores where appropriate.
- Organizations should maintain audit trails and logs to trace AI decisions, especially in high-stakes applications.

   Transparency is essential for accountability and user empowerment.

3. **Privacy and Data Protection**
   LLMs often train on or ingest sensitive data. Protecting user privacy

must be non-negotiable:

- Employ data anonymization, differential privacy, and federated learning approaches to minimize exposure of personally identifiable information.
- Ensure compliance with global data protection regulations such as GDPR, CCPA, and others.
- Design systems that collect only the data necessary for their function and provide users with clear consent mechanisms and control over their data.

Respecting privacy fosters user confidence and legal compliance.

4. **Safety and Robustness**
   AI systems must perform reliably under diverse conditions, resist adversarial attacks, and avoid causing harm:

- Rigorous testing and validation on diverse datasets, including edge cases.
- Monitoring models post-deployment to detect drifts or unexpected behaviors.
- Implementing guardrails against harmful or misleading outputs, such as hate speech, misinformation, or unsafe instructions.
- Providing human-in-the-loop mechanisms for oversight and intervention.

Safety protocols ensure that AI contributes positively without unintended consequences.

5. **Inclusivity and Accessibility**
   AI should be designed for the full spectrum of users, including those with different languages, abilities, and cultural backgrounds:

- Support multiple languages and dialects beyond dominant ones.
- Consider accessibility features for people with disabilities (e.g., screen readers, voice commands).
- Engage diverse user groups during design and testing phases.
- Tailor AI outputs to cultural sensitivities and local norms.

Inclusive AI empowers a wider population and avoids reinforcing digital divides.

Governance: The Framework for Responsible AI

Ethics and principles must translate into practice through robust governance frameworks that define roles, responsibilities, and processes:

- **Organizational Policies:** Clear AI ethics guidelines embedded within corporate governance ensure alignment from leadership to engineering teams.
- **Multidisciplinary Oversight:** Ethics committees or AI review boards including technologists, ethicists, legal experts, and community representatives provide diverse perspectives on risk and impact.
- **Continuous Monitoring:** AI models and applications require ongoing evaluation throughout their lifecycle to detect emergent issues and update policies accordingly.
- **Stakeholder Engagement:** Regular dialogue with users, customers, regulators, and affected communities builds transparency and responsiveness.

Governance makes responsible AI a living practice rather than a one-time effort.

The Human Element: Collaboration and Accountability

Despite advances in autonomous AI, human judgment remains essential. AI should augment, not replace, human decision-making—especially in critical domains like healthcare, finance, and justice.

- Humans should retain oversight authority, with clear escalation paths for AI failures or ethical concerns.
- Training and awareness programs equip employees to understand AI risks and ethical dilemmas.
- Cultivating a culture of responsibility and empathy within AI teams helps anticipate societal impact.

Building trustworthy AI is as much about people and culture as it is about technology.

Real-World Implications and Challenges

The road to responsible AI is complex and often fraught with trade-offs:

- Balancing transparency with intellectual property or security concerns.
- Navigating conflicting cultural norms and ethical standards across regions.
- Ensuring smaller enterprises and developing countries can access ethical AI tools without disproportionate burden.
- Dealing with evolving regulatory landscapes and legal uncertainties.

These challenges demand collaboration across industries, governments, academia, and civil society.

Looking Ahead: Toward a Future of Ethical AI

The journey to building trustworthy and inclusive AI is ongoing and iterative. It requires vigilance, humility, and innovation.

By embedding ethics, safety, and governance into the DNA of AI development, we not only mitigate risks but also unlock the full potential of language models and AI agents to empower individuals, enhance enterprises, and foster global progress.

Responsible AI is not merely a constraint—it is a catalyst for innovation that aligns technology with human values and dignity.

CHAPTER ELEVEN

Beyond the Horizon — The Future of LLMs and Agentic AI

Emergence of Agentic Architectures

As we stand on the cusp of a new era in artificial intelligence, the journey of Large Language Models (LLMs) is evolving from powerful but passive tools into dynamic, autonomous agents capable of complex reasoning, decision-making, and real-world interaction. This transformation marks the emergence of **agentic architectures** — AI systems designed not merely to respond, but to **act, plan, learn, and collaborate** in ways that resemble human intelligence, yet extend far beyond it.

From Language Models to Agents

Traditionally, LLMs have been phenomenal at **generating text** and **predicting language patterns** based on vast training data. However, they operate primarily as reactive systems: given an input prompt, they produce a relevant output. This "input-output" model, while powerful, is limited by its lack of ongoing intentionality, memory, or autonomous goal pursuit.

Agentic architectures seek to transcend this limitation by embedding LLMs within broader cognitive frameworks. These frameworks enable AI to **initiate actions proactively**, **manage multiple tasks concurrently**, and **adapt over time** through experience and interaction with their environments. This shift is akin to moving from a calculator that solves isolated equations to an assistant that organizes your day, negotiates on your behalf, and anticipates your needs.

Key Characteristics of Agentic AI

Agentic AI systems combine multiple core capabilities, which together define their intelligence and autonomy:

1. **Goal-Oriented Reasoning:** Unlike simple language models, agentic AI can maintain explicit objectives and strategize to achieve them. For example, a customer service agent might prioritize resolving a customer's issue while minimizing wait time and escalating complex cases to human experts.
2. **Planning and Sequential Decision Making:** Agents can formulate multi-step plans, forecast potential outcomes, and revise strategies dynamically. This allows them to navigate complex problem spaces, such as managing supply chains, coordinating logistics, or performing research synthesis.
3. **Memory and Contextual Awareness:** Agentic architectures incorporate persistent memory modules that retain knowledge across interactions, enabling continuity and learning. This memory is not just passive storage but actively shapes decision-making, allowing agents to learn user preferences, past errors, and domain-specific nuances.
4. **Multi-Modal and Cross-Domain Integration:** Agents leverage data from diverse sources — text, images, audio, video, sensor data, and even structured databases — synthesizing information to generate comprehensive insights and actions. This multimodal fluency enables applications ranging from autonomous vehicles to personalized education platforms.
5. **Interactive and Collaborative Behavior:** Rather than working in isolation, agentic AI systems engage in dialogue, negotiate, and cooperate with humans and other agents. This social intelligence is critical for deployment in real-world scenarios where communication and coordination are paramount.
6. **Self-Monitoring and Adaptation:** Agentic systems continually assess their performance, detect failures or uncertainties, and self-correct or escalate when necessary. This metacognitive ability fosters robustness

and reliability in unpredictable environments.

Architectures Driving Agentic AI

The emergence of agentic AI is powered by innovations that integrate large language models with modular cognitive architectures:

- **LLM-Based Reasoning Engines:** At the core, advanced LLMs provide natural language understanding and generation, allowing agents to interpret instructions, generate explanations, and reason about complex scenarios.
- **Memory and Knowledge Graphs:** External or integrated memory systems allow agents to maintain state across sessions, retrieve facts, and build knowledge representations that extend beyond training data.
- **Planner and Scheduler Modules:** These components enable agents to break down goals into actionable steps, manage resources, and optimize workflows, often borrowing from classic AI planning techniques enhanced by neural models.
- **Perception and Sensor Integration:** For agents operating in physical or sensory-rich domains, perception modules process inputs from cameras, microphones, and other sensors, converting raw data into actionable understanding.
- **Reinforcement Learning and Feedback Loops:** Continuous learning from interactions allows agents to refine their behavior over time, adapting to user feedback, changing contexts, and evolving goals.
- **Multi-Agent Coordination:** In complex environments, multiple agents may collaborate, share knowledge, or negotiate, forming distributed systems that mimic human teamwork and organizational dynamics.

Why Agentic AI Matters

The agentic transformation of LLMs represents a leap from passive automation to **proactive intelligence** with profound implications across industries and societies:

- **Enterprise Transformation:** Agentic AI can autonomously manage end-to-end business processes, from sales outreach to supply chain optimization, reducing operational costs and enabling rapid innovation.
- **Personalized User Experiences:** Intelligent agents can act as personalized assistants, not only understanding requests but anticipating needs, managing schedules, and offering proactive recommendations tailored to individual preferences.
- **Scientific Discovery and Research:** Agentic AI accelerates knowledge synthesis, hypothesis generation, and experiment planning, democratizing access to cutting-edge research tools and speeding up innovation cycles.
- **Autonomous Systems:** From self-driving vehicles to smart cities, agentic architectures underpin systems that can navigate complex environments safely and efficiently, interacting with humans and other agents seamlessly.
- **Ethical and Responsible AI:** Agentic AI's autonomous nature necessitates rigorous frameworks for transparency, fairness, and control. These systems must be designed to respect privacy, avoid biases, and align with human values, making ethics foundational to their development and deployment.

Challenges on the Horizon

Despite their promise, agentic architectures face significant challenges:

- **Complexity and Interpretability:** As agents grow more autonomous, understanding their decision-making becomes harder. Building explainable AI that users and regulators can trust is critical.
- **Robustness and Safety:** Agents must perform reliably in unpredictable real-world conditions, handling failures gracefully and avoiding unintended consequences.
- **Alignment with Human Intent:** Ensuring that agentic AI acts in accordance with human goals, ethics, and legal norms is a complex, ongoing research frontier.
- **Scalability and Resource Efficiency:** Agentic systems often require massive computational resources. Making them accessible and efficient enough for widespread deployment, including on edge devices and in

resource-constrained settings, remains a challenge.

Toward a Collaborative Future

The rise of agentic architectures signals a future where AI moves beyond tools to become collaborators — partners in creativity, problem-solving, and decision-making. By combining the linguistic fluency of large language models with goal-directed autonomy, persistent memory, and interactive capabilities, these agents will empower humans to tackle complexity at unprecedented scales.

In the coming years, the integration of agentic AI with advances in multimodal perception, knowledge graphs, and real-time interaction will create intelligent ecosystems. These ecosystems will be capable of continuous learning, self-improvement, and ethical action — ultimately ushering in a new paradigm where humans and machines co-create solutions for the world's most pressing challenges.

Memory, Planning, and Goal-Oriented Agents

As we stand at the frontier of artificial intelligence, large language models (LLMs) have already demonstrated an extraordinary ability to generate human-like language, understand context, and perform an impressive variety of tasks. Yet, the future of LLMs is not merely about generating text or answering queries. It lies in transcending isolated interactions and evolving into **agentic AI** — systems that can remember, plan, and pursue complex goals autonomously over time.

This shift marks a profound evolution from reactive, single-turn language understanding to proactive, multi-turn intelligence capable of sophisticated reasoning, decision-making, and collaboration. In this chapter, we explore the emerging capabilities of memory, planning, and goal-oriented behavior in LLM-driven agents, illuminating how these advances will redefine AI's role across industries, applications, and societies.

The Role of Memory in Agentic AI

Human intelligence is deeply rooted in memory. Our ability to recall past experiences, learn from history, and adapt behavior accordingly is what enables long-term planning, contextual understanding, and creativity. For LLMs and AI agents, integrating effective memory systems is pivotal to moving beyond isolated question-answering toward continuous, context-rich interaction.

Memory in AI can be understood in two primary forms:

- **Short-term memory:** This holds information relevant to the current session or task — for example, remembering details from a conversation or recent actions.
- **Long-term memory:** This involves persistent storage of knowledge, preferences, past decisions, and learned skills across multiple interactions or even extended periods.

In practice, current LLMs operate with limited short-term context windows—typically a few thousand tokens—restricting how much prior conversation or information they can retain. Overcoming this limitation involves novel architectures and mechanisms such as:

- **External memory modules:** These allow the AI to read from and write to a memory store outside of the core model weights. This can include databases, knowledge graphs, or specialized memory networks that store facts, documents, or user preferences.
- **Memory retrieval systems:** Using intelligent indexing and search methods, agents can retrieve relevant information from vast data stores to inform their responses dynamically.
- **Continual learning frameworks:** These enable models to update their knowledge base and skills without forgetting prior training, essential for evolving environments like enterprise workflows or regulatory compliance.

For enterprises, embedding memory means AI agents can maintain **user profiles, historical interaction logs, and evolving knowledge**—offering truly personalized, consistent, and context-aware assistance. For example, a customer support agent that remembers previous tickets and user preferences can resolve issues faster and with more empathy.

Planning: From Reactive Responses to Proactive Strategies

While current LLMs excel at generating plausible text given a prompt, their reasoning is largely **reactive**—they respond to inputs without an explicit notion of future states or objectives beyond the immediate turn. The next generation of agentic AI must integrate **planning capabilities** that enable foresight, strategy formulation, and adaptive behavior aligned with long-term goals.

Planning in AI involves several layers:

- **Task decomposition:** Breaking complex goals into manageable subtasks or steps.
- **Sequencing:** Determining the optimal order of actions to achieve objectives.
- **Conditional reasoning:** Adjusting plans based on new information, constraints, or unexpected changes.
- **Resource management:** Allocating time, computational power, or external tools effectively.

Integrating planning with LLMs often entails coupling them with **symbolic reasoning modules, reinforcement learning, or hierarchical controllers** that guide the language model's output according to a global strategy. These hybrid systems enable agents to:

- Generate detailed action plans.
- Anticipate potential obstacles.
- Adjust tactics dynamically in response to evolving scenarios.

In business contexts, planning enables AI systems to act as **intelligent assistants** that can manage projects, automate workflows, or optimize operations autonomously. For instance, an AI agent might plan a marketing campaign by sequencing tasks—content creation, budget allocation, audience segmentation—while adapting in real time to market feedback.

Goal-Oriented Agents: Autonomy and Adaptivity

The synthesis of memory and planning culminates in **goal-oriented agents**—AI systems that not only understand and generate language but also possess a sense of purpose and direction. These agents are designed to **pursue objectives autonomously**, monitor their own progress, and learn from outcomes, thereby mimicking aspects of human problem-solving and initiative.

Key characteristics of goal-oriented LLM agents include:

- **Explicit goal representation:** Agents maintain a clear understanding of what they aim to achieve, whether that is completing a customer request, optimizing a process, or providing strategic recommendations.
- **Self-monitoring and feedback loops:** They evaluate their performance continuously, using internal metrics or external feedback to refine actions.
- **Multi-modal integration:** Beyond text, these agents can interpret and incorporate data from images, audio, sensor inputs, or business systems, enabling more holistic decision-making.
- **Collaboration:** They can interact with other agents, humans, or software tools, coordinating efforts toward shared objectives.

Developing truly autonomous, goal-oriented agents requires breakthroughs in **reinforcement learning with human feedback (RLHF), causal reasoning, and explainability**, ensuring agents act reliably and transparently.

For enterprises, such agents herald a new era of productivity — AI that not only assists but anticipates needs, autonomously executes complex tasks, and continuously learns to improve. Imagine virtual legal assistants drafting contracts while negotiating with counterparties, or intelligent operations agents dynamically adjusting supply chains in response to demand shifts, all with minimal human intervention.

Challenges and Ethical Considerations

While the promise of memory-enhanced, planning-capable, goal-oriented agents is immense, realizing it at scale involves addressing significant challenges:

- **Data privacy and security:** Memory systems must handle sensitive information with strict safeguards to prevent misuse or leaks.
- **Bias and fairness:** Autonomous agents must be designed to avoid reinforcing societal biases embedded in training data.

- **Transparency and explainability:** As agents make decisions, especially in high-stakes domains like healthcare or finance, their reasoning must be interpretable and auditable.
- **Alignment with human values:** Ensuring that agents pursue goals aligned with ethical norms and user intentions is critical to avoid unintended consequences.
- **Robustness and reliability:** Agents must gracefully handle ambiguous, conflicting, or incomplete information without catastrophic failure.

Addressing these challenges will require multi-disciplinary collaboration across AI research, policy, law, and ethics.

The Path Ahead

The integration of memory, planning, and goal-oriented behavior into LLMs is rapidly progressing, driven by innovations in model architectures, training paradigms, and computational infrastructure. Hybrid systems that combine neural networks with symbolic reasoning, external knowledge bases, and real-world data streams will become the norm.

This evolution will unlock AI agents that are not just conversational partners but **trusted collaborators and autonomous decision-makers** — capable of navigating complex environments, learning from experience, and delivering tailored value across sectors.

In the coming years, the fusion of language understanding with memory and planning will transform AI from reactive tools into proactive, goal-driven partners — amplifying human creativity, efficiency, and problem-solving at scales previously unimaginable.

Specialized Models and Industry-Specific LLMs

As large language models (LLMs) evolve, their transformative potential hinges not just on scale or generality but increasingly on specialization. While foundational LLMs like GPT-4 have showcased extraordinary versatility across myriad tasks and domains, the future of AI lies in tailoring these powerful engines to meet the nuanced demands of specific industries, disciplines, and applications. This drive toward specialization reflects both practical needs and the maturation of AI from experimental innovation to indispensable business asset.

The Case for Specialization

General-purpose LLMs are trained on vast and diverse datasets spanning the internet, books, code repositories, conversations, and more. Their broad knowledge base enables impressive zero-shot and few-shot capabilities, allowing them to perform well even in domains they were not explicitly trained for. However, this breadth is also a limitation when addressing highly technical, regulated, or domain-specific tasks.

Industries such as healthcare, finance, legal, manufacturing, telecommunications, and energy possess unique languages — jargon, acronyms, regulatory frameworks, and knowledge structures — that generalist models struggle to fully master without explicit adaptation. Furthermore, these sectors demand rigorous accuracy, explainability, compliance, and integration with existing workflows, which off-the-shelf models often cannot guarantee.

By developing specialized LLMs, organizations can harness the raw power of language modeling while embedding deep domain knowledge, compliance constraints, and industry-specific context into the AI's architecture and training. This approach enhances performance, trust, and usability — transforming AI from a generic assistant into a strategic partner.

Forms of Specialization

Specialized LLMs can take several forms depending on their design and intended use:

1. **Domain-Focused Pretraining:**
   Instead of—or in addition to—starting from a generic foundation model, these LLMs are pretrained or continuously trained on vast corpora of domain-specific text. For example, a healthcare-specialized model might be trained extensively on medical journals, clinical notes, drug databases, and patient records (appropriately anonymized). This imbues the model with in-depth terminology, common patterns, and medical reasoning capabilities far beyond a generalist's scope.
2. **Fine-Tuning with Industry Data:**
   Fine-tuning is the most common route to specialization. Organizations take a foundational LLM and refine it using carefully curated datasets

from their domain, such as financial reports, legal contracts, technical manuals, or customer interactions. This sharpens the model's ability to handle domain-specific queries, interpret ambiguous language, and generate precise responses. Fine-tuning also enables models to respect regulatory and compliance standards embedded in the training data.

3. **Prompt Engineering and Few-Shot Learning for Domain Adaptation:** Even without retraining the entire model, tailored prompt designs and few-shot examples enable contextual steering toward specialized behaviors. While this method offers agility and cost-effectiveness, it may not reach the precision of dedicated specialized models but remains valuable for rapid prototyping and flexible deployment.
4. **Hybrid Architectures Combining Symbolic and Neural Models:** For some industries with structured rules and logic, combining LLMs with symbolic AI, knowledge graphs, or rule engines can enhance reasoning, compliance, and interpretability. Hybrid systems can leverage the generative prowess of LLMs alongside precise, verifiable business logic.
5. **Multimodal Specialization:** Certain industries require understanding not just language but other data types simultaneously — medical imaging with clinical notes, manufacturing sensor data with maintenance logs, or multimedia content with metadata. Multimodal specialized LLMs integrate language with vision, audio, and structured data to deliver comprehensive intelligence in industry workflows.

Industry Examples: Where Specialized LLMs Make an Immediate Impact

- **Healthcare:** Specialized medical LLMs can assist in clinical decision support, summarizing patient histories, generating discharge notes, and extracting insights from scientific literature. They help reduce physician burnout, enhance diagnostics, and enable personalized medicine. Privacy, safety, and regulatory compliance are paramount, necessitating rigorous model validation and explainability.

- **Finance and Banking:**
  Financial institutions deploy specialized LLMs for risk assessment, fraud detection, regulatory reporting, and client interactions. These models are trained on market data, legal regulations, and proprietary transaction records. Precision and auditability are critical to meet compliance standards like AML (Anti-Money Laundering) and GDPR.
- **Legal Sector:**
  Legal LLMs streamline contract review, case law research, and compliance monitoring. They understand legal terminology, jurisdictional nuances, and document structures. By automating repetitive tasks, legal professionals can focus on higher-value strategy and client advisory.
- **Telecommunications:**
  Telecom-specific LLMs analyze call transcripts, SMS, and customer feedback to detect spam, fraud, and service issues in real time. Integration with call routing and customer experience systems enables proactive issue resolution and churn reduction.
- **Manufacturing and Industry 4.0:**
  Models tuned on technical manuals, sensor logs, and maintenance records support predictive maintenance, troubleshooting, and process optimization. They help engineers quickly access relevant knowledge and generate precise repair instructions.
- **Energy and Utilities:**
  These models assist with monitoring infrastructure, interpreting regulatory documents, and analyzing environmental data. They support decision-making for asset management and sustainability initiatives.

Challenges in Building and Deploying Specialized LLMs

Despite the promise, specialized LLM development is not without challenges:

- **Data Quality and Availability:**
  High-quality, domain-specific training data can be scarce, sensitive, or proprietary. Ensuring data privacy and compliance while sourcing enough examples for effective model training is a delicate balance.

- **Model Validation and Explainability:**
  Industry-specific LLMs often power high-stakes decisions. Ensuring their outputs are reliable, interpretable, and auditable is essential to avoid risks and build trust with end users.
- **Regulatory Compliance:**
  Industries like healthcare and finance are heavily regulated. Specialized LLMs must incorporate these rules and constraints to avoid legal exposure.
- **Integration into Legacy Systems:**
  Enterprises often operate complex IT ecosystems. Specialized LLMs must be engineered for seamless integration, API compatibility, and scalability.
- **Continuous Learning and Adaptation:**
  Domains evolve — regulations change, language usage shifts, new products emerge. Maintaining specialized models requires continuous retraining, monitoring, and updating.

The Path Forward: Towards Industry-Centric AI Ecosystems

The future will see a flourishing ecosystem of specialized LLMs tailored for verticals and even specific enterprises, sometimes coexisting with or built atop generalized foundation models. Enterprises will benefit from:

- **Custom AI Solutions:** Purpose-built LLMs fine-tuned to their data, processes, and goals.
- **Plug-and-Play AI Modules:** Specialized LLM APIs designed for quick deployment within industry workflows.
- **Collaborative Model Development:** Industry consortia sharing anonymized data and expertise to co-develop robust models.
- **Hybrid Human-AI Teams:** Where human expertise and AI insights complement each other in decision-making.

This landscape will empower businesses to unlock new efficiencies, innovations, and competitive advantages while addressing ethical, legal, and operational imperatives.

Conclusion

Specialized and industry-specific LLMs represent a critical frontier in the evolution of artificial intelligence. By marrying the raw linguistic and reasoning power of large language models with deep domain expertise, these AI systems transcend generic capabilities to become trusted partners in sectors that shape economies and societies. Their impact will be felt not only in automating routine tasks but in enabling smarter, more inclusive, and more responsible AI-driven transformations.

As we look beyond the horizon, the journey from generalist to specialist is not merely an evolution of technology but a reflection of AI's growing maturity — a move from tool to collaborator, from possibility to proven value.

Open Source Ecosystems and Democratization

As we stand at the threshold of unprecedented advances in large language models (LLMs) and agentic AI, one of the most transformative forces shaping this future is the rise of **open source ecosystems**. The democratization of AI through open source is not just a technological trend — it is a paradigm shift with profound implications for innovation, inclusion, ethics, and global development.

The Power of Openness in AI

Historically, breakthroughs in artificial intelligence have often been closely guarded within proprietary walls of tech giants and elite research institutions. While this model enabled rapid innovation fueled by massive investments, it also concentrated power and influence in a few hands, limiting accessibility for smaller players, startups, academia, and underrepresented regions.

Open source changes this dynamic by making the core tools, models, and frameworks freely available for anyone to use, modify, and build upon. This openness accelerates progress by:

- **Lowering barriers to entry:** Smaller companies, developers, and researchers can experiment without prohibitive costs or licensing restrictions.

- **Enabling collaboration:** Diverse communities worldwide contribute code, datasets, benchmarks, and ideas, driving collective improvement.
- **Increasing transparency:** Open codebases and model architectures invite scrutiny, helping identify and mitigate biases, errors, and vulnerabilities.
- **Fostering innovation:** Open ecosystems serve as fertile ground for unexpected breakthroughs, novel applications, and localized adaptations.

For LLMs and agentic AI, this democratization means that the technology is no longer the exclusive domain of large corporations or governments. Instead, it becomes a shared resource, empowering a broad spectrum of creators, entrepreneurs, and users.

Notable Open Source Contributions to LLMs

The recent surge in open source LLM initiatives exemplifies this transformation. Projects such as Meta's **LLaMA**, EleutherAI's **GPT-Neo** and **GPT-J**, Hugging Face's extensive model hub, and many community-led efforts have made powerful language models accessible beyond corporate firewalls.

These projects:

- Provide pretrained models of varying sizes tailored for different use cases and resource constraints.
- Offer training pipelines, datasets, and fine-tuning tools that enable customization for specific languages, industries, or tasks.
- Encourage ethical considerations by fostering transparent documentation and open discussions about potential risks.

Open source LLMs enable enterprises, especially those in emerging markets or specialized fields, to build AI solutions that are culturally relevant, linguistically diverse, and ethically aligned with their communities.

Democratization Beyond Code: Building Inclusive AI Ecosystems

True democratization extends beyond releasing code. It requires building an ecosystem where diverse voices have the tools, knowledge, and agency to participate fully. This involves:

- **Education and capacity-building:** Open source AI must be paired with accessible learning resources, tutorials, and community support to help newcomers acquire the necessary skills.
- **Infrastructure access:** Running LLMs demands significant compute power. Democratization efforts include providing cloud credits, optimized lightweight models, and tools for on-device AI to reduce dependency on expensive hardware.
- **Multilingual and culturally-aware AI:** Democratized AI must serve the billions of people who speak less-resourced languages or live in underrepresented regions. Open source initiatives can adapt models to local dialects, idioms, and social norms.
- **Ethical frameworks and governance:** Communities engaged in open AI development often pioneer ethical guidelines, best practices, and mechanisms for accountability that balance innovation with safety and fairness.

Through these interconnected efforts, democratization can help bridge the global digital divide rather than deepen it.

The Role of Agentic AI in a Democratized Future

Agentic AI — systems capable of autonomous reasoning, decision-making, and learning — magnifies both the promise and responsibility of open source democratization.

When AI agents can act independently, the need for transparent, auditable, and controllable systems becomes paramount. Open source ecosystems provide fertile ground for collaborative development of:

- **Explainability tools:** To understand agent decisions.
- **Safety layers:** To prevent harmful or unintended behavior.
- **Customization frameworks:** Allowing users to align AI behavior with their values and operational needs.

Democratized agentic AI empowers individuals and organizations not only to use AI but to co-create it, shaping the agents to reflect diverse human priorities and ethical standards.

Challenges on the Path to Democratization

Despite its promise, open source AI democratization faces significant challenges:

- **Resource imbalances:** Even with open models, the cost of training, fine-tuning, and deploying LLMs remains high for many.
- **Data access:** Quality datasets, especially for underrepresented languages and domains, are scarce or siloed.
- **Security risks:** Open source models can be misused to generate misinformation, spam, or malicious content.
- **Governance complexity:** Decentralized development makes it harder to enforce consistent standards or quickly address emergent risks.

Addressing these challenges demands coordinated efforts between governments, academia, industry, and civil society to create equitable infrastructures, data-sharing agreements, and ethical oversight frameworks.

The Democratization Dividend: What the Future Holds

Looking ahead, the open source ecosystem will continue to drive LLM and agentic AI innovation in ways we can only begin to imagine. The democratization of language intelligence promises to:

- Empower startups and local innovators to solve region-specific problems with AI.
- Foster cross-cultural exchange and collaboration, enriching AI models with diverse knowledge and perspectives.
- Catalyze new forms of creative expression, education, and digital empowerment.
- Enable transparent, community-driven governance that aligns AI's evolution with human values.
- Accelerate AI adoption in industries like healthcare, agriculture, finance, and public services worldwide.

Ultimately, the future of LLMs and agentic AI is a future shared. Open source and democratization unlock this shared potential, transforming AI from a tool of a few into a resource for all — where the intelligence of machines amplifies the creativity, wisdom, and compassion of humanity.

Multilingual and Cross-Cultural Models

In an increasingly interconnected world, language is both a bridge and a barrier. While English remains a dominant language in technology and business, billions of people communicate primarily in other languages—often many different languages within the same country or region. This linguistic diversity presents one of the most significant frontiers for large language models (LLMs) and agentic AI systems. To truly realize the transformative potential of AI on a global scale, these models must transcend language boundaries and cultural contexts, embracing multilingualism and cross-cultural understanding at their core.

The Challenge of Linguistic Diversity

Human languages are complex, nuanced, and deeply tied to culture, history, and identity. Each language carries idioms, dialects, grammar, and cultural references that do not translate easily or directly into others. This complexity poses formidable challenges for AI systems designed to understand and generate language:

- **Vocabulary and Grammar Variability:** Languages differ widely in their phonetics, syntax, and semantics. For example, some languages have gendered nouns, others use tone to distinguish meaning, and some rely heavily on context to convey tense or mood.
- **Cultural Nuance and Context:** Meaning is often grounded in shared cultural knowledge—references, humor, values, and social norms—that can be invisible to outsiders. A phrase considered polite in one culture may be offensive in another.
- **Resource Imbalance:** While languages like English, Mandarin, Spanish, and French have abundant digital text and linguistic resources, many others—especially those spoken by smaller or marginalized communities—lack sufficient training data. This imbalance risks perpetuating technological divides.

- **Code-Switching and Multilingual Speech:** In many parts of the world, people mix languages fluidly in speech and text. AI models need to handle such code-switching seamlessly to serve real-world communication needs.

Multilingual LLMs: Bridging the Language Divide

The future of LLMs is inherently multilingual. Unlike early models trained primarily on English data, today's next-generation models are designed to understand and generate text across dozens or even hundreds of languages. These multilingual LLMs offer several advantages:

- **Unified Model for Many Languages:** Instead of building separate models for each language, multilingual LLMs leverage shared linguistic patterns and representations to process multiple languages within a single architecture. This reduces complexity and cost.
- **Cross-Lingual Transfer Learning:** Knowledge learned from high-resource languages can benefit lower-resource ones. For example, understanding syntax or semantics in one language can help the model perform better on structurally similar languages.
- **Seamless Translation and Interaction:** Multilingual models can enable real-time translation, cross-language information retrieval, and communication, breaking down language barriers in global business, healthcare, education, and diplomacy.
- **Inclusive AI Access:** By supporting a wide array of languages, LLMs can empower users from diverse linguistic backgrounds to access AI-powered tools, ensuring technology serves a truly global population.

Cross-Cultural Intelligence: Beyond Language

While language is a critical factor, understanding culture is equally essential for creating AI that interacts meaningfully across borders. Cross-cultural models aim to embed cultural awareness and sensitivity into AI systems, addressing:

- **Contextual Interpretation:** Cultural context influences not only language but also how information is perceived. An AI assistant's responses in one country must be adapted to local customs, legal norms, and communication styles.
- **Bias Mitigation:** AI models trained on global datasets risk amplifying cultural biases or stereotypes if not carefully designed. Cross-cultural awareness helps identify and reduce such biases, promoting fairness and respect.
- **Personalization and Localization:** Agentic AI systems must adapt their behavior and content to individual user preferences and cultural expectations, enhancing relevance and trust.
- **Ethical Considerations:** Respect for cultural values and norms is paramount in deploying AI responsibly. This includes sensitivity to privacy, consent, and content appropriateness across regions.

Technical Approaches to Multilingual and Cross-Cultural AI

Developing robust multilingual and cross-cultural LLMs involves multiple cutting-edge techniques:

- **Massive Multilingual Corpora:** Training on diverse, high-quality datasets from many languages, including books, websites, social media, and transcribed speech, is foundational. Efforts are underway to collect and curate data for underrepresented languages, often involving collaboration with local communities.
- **Language-Agnostic Architectures:** Models are designed to learn language representations that capture universal linguistic features, enabling effective transfer across languages with minimal additional training.
- **Cross-Lingual Embeddings:** Embeddings map words or phrases from different languages into a shared semantic space, allowing the model to relate concepts across languages even when direct translations don't exist.
- **Cultural Metadata and Conditioning:** Incorporating metadata about cultural context—such as region, formality level, or local conventions—enables models to adjust responses appropriately.

- **Continual Learning and Adaptation:** Multilingual and cross-cultural AI must adapt over time to evolving language use, emerging dialects, and shifting cultural norms. Continuous retraining and feedback loops from diverse user bases are crucial.

Applications Empowering Global Inclusion

The impact of multilingual and cross-cultural LLMs is already visible and poised to accelerate:

- **Global Customer Support:** Enterprises can deploy AI chatbots and voice assistants capable of fluent, culturally sensitive interaction across multiple languages, improving customer satisfaction worldwide.
- **Healthcare Access:** AI-driven translation and summarization help medical professionals communicate with patients in their native languages, overcoming critical barriers in emergency and routine care.
- **Education and Literacy:** Multilingual AI tools personalize learning experiences, deliver content in local languages, and support literacy efforts in underserved communities.
- **Legal and Regulatory Compliance:** Cross-lingual models assist in analyzing and harmonizing legal texts, helping multinational companies navigate diverse regulatory landscapes.
- **Content Moderation and Social Media:** Understanding language and cultural nuance aids in detecting harmful content and misinformation across global platforms.

The Road Ahead: Challenges and Opportunities

Despite impressive progress, multilingual and cross-cultural AI faces ongoing challenges:

- **Data Scarcity for Low-Resource Languages:** Many languages still lack sufficient digitized text, impacting model performance and perpetuating inequality.
- **Evaluation Metrics:** Measuring AI effectiveness across languages and cultures requires new benchmarks that consider linguistic and cultural

nuances.
- **Ethical Stewardship:** Ensuring AI respects local customs without reinforcing harmful stereotypes or censorship demands nuanced governance.
- **User Trust and Adoption:** Building confidence in AI systems across cultures means transparent communication about capabilities, limitations, and data privacy.

Yet, these challenges also present opportunities for innovation, collaboration, and impact. By partnering with linguists, anthropologists, technologists, and local communities, the AI field can create models that truly serve the world's linguistic and cultural mosaic.

Conclusion

Multilingual and cross-cultural capabilities are not optional extras for the future of AI — they are fundamental prerequisites for building intelligent, ethical, and inclusive systems. As large language models evolve beyond English-centric paradigms, they will become catalysts for global understanding and cooperation, enabling agentic AI that respects diversity and amplifies human potential everywhere.

The journey towards this horizon requires commitment, ingenuity, and responsibility. But the reward is a world where AI is a genuine partner to all people, speaking their languages, honoring their cultures, and helping them unlock new possibilities — wherever they are, whoever they are.

Efficiency: Sparse Models, Quantization, and Energy Awareness

As large language models (LLMs) continue to revolutionize artificial intelligence, one of the most pressing challenges shaping their future is **efficiency**. Today's state-of-the-art LLMs, such as GPT-4 and beyond, achieve remarkable performance through vast numbers of parameters—often measured in the hundreds of billions. However, this scale comes with steep computational and energy costs, limiting their accessibility, environmental sustainability, and real-time deployment, especially on resource-constrained devices.

To unlock the full transformative potential of LLMs and agentic AI—particularly for global enterprises and billions of users across diverse devices and geographies—efficiency is not merely a technical optimization but a fundamental enabler. This section explores three pivotal directions in making LLMs more efficient: **sparse modeling**, **quantization**, and **energy-aware computing.**

Sparse Models: Doing More with Less

The principle of **sparsity** is inspired by the observation that not all parts of a model need to be active at all times. In large neural networks, many parameters or neurons contribute little or redundant information for a given input. Sparse models leverage this by activating only the most relevant components during inference, dramatically reducing computational load.

- **Mixture of Experts (MoE):** A leading approach to sparsity in LLMs is the Mixture of Experts architecture. Instead of a dense network where every parameter processes every input, MoE models contain multiple "expert" subnetworks, but only a small subset of these experts is activated for each input. This conditional computation approach reduces the effective number of operations, allowing the model to scale in size without a linear increase in inference cost.
- **Dynamic Sparsity:** Beyond static sparse architectures, dynamic sparsity adjusts which parts of the network are used in real time, guided by the input or intermediate results. This enables fine-grained control of computation and potentially improves efficiency without sacrificing accuracy.
- **Pruning:** Another technique is pruning, where after training, parameters deemed less critical are removed. Pruned models maintain performance while significantly reducing size and computation.

The rise of sparse models means that future LLMs will be capable of maintaining or improving their reasoning and generation capabilities while dramatically lowering the resources needed for inference. This is crucial for on-device AI and real-time applications where latency and energy consumption are critical.

Quantization: Shrinking Models for Speed and Scale

Quantization is the process of reducing the precision of the numbers representing model weights and activations, for example, converting 32-bit floating-point numbers to 8-bit or even lower-bit integers.

- **Reduced Memory Footprint:** By lowering numerical precision, quantization compresses models, reducing memory requirements and bandwidth needed for loading and transferring parameters.
- **Faster Computation:** Lower-bit arithmetic operations require less energy and are faster to execute on modern hardware, enabling real-time inference on devices with limited computational power.
- **Quantization-Aware Training (QAT):** To counteract the potential loss in model accuracy from reduced precision, QAT trains the model while simulating quantization effects, allowing the network to adapt and maintain high performance even in low precision.
- **Post-Training Quantization (PTQ):** This method applies quantization after a model is trained, providing a faster way to compress existing models for deployment, albeit sometimes with a slight accuracy trade-off.

For LLMs, aggressive quantization strategies are being developed that push precision down to 4-bit and even 2-bit representations without significant degradation in quality. Such breakthroughs allow massive models to run on consumer hardware, mobile devices, and edge environments—greatly expanding the reach of AI capabilities.

Energy Awareness: Sustainable and Responsible AI

The energy consumption of large-scale AI training and inference is no longer a niche concern—it's a global imperative. Training a single large LLM can consume megawatt-hours of electricity, comparable to the annual consumption of dozens of households. Similarly, running millions of inference requests at scale translates into substantial carbon footprints.

- **Green AI Initiatives:** The AI research community and industry leaders are increasingly prioritizing "Green AI," focusing on measuring and reducing the energy impact of models throughout their lifecycle. This includes adopting energy metrics alongside accuracy benchmarks to guide model design and deployment.

- **Hardware-Software Co-Design:** Energy efficiency gains come not just from algorithms but from close integration with specialized hardware. AI accelerators, such as tensor processing units (TPUs) and neural processing units (NPUs), are being designed with low-power modes, adaptive voltage scaling, and optimized data movement to minimize wasted energy.
- **On-Device Processing:** Running LLMs directly on user devices — such as smartphones, IoT nodes, or edge servers — reduces data transmission energy and latency. Combined with sparse and quantized models, on-device AI offers an energy-efficient alternative to cloud-dependent systems.
- **Adaptive Inference:** Energy-aware AI can dynamically adjust its computational effort depending on the complexity of the input or the task's criticality. For instance, a spam detection model on a mobile device might perform a quick heuristic check before invoking a more expensive, detailed analysis only if necessary.
- **Lifecycle Optimization:** Beyond training and inference, energy awareness encompasses dataset curation, model fine-tuning, and even data center cooling and resource allocation strategies.

Synergy and Impact

Sparse modeling, quantization, and energy-aware design are not isolated strategies but complementary pillars that collectively enable sustainable, scalable, and accessible AI. Together, they promise to:

- Democratize LLM technology by making it viable on low-cost, low-power devices worldwide, supporting inclusion and bridging digital divides.
- Reduce the environmental footprint of AI, aligning technological progress with global climate goals.
- Enable real-time, on-device, and continuous AI services for applications ranging from healthcare diagnostics to fraud detection, customer engagement, and personalized learning.

- Facilitate agentic AI systems that can operate autonomously and responsibly within resource constraints, adapting their compute and energy consumption dynamically based on context.

Looking Ahead

The future of LLMs will be defined not just by bigger models but by smarter, leaner, and greener architectures. Efficiency innovations will unlock new domains where AI can seamlessly integrate into daily life and enterprise operations — from rural healthcare clinics in emerging economies to mobile financial services in the developing world, from augmented creativity tools to intelligent automation at the network edge.

As we build towards agentic AI that learns, plans, and acts autonomously, efficiency will ensure that these systems remain practical, ethical, and impactful at scale. Embracing sparse models, quantization, and energy awareness is therefore not just an engineering necessity but a moral and strategic imperative on the horizon of AI evolution.

Explainability and Interpretability Research

As large language models (LLMs) become increasingly embedded in critical decision-making processes, enterprise workflows, and even in shaping public discourse, a pressing question emerges: **How and why do these models make the predictions they do?** This is the domain of **explainability** and **interpretability** research — a rapidly growing field that seeks to open the "black box" of complex AI models, bringing clarity and trust to their inner workings.

Why Explainability Matters

LLMs, particularly those based on deep neural networks like Transformers, operate by processing vast amounts of data and learning statistical patterns at scales beyond human comprehension. While their outputs often appear remarkably coherent and insightful, the reasoning behind these outputs is opaque. Unlike traditional rule-based systems where logic flows are explicit, LLMs rely on millions or billions of parameters whose interactions produce results that are difficult to trace or justify.

In enterprise contexts, this opacity creates a barrier to adoption and responsible use. When decisions have significant consequences — in healthcare, finance, legal judgments, or customer interactions — organizations need to understand:

- **Why a model recommended a particular course of action?**
- **What data or features influenced the output most?**
- **Are there biases or errors baked into the model's reasoning?**
- **Can the model's behavior be audited or explained to regulators, customers, or end-users?**

Without transparency, trust in AI remains fragile. Explainability is not a luxury; it is a requirement for safety, fairness, and accountability.

Defining Explainability and Interpretability

While often used interchangeably, **explainability** and **interpretability** have subtle distinctions:

- **Interpretability** refers to the extent to which a human can understand the internal mechanics of a system directly. For example, a linear regression model with a few coefficients is interpretable because each weight directly corresponds to a feature's importance.
- **Explainability** involves creating tools or methods that help elucidate how a model arrived at a particular decision, often post hoc, especially when the model itself is too complex to be fully interpretable. It may involve generating simplified explanations, visualizations, or natural language summaries.

LLMs, by virtue of their complexity, are largely uninterpretable in the purest sense, which means explainability techniques are essential for providing actionable insights about their behavior.

Techniques and Approaches

Explainability research encompasses a spectrum of methods, each with strengths and trade-offs:

1. **Feature Attribution Methods:**
   These techniques identify which parts of the input most influenced the

model's output. Examples include attention visualization, saliency maps, SHAP (SHapley Additive exPlanations), and LIME (Local Interpretable Model-agnostic Explanations). For LLMs, this might mean highlighting specific words or phrases that steered a classification or generation.

2. **Probing Models and Diagnostic Classifiers:**
   Researchers train small auxiliary models on LLM internal states (like hidden layers or attention weights) to reveal what linguistic or factual knowledge the model encodes. For instance, probing can show whether an LLM understands syntax, semantics, or factual relationships.
3. **Counterfactual and Perturbation Analysis:**
   By systematically modifying inputs and observing changes in outputs, these methods reveal sensitivity and decision boundaries. This can help identify fragile or biased model behavior.
4. **Model Distillation and Simplification:**
   Complex LLMs can be approximated by simpler, more interpretable models for particular tasks. While distilled models lose some nuance, they offer a window into high-level decision rules.
5. **Natural Language Explanations:**
   Some research explores enabling LLMs themselves to generate human-readable explanations for their outputs. This "self-explaining AI" promises a more intuitive bridge between machine reasoning and human understanding.

Challenges Unique to LLMs

Despite progress, explainability for LLMs presents unique hurdles:

- **Scale and Complexity:**
  With hundreds of billions of parameters, interactions within LLMs are highly non-linear and context-dependent. This sheer scale complicates attribution and understanding.
- **Contextual and Dynamic Behavior:**
  LLM responses depend heavily on subtle contextual cues and prompt phrasing. Explaining why a model responded one way versus another often requires modeling these prompt-dependent dynamics.
- **Emergent and Implicit Knowledge:**
  LLMs store vast factual, commonsense, and linguistic knowledge

implicitly. Extracting these latent concepts in human terms is inherently difficult.

- **Bias and Fairness Concerns:**
  Explanation tools must help surface biases — including those related to gender, race, culture, or socioeconomic status — embedded in training data and model behavior. But explaining bias requires sophisticated approaches that connect statistical patterns to real-world harms.

The Role of Explainability in Responsible AI

Explainability is foundational to several pillars of responsible AI:

- **Accountability:**
  Organizations must be able to justify AI-driven decisions to stakeholders and regulators, ensuring compliance with legal and ethical standards.
- **Debugging and Improvement:**
  Clear explanations reveal model weaknesses, enabling targeted retraining, data augmentation, or architectural changes.
- **User Trust and Adoption:**
  End-users are more likely to trust and adopt AI systems that transparently communicate their reasoning, especially in sensitive domains like healthcare or finance.
- **Bias Mitigation:**
  Explanation tools can identify when a model's output is influenced by undesirable or unethical factors, helping teams take corrective action.

Cutting-Edge Research Directions

The future of explainability research is vibrant and rapidly evolving. Some promising directions include:

- **Interactive Explainability:**
  Developing tools that allow users to query models iteratively, drilling down into reasoning and testing "what-if" scenarios.
- **Multimodal Explanation:**
  As LLMs integrate vision, audio, and other modalities, explanations must

span multiple input types, requiring new frameworks for cross-modal interpretability.

- **Causal Explainability:**
  Moving beyond correlation-based explanations to uncover causal relationships embedded in model decisions, enabling deeper insights.
- **Standardization and Benchmarks:**
  Creating universally accepted metrics and evaluation protocols to compare explanation methods and ensure robustness.
- **Explainability at Scale:**
  Engineering solutions to generate fast, comprehensible explanations even in large-scale, real-time applications.

Balancing Transparency and Usability

A critical tension exists between making models fully transparent and maintaining usability:

- **Too much detail** can overwhelm or confuse users.
- **Too little explanation** undermines trust and actionable insight.

Effective explainability solutions must tailor explanations to different audiences — from AI researchers needing granular model internals, to business leaders requiring high-level rationales, to end-users needing intuitive and actionable feedback.

Conclusion

Explainability and interpretability research represent the gateway between opaque algorithmic intelligence and human understanding. As LLMs and agentic AI systems become more powerful and widespread, the demand for trustworthy, transparent, and auditable AI will only intensify.

The journey toward truly explainable AI is as much social and ethical as it is technical. It challenges us to rethink how we design, deploy, and govern intelligent systems — ensuring that these transformative technologies empower humans, enhance decision-making, and uphold the values of fairness, accountability, and respect.

By investing in explainability research today, we pave the way for a future where AI is not just intelligent but also **understandable** and **trusted** — a future where human and machine intelligence collaborate openly, responsibly, and effectively.

Federated and Collaborative Learning

As we look ahead to the future of large language models (LLMs) and agentic AI systems, one of the most transformative shifts will come from **federated and collaborative learning paradigms**. These approaches are redefining how AI systems learn, adapt, and evolve — moving away from centralized, data-hungry training toward distributed, privacy-preserving, and cooperative models of intelligence.

The Limits of Centralized Learning

To appreciate the significance of federated and collaborative learning, it helps to understand the limitations of traditional centralized AI training. Most state-of-the-art LLMs today rely on massive centralized datasets, often gathered from the internet, corporate servers, or cloud platforms. These datasets, while extensive, are typically siloed, sensitive, and laden with privacy and security concerns.

Centralized training requires aggregating data into a single location, raising risks such as:

- **Data privacy breaches:** Sensitive information (personal, medical, financial) may be exposed during collection, transfer, or storage.
- **Regulatory constraints:** Laws like GDPR, HIPAA, and others limit the ability to move or share certain data across borders or entities.
- **Data imbalance and bias:** Centralized data may underrepresent certain populations or contexts, limiting model fairness and performance.
- **High infrastructure costs:** Collecting, storing, and processing exabytes of data centrally demands enormous computational and energy resources.

These challenges create bottlenecks that limit the scalability, inclusivity, and trustworthiness of LLMs.

What Is Federated Learning?

Federated learning (FL) offers a groundbreaking alternative. Instead of bringing data to the model, FL brings the model to the data — distributed across many devices or organizations. In this approach:

- AI models are trained locally on user devices, edge servers, or institution-owned infrastructure.
- Only the model updates (like gradients or parameters), not the raw data, are sent back to a central aggregator.
- The aggregator combines these updates to refine a global model that benefits from all participants without exposing their data.

Federated learning thus enables collaborative model training **without compromising data privacy or security**.

How Federated Learning Works in Practice

Imagine thousands — or millions — of smartphones, IoT devices, or enterprise nodes each holding valuable proprietary data. Instead of uploading all that data to a centralized cloud:

- Each device trains the shared LLM locally on its own data, adapting it to personal or domain-specific needs.
- Periodically, devices send encrypted model updates to a server that aggregates them securely.
- The global model improves by learning from diverse data distributions, representing many languages, dialects, cultures, and industries.
- The updated global model is pushed back to devices, continuously improving their local AI capabilities.

This cycle repeats iteratively, enabling scalable, privacy-preserving AI that is personalized and inclusive.

Benefits for Large Language Models and Agentic AI

Federated learning unlocks several critical advantages for the future of LLMs and agentic AI:

- **Data privacy and compliance:** Sensitive information remains on-device or within institutional firewalls, meeting strict privacy regulations and building user trust.
- **Personalization at scale:** Models can adapt to individual users' language, preferences, and behavior patterns, improving relevance and accuracy.
- **Cross-domain generalization:** Aggregating updates from varied domains helps build more robust, versatile language models that can serve diverse sectors such as healthcare, finance, telecom, and education.
- **Reduced latency and bandwidth use:** Training locally cuts down the need to transfer large data volumes over networks, critical for low-resource settings and edge computing environments.
- **Democratized AI development:** Smaller organizations or regions with limited data can participate in collaborative model training, leveling the playing field in AI access and innovation.

Collaborative Learning: Beyond Federated Learning

Federated learning is a cornerstone, but the future will see even richer forms of **collaborative learning** that go beyond just aggregating model updates. These include:

- **Multi-stakeholder collaboration:** Different organizations or industries can jointly train domain-specific LLMs, sharing knowledge while protecting proprietary information. For example, hospitals across regions can collaborate on a medical LLM without exposing patient data.
- **Cross-lingual and cross-cultural adaptation:** Collaborative frameworks can enable models to learn from diverse linguistic and cultural data sets dispersed globally, improving inclusivity and reducing language bias.
- **Knowledge distillation and transfer:** Participants can exchange distilled knowledge or trained model components rather than raw data or full models, optimizing efficiency and protecting intellectual property.
- **Decentralized governance and incentives:** Emerging blockchain and decentralized frameworks could facilitate transparent, fair, and auditable collaboration, rewarding contributors and ensuring ethical AI development.

Challenges and Considerations

While promising, federated and collaborative learning introduce unique challenges that must be addressed:

- **Communication efficiency:** Aggregating updates from millions of devices or organizations requires efficient protocols to minimize bandwidth and computation.
- **Model heterogeneity:** Devices or participants may have different hardware capabilities or data distributions, complicating model convergence and performance.
- **Security threats:** Despite privacy safeguards, federated systems are vulnerable to adversarial attacks like model poisoning or inference attacks that must be actively mitigated.
- **Coordination and trust:** Effective collaboration requires robust frameworks for participant verification, contribution weighting, and conflict resolution.
- **Ethical and regulatory compliance:** Even with data privacy, federated models must be designed to avoid bias, ensure fairness, and respect user consent.

The Road Ahead

Federated and collaborative learning represent a paradigm shift toward AI systems that are **distributed, democratized, and human-centric**. For LLMs and agentic AI, this means:

- Models that are continuously updated in the wild, learning from real-world diverse interactions without compromising privacy.
- AI systems personalized for individuals, communities, and industries while grounded in a collective intelligence.
- A future where innovation is decentralized, driven by collaborative ecosystems spanning countries, sectors, and stakeholders.

This future aligns perfectly with emerging needs:

- Empowering users in developing countries with on-device AI that respects privacy.
- Enabling enterprises to leverage proprietary data without risk.
- Promoting ethical AI that prioritizes inclusion and fairness.

Conclusion

The journey beyond the horizon of AI and large language models will be marked by collaboration — not just between humans and machines, but among machines themselves, learning together without centralized control. Federated and collaborative learning are the foundations of this next wave, offering a powerful vision where AI is not only smarter but also safer, fairer, and more accessible.

As we continue exploring agentic AI's potential — where machines autonomously learn, plan, and act — these distributed learning paradigms will be critical. They hold the promise of truly democratizing AI, enabling a future where intelligence is collective, privacy-respecting, and universally beneficial.

Standards, APIs, and Ecosystem Interoperability

As large language models (LLMs) and agentic AI systems evolve at an extraordinary pace, the future of these technologies hinges not only on breakthroughs in model architecture or training data but equally on the frameworks that enable their seamless integration and ethical deployment at scale. Beyond the raw power of any single model lies a vast ecosystem of tools, platforms, and services that must interact cohesively to deliver reliable, responsible, and scalable AI solutions. This is where standards, APIs, and ecosystem interoperability become critical pillars for the next era of AI innovation.

The Need for Standards: Building Trust and Consistency

Standards in AI are the foundational agreements that define how systems communicate, share data, and operate within a broader technological and ethical landscape. Unlike in traditional software development where standards have long been established for protocols, formats, and security,

AI—and particularly LLMs—introduces new challenges that demand fresh approaches to standardization.

At the core, standards ensure **compatibility** and **consistency** across diverse AI systems. With multiple organizations, cloud providers, and startups developing their own LLMs, models vary in architecture, data handling, inference protocols, and output formats. Without agreed-upon standards, integrating these models into existing enterprise workflows or combining their outputs into composite solutions becomes cumbersome or error-prone.

But standards go beyond technical specifications. They also provide frameworks to address **ethical considerations** like transparency, bias mitigation, and privacy compliance. For example, defining standards for model auditability—how a model's decisions and training data provenance are documented—enables enterprises and regulators to hold AI systems accountable.

Industry consortia and international bodies are already working to create such frameworks. Initiatives like the IEEE's *Ethically Aligned Design*, the Partnership on AI, and emerging government policies focus on establishing principles for trustworthy AI. However, the next frontier is creating **operational standards** that govern how LLMs can be developed, deployed, and interacted with in a global, multi-vendor ecosystem.

APIs: The Language of AI Integration

If standards provide the rules of the road, **Application Programming Interfaces (APIs)** are the vehicles that carry AI capabilities into the hands of developers, enterprises, and users.

APIs for LLMs abstract away the immense complexity of model training, hardware optimization, and infrastructure management. They allow developers to plug into pre-trained models and access capabilities such as text generation, summarization, question answering, and more through simple calls.

In the future, API design will be pivotal in enabling **modularity and composability** within AI ecosystems. Instead of monolithic "black box" models, AI platforms will expose granular services—language understanding, context memory, intent recognition, knowledge retrieval—that can be orchestrated dynamically depending on use case.

For agentic AI, which involves models autonomously planning, executing tasks, and learning, APIs will need to support:

- **Stateful interactions**: Maintaining memory across sessions or conversations to enable continuity and personalization.
- **Tooling interfaces**: Allowing AI agents to call external services (e.g., calendars, databases, IoT devices) safely and efficiently.
- **Multi-modal data handling**: Managing inputs and outputs across text, voice, images, video, and sensor data.
- **Feedback loops**: Enabling users or systems to provide real-time corrections or updates that the agent can learn from or adapt to.

Standardizing such APIs will ensure interoperability between agentic AI components from different vendors, allowing enterprises to build complex workflows without vendor lock-in.

Ecosystem Interoperability: The Web of AI Collaboration

The true promise of LLMs and agentic AI lies not in isolated capabilities but in their integration within diverse ecosystems of applications, devices, and users. Ecosystem interoperability refers to the ability of AI systems to work together seamlessly, exchanging data, capabilities, and insights across organizational and technological boundaries.

Interoperability facilitates:

- **Cross-platform deployment**: Ensuring AI services work across cloud providers, on-premises environments, edge devices, and mobile platforms.
- **Multi-vendor collaboration**: Allowing components from different AI vendors—language models, knowledge graphs, analytics tools—to combine in composite solutions.
- **Domain specialization**: Integrating generalist LLMs with specialized models trained for healthcare, finance, legal, or other industries to deliver precise, contextual outcomes.
- **Global reach**: Supporting cross-lingual and cross-cultural AI that respects regional data sovereignty and regulatory frameworks.

Achieving this interoperability requires open standards but also robust **data exchange protocols**, **semantic interoperability** (common understanding of concepts and metadata), and **security frameworks** to protect sensitive information.

For example, in telecommunications — your domain of expertise — interoperability enables AI-driven spam detection, customer experience personalization, and fraud prevention systems to work across different network operators, handset manufacturers, and software platforms. It allows new AI services to plug into existing infrastructure and evolve as subscriber behaviors and threat landscapes change.

Challenges on the Path Forward

Despite the clear benefits, several challenges stand in the way of realizing fully interoperable AI ecosystems:

- **Fragmentation**: With numerous proprietary LLMs and APIs, consolidating standards is difficult amid competing commercial interests.
- **Rapid innovation cycles**: AI models and methods evolve quickly, making it hard for standards to keep pace without stifling innovation.
- **Privacy and security**: Sharing data and models across ecosystems raises significant concerns over data leakage, misuse, and compliance with laws like GDPR.
- **Ethical alignment**: Ensuring interoperable systems do not amplify biases or unethical behaviors requires continuous oversight and transparent auditing.

Overcoming these requires cooperation across industry, academia, and regulators — an inclusive approach that balances innovation, trust, and social responsibility.

The Vision: A Harmonized AI Future

Imagine a future where:

- Enterprises can select and combine best-in-class LLMs from multiple providers via standardized APIs, creating tailored AI assistants for every department.

- Agentic AI systems communicate fluently with enterprise applications, IoT devices, and human users, orchestrating complex workflows while respecting privacy and ethical boundaries.
- Developers worldwide contribute interoperable components and datasets to a shared AI ecosystem, accelerating innovation through collaboration rather than competition.
- Regulators and watchdogs access transparent audit trails built into AI standards, ensuring AI systems operate fairly and without harm.
- Cross-lingual, multicultural AI agents operate globally, bridging language barriers and fostering inclusive digital societies.

Standards, APIs, and ecosystem interoperability are not just technical necessities—they are the infrastructure of this AI future. They transform LLMs and agentic AI from isolated marvels into trusted, scalable, and ethical collaborators that amplify human potential.

Redefining Human-Machine Collaboration

The relationship between humans and machines is undergoing a profound transformation. For most of history, machines have functioned as tools — fast, powerful, obedient, but fundamentally passive. They did what they were programmed to do. Even the early wave of automation in factories and software systems largely followed this paradigm: rule-based, task-specific, and deterministic.

But with the rise of **large language models (LLMs)** and **agentic AI**, we are entering a new era where machines are no longer just tools — they are **collaborators**. These systems don't just execute instructions; they interpret intent, adapt to new contexts, and assist proactively. The boundaries between tool, assistant, and colleague are beginning to blur.

From Command Execution to Intent Understanding

In traditional software systems, humans had to adapt to the logic of machines. We learned command-line syntax, navigated rigid user interfaces, and struggled with software that lacked flexibility or common sense.

LLMs invert this paradigm. They adapt to *us*. Through natural language prompts — whether typed or spoken — users can express goals, preferences, constraints, and ambiguity. The system doesn't just respond to what was said literally; it attempts to grasp what was *meant*.

This shift, from command execution to intent understanding, is a foundational breakthrough. It allows AI to be used by non-technical users in enterprise, government, education, and healthcare without specialized training. It enables people to collaborate with systems in their own language, rather than learning the language of machines.

The Emergence of Agentic AI: From Assistants to Autonomous Agents

What makes this new generation of AI so transformative isn't just the ability to generate coherent text. It's the ability to reason, plan, and act on behalf of users.

Agentic AI refers to AI systems that are not merely reactive but can take initiative. They can:

- Decompose a goal into sub-tasks.
- Search and synthesize information across domains.
- Invoke external tools and APIs.
- Make decisions under uncertainty.
- Learn from feedback and adapt behavior over time.

These are no longer just autocomplete engines. They are emerging as **cognitive partners** — capable of carrying out complex, multi-step tasks, with memory, situational awareness, and even a sense of "persona" or style tuned to the user.

In a corporate setting, this means an AI agent could:

- Monitor market trends, detect emerging risks, and draft strategy briefs.
- Handle an entire customer interaction lifecycle — from inquiry to resolution to follow-up.
- Prepare customized learning modules for employees based on their performance data.
- Automatically triage, escalate, and respond to compliance and security alerts.

And it can do all this not through rigid automation workflows, but through a flexible understanding of goals, language, and context.

Collaboration, Not Competition

There is a common concern that intelligent systems will replace human workers — that AI is here to take jobs. But the deeper, more nuanced reality is this: **AI is redefining jobs, not just replacing them.**

The future of work is not AI *vs.* humans — it is **humans + AI**.

We are entering an era of **collaborative intelligence**, where machines augment our thinking, creativity, and execution. Just as calculators didn't eliminate mathematicians, and spreadsheets didn't make accountants obsolete, LLMs will not make professionals redundant — but they *will* redefine what those professionals do.

- **Writers** will become editors, curators, and ideators — working with AI to brainstorm, outline, and refine.
- **Doctors** will use AI to sift through medical histories, suggest differential diagnoses, and stay updated on new research.
- **Lawyers** will delegate document review and legal research to AI, focusing instead on strategic interpretation and client interaction.
- **Educators** will use AI to deliver personalized learning while spending more time mentoring and inspiring.

The essence of collaboration is **mutual adaptation**. Just as we teach and fine-tune AI models, they will shape how we think, make decisions, and solve problems. The most successful organizations and individuals will not be the ones who resist AI, but those who integrate it — thoughtfully, ethically, and strategically.

Designing Collaborative Experiences

Redefining human-machine collaboration requires more than technical capability. It requires thoughtful design of **interactions**, **interfaces**, and **boundaries**.

- **Explainability** becomes essential. A model should not only give an answer but explain *why* it gave that answer.

- **Memory and personalization** allow systems to understand a user's history, preferences, and patterns — providing continuity across sessions.
- **Controllability** ensures the user remains in charge — defining constraints, objectives, and risk thresholds.
- **Transparency** helps build trust. Users must know what the model can and cannot do, and when to defer to a human expert.

In this sense, human-machine collaboration is not just a feature of future software. It is a **design philosophy** — one that prioritizes empathy, agency, and shared responsibility.

The Social and Cultural Shift

As AI becomes a co-pilot in more aspects of daily life — from email drafting to financial planning to medical decision-making — a broader social shift is underway. We will need to redefine:

- **What it means to be an expert** when machines can replicate expert-level output.
- **What we teach and learn** when factual recall is outsourced to AI.
- **What collaboration looks like** when some team members are human, and others are software agents.

This will require **digital literacy at a new level** — not just how to use tools, but how to *collaborate* with intelligent systems. It will also require new norms, ethics, and governance frameworks to ensure that collaboration remains equitable, respectful, and accountable.

The Road Ahead: Symbiotic Intelligence

Ultimately, the vision is not of humans enslaved by machines, nor machines micromanaged by humans, but of **symbiotic intelligence** — where each party brings its strengths:

- Humans: empathy, values, judgment, ethics, and imagination.
- Machines: speed, memory, consistency, and scale.

Together, they can solve problems neither could solve alone — from climate change modeling and healthcare access to real-time fraud detection and universal education.

The collaboration is not merely transactional — it is transformational. It changes how we work, learn, govern, and dream.

End of the Book but learning continuous.

www.ingramcontent.com/pod-product-compliance
Ingram Content Group UK Ltd.
Pitfield, Milton Keynes, MK11 3LW, UK
UKHW040242300726
14061UKWH00002BD/114